Practical Approaches in the Treatment of Women Who Abuse Alcohol and Other Drugs

U.S. Department of Health and Human Services
Public Health Service
Substance Abuse and Mental Health Services Administration
Center for Substance Abuse Treatment
Division of Clinical Programs
Women and Children's Branch

Rockwall II, 5600 Fishers Lane
Rockville, MD 20857

This publication was prepared under contract No. CSAT-93-0006 from CSAT. Maggie Wilmore served as the Government project officer.

The opinions expressed herein are those of the contributors to the report and the contractor, Policy Research Incorporated, and do not reflect the official position of SAMHSA or any other part of the U.S. Department of Health and Human Services (DHHS). No official support or endorsement of the Substance Abuse and Mental Health Services Administration (SAMHSA) or DHHS is intended or should be inferred. The recommendations presented in this document should not be considered as substitutes for individualized patient care and treatment decisions.

"When a woman is unconscious about her starvation, about the consequences of using death-dealing vehicles and substances, she is dancing, she is dancing. Whether these are such things as negative thinking, poor relationships, abusive situations, drugs or alcohol—they are like the red shoes, hard to pry a person away from once they've taken hold."

"Yes there is pain in being severed from the red shoes. But it is our only hope. It is a severing that is filled with absolute blessing. The feet will grow back, we will find our way, we will recover, we will run and jump and skip again some day. By then our handmade life will be ready. We'll slip into it and marvel that we could be so lucky to have another chance."

Women Who Run With the Wolves, by Clarissa Pinkola Estés

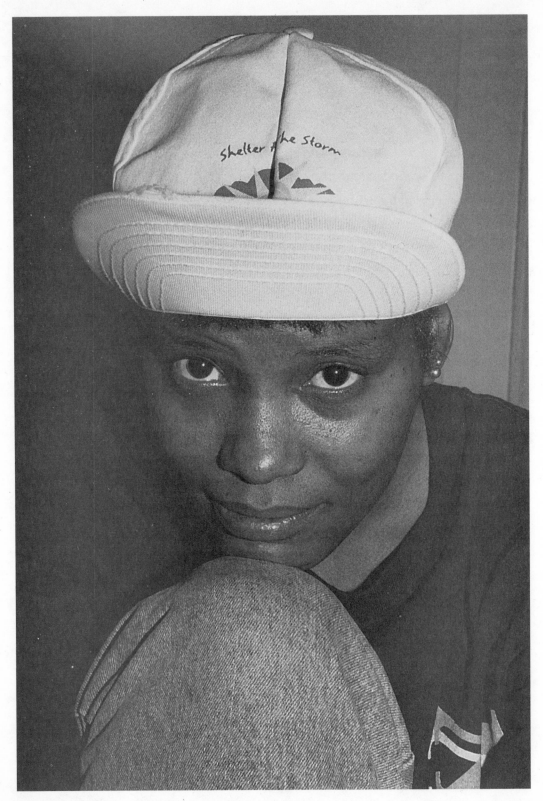

Photo by Ellen Shapiro

This document is dedicated to women with substance abuse problems and to those who support them—

- women who, despite fear and uncertainty, have said "yes" to the journey of recovery - we wish them continued growth;

- women who, because of fear, denial, and other obstacles, have not yet been released from the hold of addiction - we send them encouragement and support; and

- the families, friends, and clinicians who have supported women in treatment with compassion, competency, and concern - we commend them.

Table of Contents

Practical Approaches in the Treatment of Women Who Abuse Alcohol and Other Drugs

Table of Contents

Dear Colleague:

The Center for Substance Abuse Treatment (CSAT) is pleased to offer this guide: *Practical Approaches in the Treatment of Women Who Abuse Alcohol and Other Drugs.* Since its inception in 1990, CSAT has been acutely aware of the lack of access to treatment for women and the need for appropriate and high quality services that address women's specific treatment needs.

This guide is designed to address issues and offer strategies for effective care for women with substance abuse problems. It begins with an assessment of the extent of the problem, pointing to the enormity of attendant health and social issues faced by women who abuse alcohol and other drugs. It then presents strategies related to engaging women in the treatment process, providing comprehensive services to women, and ensuring a continuum of care during the recovery process. In addition to providing information that can be used with women in general, the manual speaks to diverse population groups of women, including women of various racial and ethnic groups, women in the justice system, and women with disabilities. The manual also specifically addresses issues relevant to many women in treatment, including violence, sexual abuse, and co-occurring mental health problems.

In most communities, there is a dearth of technical, financial, and human resources dedicated to the treatment of women with alcohol and other drug problems. Therefore, it is critical that administrators, health care professionals, and social service providers become knowledgeable about how to more effectively and efficiently use existing resources to design and implement programs that are specific to the needs of women.

CSAT highly recommends this document as a resource for all professionals involved in the assessment and treatment of women with alcohol and other drug problems, in the hope that its use will promote the development of cost-effective, gender-specific treatment and recovery services for women.

Lisa W. Scheckel

Lisa W. Scheckel
Acting Director
Center for Substance Abuse Treatment

Preface

In early 1992, the Center for Substance Abuse Treatment (CSAT) Division of Clinical Programs (the Division) determined that as part of its effort to expand the availability of quality treatment services for women, it would be necessary to make available to substance abuse treatment providers a comprehensive document on substance abuse treatment of women. To that end, CSAT initiated preparation of the document under the leadership of Maggie Wilmore, Chief of the Women and Children's Branch (the Branch). She established and involved in this process a Women's Treatment Task Force comprising 18 individuals specializing in the treatment of women for problems with alcohol and other drugs. This Task Force identified issues related to treatment of women as well as strategies that can be used by programs serving this population.

Given the paucity of published materials available on substance abuse among women and on the relative effectiveness of treatment modalities for female clients, development of the document was designed to utilize the knowledge and expertise of experts in the field insofar as possible, as well as published and unpublished documents. The involvement of experts knowledgeable about and experienced in treatment of women in general as well as specific populations of women enriched and expanded the document, which included not only basic epidemiological data, but strategies that address the specific needs of a number of populations of women. In late 1993, the first complete draft of the manual in its present form was prepared by Policy Research Incorporated and disseminated to experts in the field, including members of the Task Force and CSAT, for review and comment. Revisions were made, and the manual was again reviewed by CSAT staff, members of the Task Force, and others knowledgeable about substance abuse treatment for women. In all, more than 50 women and men of diverse cultures, viewpoints, training, and experience contributed to the preparation of this manual.

We believe that this document can contribute to improving the quality of treatment services for women. It is part of the larger effort of the Division and its Women and Children's Branch to expand quality services. These other activities include, for example, expanding services through two grant programs (the Residential Women and Children's Treatment Program and the Residential Pregnant and Postpartum Women's Program) and sponsoring preparation of a Comprehensive Treatment Model for Women to be used by substance abuse treatment providers. The manual will be disseminated to treatment programs whose client population includes women. In the future, it will be used as a basis for developing and implementing training programs for staff and for preparation of learner-centered materials that can be readily used by practitioners in the field.

We appreciate the dedication of the Chief of the Women and Children's Branch, Maggie Wilmore, who contributed to the conceptual development of the manual and who reviewed and commented extensively on each draft. Without her, this document would not have been a reality.

Warren W. Hewitt Jr.

Warren W. Hewitt, Jr.
Acting Director
Division of Clinical Programs

Foreword

The Congressional legislation which established the Center for Substance Abuse Treatment (CSAT) provided an overall mandate to expand the availability of effective treatment and recovery services for (those with) alcohol and other drug problems. This legislation specifically called for expanding treatment and recovery services for women. The Division of Clinical Programs (the Division) Women and Children's Branch of CSAT is committed to increasing service availability (access to care) for women and to ensuring that comprehensive treatment services for women are provided that empower and sustain their recovery.

This CSAT-sponsored publication, *Practical Approaches in the Treatment of Women Who Abuse Alcohol and Other Drugs,* is one of several activities carried out by the Division's Women and Children's Branch to help treatment program staff plan and deliver quality treatment services for women. It is our hope that the manual will truly make a difference—that it will inspire and activate increased concern for and attention to women's issues on the part of all substance abuse treatment providers as well as those involved in formulating substance abuse policy. The manual includes summaries of current knowledge regarding substance abuse treatment modalities for women, the epidemiology of women and substance abuse, and factors related to substance abuse among women. Equally if not more important, it provides practical information on how to design, develop, and implement effective substance abuse outreach and treatment programs for women. As the field of substance abuse treatment for women changes and grows, CSAT will revise this publication as necessary.

Acknowledgments

The experience and knowledge of many experts in the field of substance abuse treatment for women has been synthesized in this manual. More than 35 experts participated in its development. Many of them devoted considerable time and effort as volunteers. I would particularly like to express my gratitude to Doris Amaya, Barbara Aranda-Naranjo, Naya Arbiter, Andrea Barthwell, Debbie Barsell, Virginia Borrok, Vivian Brown, Carol Casey, Stephanie Covington, Mary Patricia Donegan, Barbara Eisenstadt, Susan Galbraith, Barbara Gibson, Cora (Skip) Gordon, Annette Green, Irene Jillson, Robin LaDue, Mari Ono, Helen Rodriguez-Trias, Paula Roth, Brenda Smith, Brenda Underhill, and Marilyn Vranas. These individuals either wrote a chapter or contributed substantively to one or more of the chapters. The names and affiliations of everyone who contributed to the manual are listed alphabetically on the following pages. On behalf of CSAT, I wish to express my deep appreciation for their dedication to improving substance abuse treatment for women.

Maggie Wilmore

Maggie Wilmore
Chief
Women and Children's Branch
Division of Clinical Programs

Experts Contributing to the Development of the Substance Abuse Treatment Manual for Women

Doris Amaya
Doris Amaya and Associates
Coral Gables, Florida

Barbara Aranda-Naranjo
The University of Texas
  Health Center at San Antonio
San Antonio, Texas

Naya Arbiter
Amity
Tucson, Arizona

Debbie Barsell
Technical Resources Incorporated
Rockville, Maryland

Andrea Barthwell
Interventions
Chicago, Illinois

Lorrainne Bilodeau
Florence County Commission on
  Alcohol and Drug Abuse
Florence, South Carolina

Virginia Borrok
Gateway Community Services, Inc.
Jacksonville, Florida

Aurelia Brooks
House of the Crossroads
Pittsburgh, Pennsylvania

Vivian Brown
PROTOTYPES
Culver City, California

Claire Callahan
Consultant
Bethesda, Maryland

Carol Casey
The Columbia Recovery Center, Inc.
Washington, DC

Stephanie Covington
Consultant to the Betty Ford Center
Women's Program
LaJolla, California

Mary Patricia Donegan
Psychological and Counseling
Center, Inc.
Pittsburgh, Pennsylvania

Hope Ewing
Born Free Project
Maratinez, California

Francine C. Feinberg
Our Home Foundation, Inc.
Milwaukee, Wisconsin

Norma Finkelstein
Coalition on Addiction, Pregnancy
and Parenting
Cambridge, Massachusetts

Susan Galbraith
Legal Action Center
Washington, DC

Barbara Gibson
Urban Resource Institute
Brooklyn, New York

Skip Gordon
Policy Research Incorporated
Bethesda, Maryland

Annette Green
Allegheny County Mental Health,
Mental Retardation, Drug and
Alcohol Program
Pittsburgh, Pennsylvania

Cheryl Grills
Loyola Marymont University
Los Angeles, California

Nancy Hamilton
Operation Par
St. Petersburg, Florida

Linda Herman
The Flowering Tree Project
Oglala Sioux Tribe
Pine Ridge, South Dakota

Val Jackson
The Village
Miami, Florida

Jackie Jenkins-Scott
Dimock Community Health Center
Roxbury, Massachusetts

Irene Jillson
Policy Research Incorporated
Bethesda, Maryland

Karol Kaltenback
Thomas Jefferson University
Philadelphia, Pennsylvania

Robin LaDue
Clinical Psychologist
Renton, Washington

Davene B. McCarthy-White
Howard University Hospital
Washington, DC

Lorraine Montenegro
United Bronx Parents, Inc.
Bronx, New York

Christine Olsen
Colorado Department of Health
Denver, Colorado

Mari Ono
Hawaii State Hospital
Kaneohe, Hawaii

Kattie Portis
Women Incorporated
Boston, Massachusetts

Beth Glover Reed
University of Michigan
Ann Arbor, Michigan

Helen Rodriguez-Trias
Consultant in Health Programming
Brookdale, California

Paula Roth
Consultant
New York, New York

Harilyn Rousso
Disabilities Unlimited
Consulting Services
New York, New York

Maryanne Schretzman
Women In Need, Inc.
New York, New York

Bettina Scott
Office of Alcohol Prevention
and Treatment Policy
SAMHSA
Rockville, Maryland

Albert M. Senella
Tarzana Treatment Center, Inc.
Tarzana, California

Brenda Smith
National Women's Law Center
Washington, DC

Iris E. Smith
Gapp Family Recovery Center
Atlanta, Georgia

John W. Stauder
Prince Georges County
Health Department
Landover, Maryland

Rita Sullivan
Ontrack, Inc.
Medford, Oregon

Sushma D. Taylor
Center Point, Inc.
San Rafael, California

Brenda Underhill
Policy Research Incorporated
Bethesda, Maryland

Marilyn Vranas
Center for Substance
Abuse Treatment
Rockville, Maryland

John Wilbur
Maehnowesekiyah Treatment
Center's Residential Treatment for
Pregnant and Postpartum Women
Keshena, Wisconsin

Dooley Worth
Research Consultant
New York, New York

Joan Ellen Zweben
East Bay Community
Recovery Project
Oakland, California

Chapter 1

Introduction

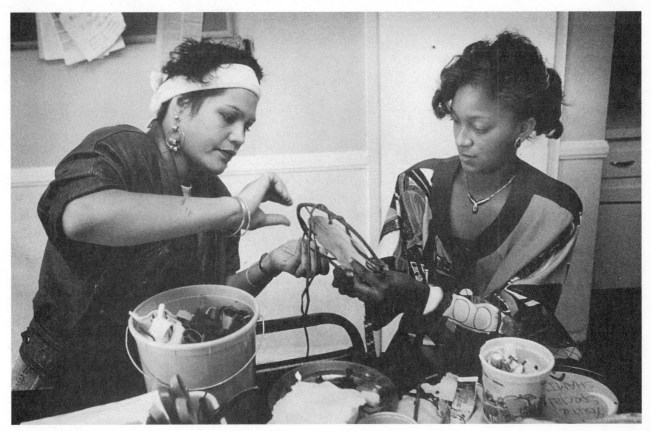

Photo by Larry Crowe

*The compilation
and presentation of the
information in this manual
serves as a guide to develop
and implement effective
substance abuse treatment
services for women.*

Chapter 1

Introduction

This manual is designed to help treatment program personnel meet the specific needs of women with substance abuse problems. It is for substance abuse treatment staff who work in programs that serve both men and women and for staff who serve women only. Although written for a wide audience, the manual is most relevant to federally-funded programs that mainly serve low-income populations. The manual is presented in eight chapters, including this introductory chapter. Chapters 2 through 8 are presented as follows:

- **Chapter 2** "Women and Alcohol and Other Drugs: An Overview" presents a summary of the current epidemiology of substance abuse among women, and data and information concerning factors related to substance abuse among women.

- **Chapter 3** "Treatment of Alcohol and Other Drug Abuse: An Introduction" presents approaches to the treatment of substance abuse.

- **Chapter 4** "Outreach to and Identification of Women" presents a discussion of barriers to engaging women in treatment and outreach strategies to deal with those barriers.

- **Chapter 5** "Comprehensive Treatment for Women" presents approaches to comprehensive care in each stage of the treatment process (e.g., intake, treatment, discharge).

- **Chapter 6** "Continuing Care and Follow Up" is a summary of approaches to continuing care.

- **Chapter 7** "Program Management Issues" presents an overview of program management issues.

- **Chapter 8** "Reflections" includes thoughts and reflections on the issues raised in the manual.

Unless otherwise stated, the discussion of treatment issues and strategies relates to women in substance abuse treatment in general; that is, the information applies across ethnic/racial groups and socioeconomic groups. Factors specifically related to different populations of women (age groups, ethnic/racial groups, and other populations) are addressed in chapters 2, 4, and 5. For example, in chapter 2, comparative information is presented by age and/or race where appropriate, but information regarding several populations is also summarized at the end of the chapter. Because of the critical importance of the cultural competency of staff in engaging and retaining women in treatment and the importance of the factors of culture, gender, and class in designing and delivering effective substance abuse treatment services, extensive discussions of issues unique to different population groups are presented in chapters 4 and 5. Those who are knowledgeable about the current epidemiology of substance abuse in women may wish to refer directly to chapters that present specific strategies concerning one of the phases of care (e.g., outreach, continuing care). Others may choose to read chapter 2 thoroughly before reading the other chapters or may wish to use chapter 2 as a quick reference for epidemiologic information.

There is no large body of research on which to base the design and implementation of strategies for women's substance abuse treatment, as chapter 2 will make clear, and many of the national data sets that might be useful do not have—or do not present—information separately for men and women. Those who manage treatment services for women or who are counselors in women's treatment programs do describe their programs and conduct at least informal assessments in the course of program management (e.g., completing required reports for funding or sponsoring agencies) and fund raising (e.g., preparing proposals). However, program managers often do not have the resources or the opportunity to conduct systematic evaluations or assessments of their programs or to compare their services with those of other treatment programs. Thus, program staff usually rely on experiential knowledge or the "oral tradition" in designing, developing, and implementing substance abuse treatment services for women.

This manual is based on the knowledge of experts in the field of substance abuse treatment for women as well as on published and unpublished research. Both of these information sources contribute to the knowledge base of substance abuse treatment. The compilation and presentation of the information in this manual serves as a guide to develop and implement effective substance abuse treatment services for women. This manual also serves as a guidepost for research by helping to make evident the gaps in current knowledge. As this process continues, it will provide relevant and current information to help those in the field of substance abuse treatment implement effective substance abuse treatment services for women.

Across all program components in the continuum of care for women, the mandate of providers is to do the following:

- <u>Engender</u> hope and empowerment in their clients,

- <u>Ensure</u> safe, secure, and supportive environments,

- <u>Establish</u> trusting relationships between women clients and staff,

- <u>Provide</u> advocacy in accessing all services needed,

- <u>Promote</u> self responsibility, self sufficiency, and interdependence,

- <u>Strive</u> for gender specific and culturally relevant client-driven services,

- <u>Eliminate</u> labeling of women and their children in all respects, and

- <u>Build</u> the effective linkages and networking required for model women's programs.

Chapter 2

Women and Alcohol and Other Drugs: An Overview

Photo by Larry Crowe

The effects of alcohol and other drug abuse on women's health are clear.

Chapter 2

Women and Alcohol and Other Drugs: An Overview

To encourage women who have problems with alcohol or other drugs to enter and stay in treatment programs, it is essential for all treatment providers to incorporate understanding of this population into their treatment paradigms. This chapter includes information on the following:

- the breadth and depth of alcohol and other drug problems among women of various ages, races, and socioeconomic status;

- patterns of alcohol use and other types of drugs abused most frequently by women of various ages, races, and socioeconomic status; and

- health-related issues likely to arise because of alcohol and other drug use.

With this knowledge, providers of substance abuse treatment services can do the following:

- target specific groups of women in the community who are likely to have problems with alcohol or other drugs;

- identify patterns of abuse and other health-related problems that clients may be unwilling to self-disclose;

- forecast client needs more accurately by understanding what the current trends in alcohol and other drug use indicate for the number and types of clients in treatment in the coming years; and

- gain community support for treatment initiatives by informing the public about the nature, extent, and impact of the problem of alcohol and other drugs.

The remainder of this chapter summarizes the most recent epidemiologic data on alcohol and other drug abuse among women.

2.1   The Epidemiology of Substance Use Among Women

2.1.1   Overview

Overall, adequate data and information about substance abuse by women is scarce. This scarcity exists in part because a relatively small proportion of substance abuse resources have been allocated to research designed for the understanding of women and their problems associated with substance abuse. Also, information from national data sets is not automatically broken down by gender so that comparisons of substance use can be made between men and women and among women of different ages and racial and ethnic groups. Where possible, data and information related to substance abuse is presented by type of drug and frequency of use. This helps to avoid problems associated with varying interpretations of "abuse," "addiction," and "dependence."

The following definitions derived from the Center for Substance Abuse Treatment's Treatment Improvement Protocol (TIP) for Pregnant, Substance-Using Women are used in this manual:

- Abuse—the harmful use of a specific substance including alcohol, tobacco, and other drugs.

- Addiction—a disease process characterized by the continued use of a specific substance such as alcohol, tobacco, and other drugs despite physical, psychological, or social harm.

- Dependence—the abuse of alcohol, tobacco, or other drugs such that to stop using would result in physical or psychological symptoms of withdrawal.

It should be pointed out that any use of an illegal substance is generally considered to be "abuse."

The Substance Abuse and Mental Health Services Administration's (SAMHSA) National Household Survey on Drug Abuse (NHSDA) is the largest national survey of substance abuse in the United States. The NHSDA is based on the civilian non-institutionalized population aged 12 and over living in households and institutional group quarters. These group quarters include college dormitories, rooming houses, and shelters. Together with the National Institute on Drug Abuse (NIDA)-sponsored survey of high school students, the SAMHSA survey is the primary source of national data on the use of alcohol and other drugs. The Drug Abuse Warning Network (DAWN) is another source of information on drug use patterns. Prior to 1988, DAWN was not updated in a way that would maintain randomness of selected hospitals. Since that time, the data have been based on a nationally representative probability sample of hospitals located throughout the United States, with the exception of Hawaii and Alaska. Twenty-one oversampled metropolitan areas are also included.

The limitations of these surveys, which have been noted by researchers and by the General Accounting Office, are applicable to the general population as well as to women. For example, certain groups of women who are undocumented, incarcerated, homeless, or living in residential or hospital-based treatment programs or nursing homes are not included as part of the NHSDA sample. Similarly, the high school survey does not include girls who have dropped out of school, who are runaways, or who are incarcerated—clearly high-risk populations. The surveys are also limited because of the respondents' reluctance to answer questions regarding use of any substance, particularly illegal drugs, given the stigma our society attaches to drug use, especially by women. Neither of the surveys provides data by subethnic populations (e.g., Mexican American,

Puerto Rican) or for Native Americans or Asian Americans. Finally, although increased heroin use by women is of major concern, the survey does not have a sufficient response rate to allow for disaggregations by race/ethnicity or age. These limitations must be considered when reviewing the estimates of substance abuse by women.

2.1.2   Trends in Substance Abuse Among Women

According to the 1992 SAMHSA survey, American women were less likely to abuse alcohol and other drugs in 1992 than they were in 1976, reflecting a downward trend over the previous 16 years. However, the estimated number of women who use or abuse legal or illegal substances is still startling:

The effects of alcohol and other drug abuse on women's health are clear.

- 2.1 percent of the respondents, or an estimated 2.2 million women aged 12 and over, had engaged in heavy alcohol use, which is defined as drinking 5 or more drinks per occasion on 5 or more days during the previous 30 days (see Figure 1);[1]

- 4.1 percent of the survey respondents, or an estimated 4.4 million women aged 12 and over reported using an illicit drug during the month before the NHSDA (see Figure 3);[2]

- 1.2 percent of the respondents, or an estimated 1.3 million women aged 12 and over, reported nonmedical use of a psychotherapeutic drug in the past month (see Figure 6);[3]

- 0.4 percent of the respondents, or an estimated 419,000 women aged 12 and over, reported using cocaine in the past month (see Figure 4);[4] and

- 0.3 percent of the respondents, or an estimated 300,000 women aged 12 and over, reported using crack in the past year.[5]

The effects of alcohol and other drug abuse on women's health are clear: In 1990, the death rate for alcohol-induced causes for Caucasian and African American women was 2.8 per 100,000 and 7.7 per 100,000, respectively. The death rate related to drugs other than alcohol was 2.5 per 100,000 for Caucasian women and 3.4 per 100,000 for African American women.[6] In the same year, nearly 9,200 women died of chronic liver disease or cirrhosis;[7] 4,159 infants were born with fetal alcohol syndrome (FAS);[8] and 3,279 women were diagnosed as having AIDS as a result of either injection drug use or sexual contact with an HIV-infected injecting drug user.[9] In 1992, 210,051 women presented in emergency rooms for episodes related to drugs other than alcohol; 38,194 of these involved cocaine.[10]

2.1.3   Alcohol

Alcohol is the substance most commonly abused by the general population and by women. The trends in abuse of alcohol by women are not encouraging. For example, although heavy use declined between 1985 and 1992, the decrease was slight, and reported heavy use increased by more than one-third between 1988 and 1992.[11] According to the 1992 NHSDA, 2.1 percent of women aged 12 and over had engaged in heavy alcohol use in the month prior to the survey (see Figure 1).[12] The 1988 National Health Interview Survey (the most recent one for which data are available), found that seven percent of female respondents[13] (or an estimated 6.6 million women)[14] drank at heavy levels in the two weeks prior to the survey. A 1984 national survey of alcohol problems found that six percent of women reported at least a moderate problem with alcohol and sixteen percent reported at least a minimal problem with alcohol.[15] In 1990, the National Institute on Alcoholism and Alcohol Abuse (NIAAA) estimated that "alcohol abuse and alcohol dependence are serious problems that affect about 10 percent of adult Americans."[16] Given an estimated adult female population (women aged 12 and over) of approximately 107

Figure 1

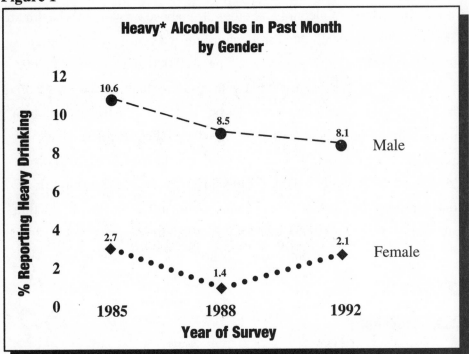

National Household Survey on Drug Abuse: Population Estimates 1992, 121. National Household Survey on Drug Abuse: Population Estimates 1998, 117. National Household Survey on Drug Abuse: Population Estimates 1985, 70.

million in 1992, it can be estimated that as many as 10.7 million American women may abuse alcohol.

Heavy alcohol use was reported by 6.5 percent of young women aged 18 to 25 and 0.5 percent of adolescent girls aged 12 to 17.[17] In terms of population estimates, this indicates that nearly 921,000 young women and more than 50,000 adolescent girls engaged in heavy drinking in 1992.[18]

The survey also reported that 12.3 million women, or 11.5 percent of women aged 12 and over, consumed alcohol at least once a week. Women 18 to 25 and 26 to 34 are more likely to consume alcohol once a week than those 35 and over (16 percent, 14.5 percent, and 10.9 percent respectively).[19] Given that these are primary childbearing years, this figure

Figure 2

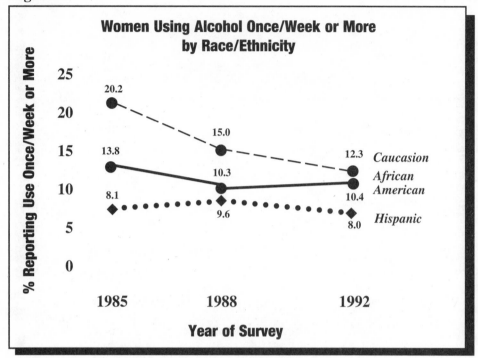

National Household Survey on Drug Abuse: Population Estimates 1992, 121. National Household Survey on Drug Abuse: Population Estimates 1998, 117. National Household Survey on Drug Abuse: Population Estimates 1985, 70.

is noteworthy. In fact, the 1992 NHSDA also found that 40.4 percent of the women aged 12 and over reported consuming alcohol in the previous month. More than half (53 percent) of the women 18-34—the prime childbearing years—reported alcohol consumption in the previous month. Also of concern is the finding that one in seven adolescent girls (14.5 percent) reported consuming alcohol in the previous month.[20]

As Figure 2 shows, Caucasian women are slightly more likely to use alcohol once a week or more than African American women (12.3 percent compared to 10.4 percent) and much more likely than Hispanic women (8 percent).[21]

Figure 3

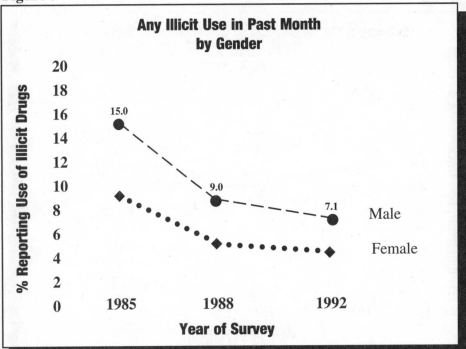

National Household Survey on Drug Abuse: Population Estimates 1992, 19. National Household Survey on Drug Abuse: Population Estimates 1998, 17. National Household Survey on Drug Abuse: Population Estimates 1985, 54.

A number of researchers report differences in drinking patterns by gender. For example, men report higher quantity, frequency, and rates of intoxication at an earlier age then do women and experience more lifetime symptoms on average.[22] As Figure 1 shows, the gender difference in reported heavy alcohol use decreased from 1985 to 1992. While heavy use by men has steadily declined during this period, heavy use by women actually increased from 1988 to 1992.

2.1.4   Illicit Drugs

According to the 1992 SAMHSA Survey on Drug Abuse, slightly more than 4 percent of female respondents over the age of 12 had used an illicit drug in the previous month, representing an estimated 4.4 million women (see Figure 3).[23] This estimate is still significantly lower than the

Figure 4

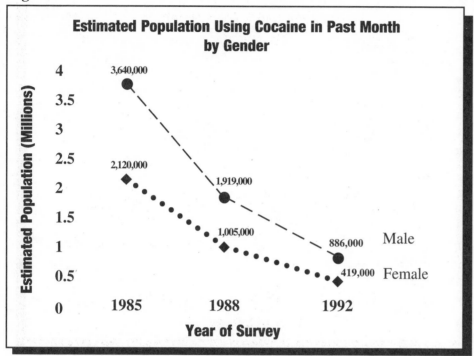

National Household Survey on Drug Abuse: Population Estimates 1992, 31. National Household Survey on Drug Abuse: Population Estimates 1998, 29. National Household Survey on Drug Abuse: Population Estimates 1985, 14.

use reported by men (7.1 percent). The use by women between 1985 and 1992 declined by 44 percent, slightly lower than the decline in use by men (47 percent).

Most of these women—2.9 percent of the female respondents or an estimated 3.1 million women—had used marijuana in the past month,[24] and an estimated 419,000 women had used cocaine in the past month (see Figure 4).[25]

According to the 1992 NHSDA, an estimated 98,000 women used crack in the past month; however, the number of responses is too small for this estimate to be reliable.[26] As Figure 4 shows, although reported cocaine use by women decreased substantially between 1985 and 1992, an esti-

Figure 5

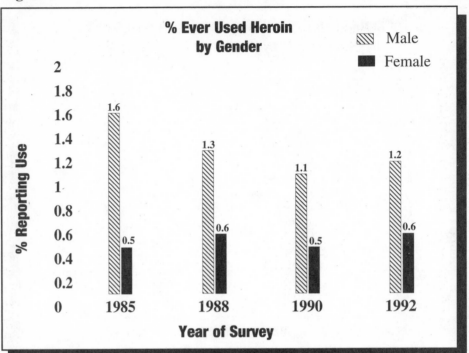

National Household Survey on Drug Abuse: Population Estimates 1992, 104. National Household Survey on Drug Abuse: Population Estimates 1998, 102. National Household Survey on Drug Abuse: Population Estimates 1985, 9.

mated 419,000 women had used this drug in the month prior to the 1992 NHSDA.

Notably, for Caucasian women and Hispanic women the decrease in cocaine-related episodes in emergency rooms between 1988 and 1991 was substantially higher (37 percent and 32.7 percent, respectively), than for the population overall (27 percent). For African American women, the decrease was substantially lower—16 percent.[27]

Only one-tenth of 1 percent (or 0.1 percent) of female respondents reported using heroin in the past year, but this translates into an estimated 88,000 women. In contrast, 0.2 percent of men (an estimated 236,000) reported using heroin in the past year. Moreover, 644,000 women, or 0.6 percent of the population of women 12 years of age and older, reported ever

Figure 6

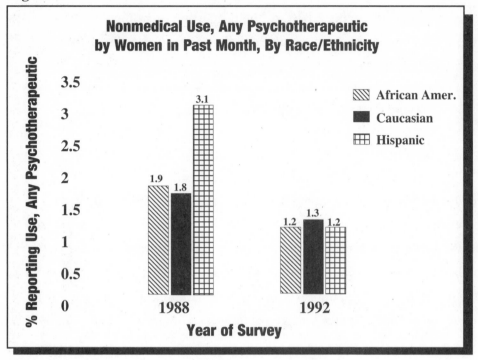

National Household Survey on Drug Abuse: Population Estimates 1992, 55. National Household Survey on Drug Abuse: Population Estimates 1998, 53.

having used heroin, compared to 1.2 million men, 1.2 percent of the male population 12 years old or older.[28]

Unfortunately, because the prevalence estimates are so small, it is not possible to compare heroin use by women and men in different age groups or among women in different age groups. However, an estimated 27,000 adolescents between the ages of 12 and 17 used heroin in the past year, as did 152,000 young adults between the ages of 18 and 25.[29] This is particularly disturbing because household surveys underreport the use of illegal drugs. As with several other estimates from the NHSDA, the samples are too small to ensure reliability.

According to the NHSDA, the proportion of women reporting lifetime heroin use has remained relatively constant over the last seven years (see Figure 5).

2.1.5   Prescription and Over-the-Counter Drugs

The 1992 NHSDA indicates that an estimated 1.3 million women (1.2 percent of female respondents) used psychotherapeutic drugs for nonmedical reasons during the month before the survey.[30] This figure indicates a 35 percent decrease in reported use since 1988 (see Figure 6). [31] These data represent rates of nonmedical use of prescription drugs, defined in the survey as "on your own, either without your own prescription from a doctor, or in greater amounts or more often than prescribed, or for any reason other than a doctor said you should take them."

Twice as many women as men receive and use prescriptions for drugs.

Although some studies have demonstrated that women are much more likely than men to abuse psychotherapeutic drugs (defined by SAMHSA to include stimulants, sedatives, tranquilizers, and analgesics), the 1992 NHSDA shows no statistically significant differences: An estimated 1.3 million men (1.3 percent of male respondents) reported nonmedical use in the previous month.[32] However, the possibility of nonmedical use of prescription drugs is greater for women than for men. Twice as many women as men receive and use prescriptions for drugs; women receive more multiple and repeat prescriptions than men; and women are more likely than men to receive prescriptions for excessive dosages.[33]

Women are twice as likely as men to be addicted to prescription drugs in combination with alcohol.

According to Roth, approximately "70 percent of the prescriptions for tranquilizers, sedatives, and stimulants are written for women." Moreover, "women are twice as likely as men to be addicted to prescription drugs in combination with alcohol." [34] Given the health risks of combining alcohol with prescription drugs, this fact represents a serious health problem for women.

2.1.6   Polydrug Use

Although only 5.3 percent of the 1991 NHSDA respondents
reported using alcohol in combination with other drugs in the previous
month, 13.9 percent were 18 to 25 years old. Moreover, 1.4 percent
reported using three or more different substances in the past month.[35]
Unfortunately, gender-disaggregated data for polydrug use (also referred to
as co-occurring drug dependencies) are not reported by SAMHSA. However, according to Ross, alcoholic women in treatment are more likely to
be abusing barbituates, sedatives, or minor tranquilizers at the time of entry
into treatment than alcoholic men, who are more likely to be abusing
marijuana.[36]

2.1.7   Women in Treatment

During 1992, 2.8 million people needed substance abuse treatment,[37] but there were fewer than 600,000 treatment slots at any given
point in time. Unfortunately, data on the number of women in treatment
versus treatment capacity needs are not readily available.

According to the 1990 Institute of Medicine report on alcohol
problems of women, specialized treatment programs for women in the U.S.
increased only slightly between 1982 and 1987 from 23 percent to 28
percent of the nearly 5,800 programs reporting to NIDA/NIAAA.[38] Nonetheless, women are increasingly entering treatment, as evidenced by several
data sets and as reported by the Institute of Medicine.[39] For example, the
1990 survey of the National Association of State Alcohol and Drug Abuse
Directors (NASADAD) revealed the following information on the 1.2
million admissions to 7,743 treatment units:

- 22.3 percent of admissions for treatment of alcoholism were
women;

- 33 percent of admissions to programs for treatment of other substance abuse were women; and

- younger clients admitted for treatment of alcoholism were more likely to be women than those in older age groups (38 percent in the under 18 age group, versus 18 percent in the 45 to 54 and 55 to 64 age groups).[40]

Of clients admitted for treatment of other substance abuse, however, 41 percent of those 18 and under were female, and women consistently represented 26 percent to 37 percent of the age cohorts. In fact, 37.2 percent of those over 65 were women.[41] Notably, these data indicate that women are under-represented in the treatment population. Moreover, because the proportion of women in treatment has not substantially changed in over a decade, it is clear that the dearth of treatment slots for women continues to be a serious problem.

According to the 1990 Drug Services Research Survey (DSRS) of 120 substance abuse treatment programs, approximately 25 percent of the 2,182 clients in the sample were women. Notably, 33.5 percent of clients in methadone treatment programs (serving heroin addicted persons) were women while 20 percent of those in programs treating alcohol addiction only were women.[42] According to the 1992 NHSDA, 27 percent of those reporting heroin use in the previous month were women,[43] and 22 percent of those reporting heavy drinking in the past month were women.[44] A 1992 evaluation of a Health Care Financing Administration (HCFA) demonstration project for Medicare coverage of alcoholism services found that 20 percent of the 2,977 clients enrolled in the study were women. In that study, women were more likely to be enrolled in outpatient programs (26 percent) and less likely to be enrolled in the combined inpatient and outpatient treatment programs (17 percent).[45] In 1992, approximately 35 percent of persons participating in Alcoholics Anonymous (AA) programs were women; 43 percent of those 30 and under were women.[46]

2.2   Correlates of Substance Use Among Women

Patterns of substance abuse for both women and men vary by sex, age, race/ethnicity, educational status, and employment status.

2.2.1   Age

Patterns of alcohol and other drug use vary by age group for both women and men. According to the 1992 NHSDA, for example, the proportion of female respondents aged 18 to 25 who reported having used any illicit drug in the month before the survey was higher than respondents in the 12 to 17 and 26 to 34 age categories: 9.5 percent versus 6.5 percent and 7.6 percent, respectively. The proportion was significantly lower for those age 35 and over (1.4 percent).[47] Women in the age groups 18 to 25 and 26 to 34 were much more likely to have abused any psychotherapeutic drug in the previous month (2.2 percent and 2.4 percent, respectively) than those 12 to 17 (1.8 percent) and over 35 (.6 percent).[48] Young women 18 to 25 were most likely to have engaged in heavy drinking: 6.5 percent versus 2.1 percent for female respondents overall.[49]

Furthermore, according to the 1992 NHSDA, adolescent girls, aged 12 to 17, were about as likely to have used an illicit drug in the previous month as adolescent boys (661,000 adolescent girls or 6.5 percent, compared to 608,000 adolescent boys or 5.7 percent).[50]

In some studies of high school students, teenage girls are less likely to identify themselves as drinkers than teenage boys, but the degrees of difference vary. Some studies show very small differences. Age of first use and age of onset of problems among girls are decreasing. Most adolescents (regardless of gender) are introduced to alcohol between the ages of 10 and 15, usually with parents at home during a meal, a celebration, or a ceremony, but without any discussion of appropriate use.[51] This method of introduction may vary by culture.

Use of alcohol, marijuana, and cocaine has decreased among female high school seniors since 1985; for example, in that year, 8.2 percent of female students reported having used cocaine in the previous month—by 1990, that proportion had decreased to 3.3 percent. However, it is important to note that there is no comparable survey of high school dropouts, a highly vulnerable population for substance abuse.[52] According to a 1992 survey of 8th and 10th grade students, there are few gender differences in the use of drugs. This may be because female students tend to date older male students who are more likely to use drugs. There is little male-female difference in 8th and 10th grades, respectively, in the use of inhalants, cocaine, and crack. As with adults, stimulant and tranquilizer use are higher among adolescent females.[53]

2.2.2 Socioeconomic Factors

Although socioeconomic factors are increasingly viewed as related both directly and indirectly to substance abuse, research-based data are scarce, and many of the published reports are based on data that are at least 10 years old. Few studies that would provide adequate data on which to ascertain socioeconomic factors related to substance abuse have been funded by either the public or private sector. However, data from the SAMHSA survey and other sources demonstrate some associations between prevalence of abuse of alcohol and other drugs and various indicators of socioeconomic status, including education, employment, and income levels. Importantly, the relationship among these factors is seen as having changed over time. For example, according to Galbraith:

> the misuse of legal drugs was once thought to be the domain of middle- and upper-class women who could afford psychiatrists. Some prevention programs, however, are reporting high rates of misuse among women in low-income communities as a result of doctors' writing prescriptions for women on Medicaid, sometimes in lieu of a thorough medical assessment.[54]

Women who are unemployed are at higher risk of becoming heavy drinkers, while women who are drinking but who work full-time outside the home evidenced fewer alcohol dependence symptoms than those working in part-time jobs.[55] However, this finding may be misleading because women who are at higher risk of becoming heavy drinkers may be more likely to be unemployed because they have already begun to experience problems associated with drinking (e.g., tardiness or absence from work). In a study that included both Caucasian and African American women entering treatment for heroin addiction, most of the women lacked education and job experience.[56]

Among older women, there are clear relationships between abuse of prescription drugs and education and income. One researcher reports "higher rates of frequency and duration of use among older, unemployed, and less educated women."[57] However, the author does not indicate how "unemployed" is defined; that is, whether this term includes retirees or those whose income is normally derived from employment; nor does she indicate if adjustments were made for those beyond the age of retirement (generally, 65 or over). These findings also reportedly conflict with the clinical experience of treatment program personnel.

2.3   Health Impact of Substance Use on Women

This section describes the physiological and the psychological effects of substance abuse on women. This information is critical to understanding the medical and mental health needs and service requirements of women in treatment.

Figure 7

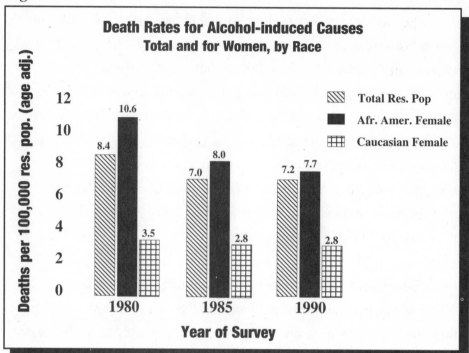

Health United States and Healthy People 2000 Review 1992, 56.

2.3.1   Physiological Effects

Women suffer severe physiological consequences as a result of substance abuse.

Women suffer severe physiological consequences as a result of substance abuse. However, because much more data are available on the effects of alcohol abuse than that of other drugs, the focus of this section focuses on physiological consequences of alcohol abuse. As was mentioned in the introduction to this chapter, in 1990, the death rate associated with alcohol-related causes was 2.8/100,000 for Caucasian females and 7.7/100,000 for African American females. The death rate for other drug induced causes was 2.5 per 100,000 for Caucasian women and 3.4 per 100,000 for African American women. Notably, the alcohol-induced death rate for African American females is higher than that for the total population (see Figure 7)[58].

The medical consequences of alcohol abuse and alcoholism
are many, as is evidenced by a number of data sources. For example,
alcohol- related medical consequences presented by 20 percent or more
of all admissions to short-stay hospitals from 1979 to 1984 included the
following: thiamine deficiency (66 percent); liver abscess and sequelae
of chronic liver disease (56 percent); varicose veins (other than lower
extremities); hemorrhoids; phlebitis or other venous thrombosis (49 percent);
spinocerebellar disease (29 percent); hypothermia (25 percent); necrosis of the
liver (23 percent); and diseases of the pancreas (20 percent).[59] Heavy alcohol
use has also been associated with peptic ulcers;[60] nutritional deficiencies
affecting anemia; neuropathy; depressed cellular and hormonal functions;[61]
hypertension; ischemic heart disease; cerebrovascular disorders;[62] cancer of
the liver; esophagus; nasopharynx; and larynx;[63] and neurologic disorders.[64]

The degree of gender disparity in the prevalence of all of these
medical consequences is not fully known. However, differences in suscep-
tibility to alcohol-related liver damage have been identified. For example,
women have been found to develop severe liver disease with shorter
durations of alcohol use and lower levels of consumption than do men, and
alcohol-dependent women have a higher prevalence and greater severity of
alcohol-related liver disease than do their male counterparts. Women with
alcohol problems are disabled more frequently and for longer periods than
are men, and women have higher death rates from alcohol-related damage.

*Women with alco-
hol problems are
disabled more
frequently and for
longer periods than
are men, and
women have higher
death rates from
alcohol-related
damage.*

In women, alcohol reaches higher peak levels in the blood faster
than it does for men, even when the same amount of absolute alcohol per
pound of body weight is consumed. There are several reasons for this
difference in alcohol metabolism. In general, a woman's body has a higher
ratio of fat-to-water composition. Women who use oral contraceptives
show slower rates of alcohol metabolism. Recent research has also identified gender differences in the stomach's capacity to oxidize alcohol.[65]

Heavy alcohol consumption also has been linked to osteoporosis (more common in women than in men)[66] and reproductive difficulties (e.g., infertility, amenorrhea, failure to ovulate, dysfunction in the post-ovulation phase of the menstrual cycle, pathologic ovary changes, premenstrual syndrome, and early menopause). However, the reasons for these links are not known.[67]

Research indicates that the chronic female drinker not only has a decrease in sexual functioning, but she also experiences serious sexual dysfunction. Researchers also have found relationships between alcoholism among women and sexual dysfunction, including high rates of anorgasm. The studies do not usually identify the onset of sexual dysfunction in terms of progression of the woman's alcoholism.

The remainder of this section (2.3.1) summarizes information on sexually transmitted diseases (STDs) and tuberculosis (TB) among women, as they relate to substance abuse.

2.3.1.1   Sexually Transmitted Diseases

STDs have a particularly significant impact on women who suffer more frequent and severe long-term consequences than men.

STDs have a particularly significant impact on women who "suffer more frequent and severe long-term consequences than men...because women tend to show fewer symptoms and as a consequence they go untreated for longer periods of time."[68] STDs are of particular concern with respect to pregnant women because the "transmission of an STD to an unborn child or during childbirth can have devastating effects."[69]

During the 1980s, reported rates of primary and secondary syphilis for both genders increased dramatically in the United States, from 13.7/100,000 population in 1981 to 20.3/100,000 in 1990.[70] In 1991, the rate began to decline; in that year, it was 17.3/100,000 and in 1992 it fell

Figure 8

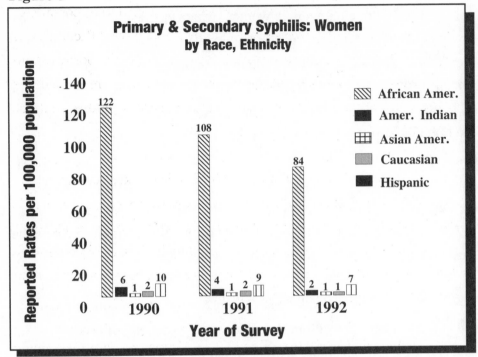

Sexually Transmitted Disease Surveillance 1992, 166-167.

again to 13.7/100,000. The rate of primary and secondary syphilis among women was 17.5, 15.4 and 12.2/100,000 in 1990, 1991 and 1992, respectively.[71] However, the rates for Caucasian women were far lower than those for African American, Hispanic, and American Indian women in the same years, as Figure 8 shows.

While the rate of gonorrhea among women decreased from 247.1/100,000 in 1988 to 175.5/100,000 in 1992, it is still a disturbing incidence. Moreover, as for syphilis, the race/ethnic differences are significant. For example, in 1992, the most recent year for which race/ethnic data are disaggregated for women, the rates per 100,000 population were: 43.0 for Caucasian women, 1,130.8 for African American women, 119.6 for American Indian women, 26.6 for Asian American women, and 92.5 for Hispanic women.[72]

The rate of chlamydia in women, which can result in serious reproductive track complications such as pelvic inflammatory disease, infertility,
and ectopic pregnancy, more than doubled in the five year period from
1988 to 1992, from 133.5/100,000 to 270.0/100,000.[73] The rate of congenital syphilis among infants less than one year of age increased from 3.0/
100,000 live births in 1980 to 44.7/100,000 in 1990.[74] The rate more than
doubled from 1989 to 1990 (to 91.0/100,000 live births),[75] although this is
reportedly in large part a result of a change in the case definition used by
the Centers for Disease Control and Prevention (CDC). After increasing to
107.5/100,000 live births in 1991, the rate of this STD, which is among the
most prevalent, decreased to 94.7/100,000 in 1992.[76]

An important consideration for prevention and treatment programs
is that STD rates differ significantly by geographic area of the country. In
New York City, for example, a 500 percent increase in reported congenital
syphilis was reported between 1986 and 1988.[77] Data are not generally
available on the incidence of STDs among women who abuse alcohol or
other drugs.

AIDS was the second leading cause of death for American women
between the ages of 25 and 44 in 1992,[78] and women constitute nearly 12
percent of cumulative diagnosed cases of AIDS.[79] According to the CDC,
as of March 1993, 32,477 women (11 percent of the total diagnosed cases)
have AIDS. More than 100,000 women are infected with HIV.[80] CDC
reports indicate that 75 percent of women and 80 percent of children with
AIDS are members of a racial or ethnic minority population. More than
half of women diagnosed with AIDS are African American (53 percent),
and 20 percent are Hispanic. Of pediatric cases, 55 percent are African
American, and 24 percent are Hispanic.[81]

Although HIV infection is a major health problem for women, many cases may be undiagnosed by physicians because they are unaware of the signs and symptoms in women. The 1992 change in the case definition of AIDS, which broadened the scope of opportunistic infections associated with AIDS, has been an important factor in recognizing the disease's impact on women. However, death rates among women who are HIV-positive are higher than those for men, perhaps because of late clinical identification of HIV infection. It should also be noted that the adverse effects of chronic alcohol use on the immune system may increase rates of progression from HIV to AIDS in women.[82] Since many women die before an HIV diagnosis is made, the numbers of women with HIV may be considerably higher than those reported.

Women who inject drugs and/or who have been the sexual partners of past and present injection drug users are at greatest risk for HIV infection. Nearly half of women with AIDS (49 percent) inject drugs. An additional 21 percent are sexual partners of injection drug users. Of the pediatric cases, 39 percent result from a mother's injection drug use and 17 percent from the mother having had sex with a partner who injected drugs.[83]

Women who inject drugs and/or who have been the sexual partners of past and present injection drug users are at greatest risk for HIV infection.

Although the public health community has concentrated on the relationship between injection drug use and HIV, there is growing evidence of a need to recognize the relationship between the use of any mind-altering substance and high-risk sexual activity. For example, one study in Florida reported a strong relationship among the number of sexual partners, drug use, condom use, and HIV-seropositivity.[84] Among the 50 drug users in the study, only one was injecting drugs. Ninety-seven percent were current users of crack, and, for the group as a whole, about 50 percent had either HIV or AIDS. In fact, numerous recent studies suggest that women who use crack cocaine may be at equal or greater risk for HIV and other

STDs than injection drug users. Accumulating evidence links increases in syphilis rates and HIV infection to the crack cocaine epidemic and indicates that crack cocaine users have significantly higher rates of STDs than nonusers.[85] According to Sterk and Elifson, for example, women who use crack cocaine may have a higher rate of sexual encounters, are more likely to engage in unsafe sex than women who use other drugs, and may trade sexual favors or engage in prostitution to obtain drugs.[86] These women are also more likely to contract STDs, which are linked with high HIV infection rates.

A woman who uses any mind-altering drug (including alcohol) can be at risk for STDs.

A woman who uses any mind-altering drug (including alcohol) can be at risk for STDs (as well as HIV and unwanted pregnancy) because her inhibitions are eased and her decision-making ability is altered. Even if she would otherwise intend to refrain from risk-taking behavior (e.g., multiple partners or unprotected sex), she might engage in such behavior while under the influence of alcohol, crack cocaine, cocaine, marijuana, or other drugs. Moreover, the compulsive use of drugs may increase a woman's risk for STDs if she engages in sex for drugs or for money to buy drugs.

2.3.1.2   Tuberculosis

Cases of tuberculosis (TB), once considered nearly eradicated in the United States, are increasing at an alarming rate for the population overall. According to the CDC, nearly 9,000 women, most between the ages of 25 and 44, were reported with verified cases of TB in 1993. African American women have the highest rates of TB followed by Asian American and Hispanic women.[87] Foreign-born women, who account for nearly one-third of reported TB cases are disproportionately represented. Women with HIV infection and homeless women are at especially high risk for contracting TB. Furthermore, injection drug users have higher rates of TB whether or not they are HIV-positive.[88]

2.3.2 Psychological Effects

The term "dual diagnosis" is applied most often to the co-occurrence with substance abuse of major psychiatric disorders; in women, these are usually depression, anxiety, and other mood disorders. It is important to note that women addicted to alcohol and/or other drugs may, early in the recovery process, present with symptoms of depression, anxiety, and mood disorders. These may be temporary conditions associated with withdrawal symptoms. For clients with bipolar affective disorder, appropriate use of lithium has not been found to interfere with recovery from addiction to alcohol or other drugs.

The concept of dual diagnosis is controversial. This controversy has been fueled by the way alcoholism treatment specialists and mental health providers perceive and treat substance abuse problems. The problem has been exacerbated by a lack of understanding of the nature of co-occurring disorders by many physicians who have prescribed sedatives/hypnotics or tranquilizers to women already experiencing alcohol and other drug problems.[89] Practitioners in both fields are now recognizing that substance abuse and mental health problems often coexist and must be addressed simultaneously, with particular interest "in the relationships between specific psychiatric syndromes and alcohol problems, primarily depression and antisocial personality disorder."[90] Clinical researchers distinguish "between those persons with an alcohol problem who were found to have a preexisting psychiatric condition and those whose psychiatric problem emerged subsequent to the onset of heavy drinking."[91] This distinction is important because in the latter group, many symptoms (especially anxiety and depression) clear within a month of cessation of drinking. Research has documented the rate and pattern of improvement: For those with a primary psychiatric disorder, improvement will be slower and will depend on effectively addressing this disorder.

Substance abuse and mental health problems often coexist and must be addressed simultaneously.

There has been little research to determine the prevalence of dual diagnosis among women. The data that does exist indicate that dual diagnosis is prevalent in the total population. For example, the 1980-1982 National Institute of Mental Health (NIMH)-sponsored Epidemiologic Catchment Area (ECA) survey of more than 20,000 adults in five communities within the United States found that more than 34 percent of the respondents had experienced a form of mental illness or chemical dependency at some time during their lives.[92] Approximately 23 percent of the respondents indicated a history of psychiatric problems, and 16 percent had a substance abuse disorder. These findings suggest that a significant number of those surveyed had two or more conditions. Approximately three out of ten individuals in the survey reporting a psychiatric illness were diagnosed as also having a substance abuse disorder at some time during their lives.[93]

Blume's 1990 discussion of Helzer's and Prybeck's analysis of the ECA concurs with Daley's findings and adds information specific to co-occurring disorders among women. According to Blume, "65 percent of female alcoholics, compared with 44 percent of males, had a second diagnosis."[94] Thirty-one percent of the women with an alcohol diagnosis had drug abuse or dependence as a co-occurring disorder, while men with an alcohol diagnosis showed a 19 percent co-occurring drug dependency.[95] Significantly, Blume also reports that not only were women with alcohol diagnoses more likely than men with alcohol diagnoses to have alcohol-related co-occurring disorders, but there were differences in the types of second diagnoses present. For women, major depression co-occurred in 19 percent (almost four times the rate for men); phobic disorder was diagnosed in 31 percent (more than twice the rate for men); and panic disorder occurred in 7 percent of the women (three and one-half times the occurrences in men). In comparing the rates of mental disorders in women with alcohol-related diagnosis to women in the general population, the rates of these second diagnoses were considerably higher in the former group (e.g., the major depression rate was nearly triple that of the general female population, the rate for phobias was nearly double, and antisocial personality occurred in 10 percent of women with an alcohol-related diagnosis, which was an astounding 12 times higher than the rate in the general population of women).[96]

2.4   Population Cohorts

This section of the manual presents summary epidemiologic data on several groups of women: older women, pregnant and postpartum women, women in the criminal justice system, homeless women, lesbians, women with disabilities, African American women, American Indian women, Asian and Pacific Islander women, and Hispanic/Latina women. It should be noted that additional information relevant to these population groups is presented in chapters 4, 5, and 6.

2.4.1   Older Women

In this manual, an "older" person is defined as a person 65 or older. Women in this age group who abuse substances have not been the subject of many research studies. The Food and Drug Administration has rarely included older women in studies evaluating medications, nor have drug companies included such women in their clinical trials,[97] in spite of the increasing awareness of the problem of substance abuse among the elderly and the consequent health and socioeconomic problems.[98]

Older people are the most frequent users of prescription medications, accounting for approximately 25 percent of all prescriptions filled, although they comprise only 12 percent of the total U.S. population according to the 1990 census.[99]

The types of drugs that generate the most substance abuse problems in older people are analgesics and benzodiazepine tranquilizers, such as Valium, which usually are prescribed for conditions of chronic pain and/or chronic depression and anxiety. Slow metabolism of a psychoactive drug can lead to interactions with alcohol that can continue for several days after the most recent consumption of the drug.[100]

Variations exist in prescribed drug use among racial/ethnic minority groups. For example, Hispanic women older than 60 years use Valium, Librium, and Tranxene more than do other women in this age group and use these drugs for longer periods and with greater frequency. However, African American women over 60 years of age report little use of psychotropic medications of any kind, in comparison with Caucasian and other women.[101] Access to health care providers who may prescribe drugs is a possible factor in this difference.

The alcohol-related cost of hospital care for the elderly was estimated at $60 billion in 1990.

An estimated 2.5 million older Americans have alcohol-related problems. Studies have shown that 21 percent of hospitalized patients over 60 who are hospitalized have a diagnosis of alcoholism. The alcohol-related cost of hospital care for the elderly was estimated at $60 billion in 1990. Of the 30,916 older Americans whose deaths in 1985 were attributed to alcohol abuse, each theoretically shortened her or his life by ten years. In addition to the loss in human terms, this translates into a productivity loss of $624 million.[102]

Research consistently indicates that alcohol consumption decreases among persons in their 60s. However, this conclusion is largely based on cross-sectional studies that compare the drinking patterns of different age groups at a given point in time. This research method often does not account for the cultural and other influences on differences in drinking attitudes and behaviors that may be present within the various groups studied. It is possible that longitudinal and cohort analyses would result in different findings with respect to alcohol consumption patterns among older Americans.[103]

2.4.2 Pregnant and Postpartum Women

Pregnant and postpartum women who use alcohol and other drugs are at risk for dangers to the fetus, HIV infection, STDs, forms of hepatitis, tuberculosis, deteriorating general health, and, in many cases, of becoming victims of violence. Specific adverse effects of maternal use of drugs during pregnancy place the fetus of the pregnant substance-abusing woman at risk for problems, including low birth weight, small head circumference, prematurity, and a variety of other medical and developmental complications. However, in the case of illegal drugs, evidence is not sufficiently broad or consistent to identify with certainty which drugs produce which effects at what levels. Nor is there evidence to untangle the environmental factors (such as poor nutrition, poverty, and lack of access to prenatal care) from substance abuse-related factors and focus on them as determinants of these problems.

More is known about the effects of alcohol consumption than about the effects of illegal drugs on pregnant women. Researchers have estimated that between 20 percent[104] and 73 percent[105] of women consume alcohol during pregnancy, although research indicates that there is no known safe level of alcohol consumption during pregnancy, or any "safe" period of gestation in which alcohol can be consumed.

Alcohol abuse during pregnancy can produce a child with Fetal Alcohol Syndrome (FAS) or Fetal Alcohol Effects (FAE), or one with low birthweight, or physical, cognitive, or behavior disabilities. The rate of FAS was 0.40/1,000 live births in 1990, nearly four times the rate in 1980. Although the National Center for Health Statistics reports improved diag-

Figure 9

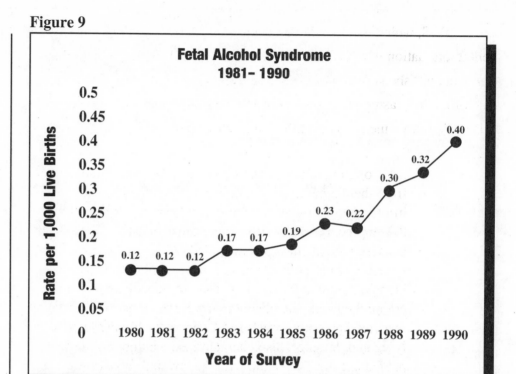

Health United States 1991, 89.

nostic and assessment techniques using the new FAS International Classifications of Diseases code for FAS, these new techniques alone would not
account for the growth in the FAS rate, which more than doubled in the
five-year period from 1985 to 1990 (see Figure 9).

Although biomedical scientists have linked alcohol use with gestational problems since at least 1899, FAS was not formally described until
1973. Clarren has summarized the clinical features of FAS:[106]

- prenatal and postnatal growth deficiency;

- central nervous system dysfunction;

- a pattern of deformed facial characteristis; and

- major organ system malformations.

FAS, which is preventable, is now considered a leading cause of mental retardation in the United States.[107] Not until 1991 was comprehensive data published concerning adolescent girls and adults with FAS, in spite of the increasing prevalence of FAS. In their report on 61 adolescent girls and adult women, Streissguth, et al., found that:

> ...although mental retardation is not necessarily predictable from the diagnoses alone, major psychosocial problems and life-long adjustment problems were characteristic....The development and cognitive handicaps persist as long in life as these patients have been studied. None of these patients were known to be independent in terms of both housing and income....Attentional deficits and problems with judgment, comprehension, and abstraction were the most frequently reported behavior problems....Conduct problems, such as lying and defiance, also characterized a number of these patients. Data on trouble with the law and substance abuse were not systematically obtained.... [108]

In another study of 92 adolescent girls and adult women with FAS, 36 percent of the patients reported having current or past experience with alcohol abuse, and 25 percent reported past abuse of other drugs.[109] While no specific data are provided in the paper reporting this study, the authors indicate that "males abused alcohol at a higher rate than females." It is important for treatment program personnel to recognize that when adolescent girls and adult women with FAS present for treatment, they have particular issues that must be addressed by both medical and mental health personnel.

Use of cocaine, heroin, methadone, and other drugs during pregnancy is widespread, but experts know less about this type of abuse. However, some direct data are available concerning cocaine use during pregnancy. According to Clark and Weinstein, "reported prevalence of use [of cocaine] rates among pregnant women in large urban teaching hospitals

FAS, which is preventable, is now considered a leading cause of mental retardation in the United States.

range from 8 to 15 percent, although frequency of use during pregnancy varies considerably."[110] In 1992, according to the SAMHSA Household Survey, an estimated 329,000 women 18 to 34 (the age group with the highest birth rates) or 1 percent of respondents in this age group, had used cocaine in the previous month, and 87,000 had used crack.[111] Data regarding women's use of heroin are not available by age group.

Researchers estimate that each year 375,000 newborns are exposed perinatally to at least one illegal drug, with significant consequences.

Only one national survey of prenatal exposure to illicit drugs has been conducted. According to that survey of 50 hospitals, an average of 11 percent of pregnant women were abusing illegal substances, with cocaine or crack as the drug of choice in 75 percent of the cases.[112] Using these data, researchers estimate that each year 375,000 newborns are exposed perinatally to at least one illegal drug,[113] with significant consequences. For example, low birthweight has been repeatedly associated with the use of heroin and methadone.[114] Heroin has also been shown to produce severe ill effects in prenatally exposed children.

In an investigation of cocaine, Chasnoff, et al., found that the infants of cocaine-abusing mothers (with or without other drugs) had significantly lower birthweights, increased prematurity, and increased incidence of intro-uterine growth retardation (IUGR) and abruptio placentae than infants of non-drug using mothers.[116] The findings of increased IUGR, prematurity, and low birthweight have been supported by other studies. [117] [118]

Although more studies of the epidemiology of drug abuse among pregnant women are clearly warranted, the growing evidence on adverse birth outcomes strongly suggests that illicit drug use contributes to high rates of infant mortality, Sudden Infant Death Syndrome (SIDS), and mental retardation. Anecdotal reports indicate that the problem may be getting worse, at least in some areas. In the District of Columbia, a sharp rise in infant mortality between 1987 and 1988—from 19.6 to 23.2—has been attributed to increased crack use among pregnant women.[119]

2.4.3 Women in the Criminal Justice System

In the past, women in the criminal justice system who had substance abuse problems received very little attention because their numbers were few and they typically served short sentences. In the last decade, however, the increased incarceration of women has shifted the focus to, at a minimum, understanding why more women are in the criminal justice system. Overall, the U.S. prison population has increased 250 percent since 1980 (from 329,821 in 1980 to 823,414 in 1991).[120] As of the end of 1991, 47,691 of the total federal and state prisoners were women.[121] The growth in the rate of women in the prison population exceeded that of men in the prison population at the state level in the 1980s, increasing 202 percent for women as compared to 112 percent for men.[122]

The major reasons for the increase in incarceration of women have been the national crisis regarding alcohol and other drug problems and the advent of mandatory minimum sentences for most drug offenses. In 1981, approximately 8 percent of state prisoners were serving sentences for drug offenses. By 1989, that number had increased to almost 30 percent.[123] Drug offenses at the federal level showed a similar increase during the 1980s, from 22 percent of all admissions to 55 percent.[124]

The major reasons for the increase in incarceration of women have been the national crisis regarding alcohol and other drug problems.

The Bureau of Justice Statistics, in a 1989 survey of inmates in local jails, collected data from interviews in a nationally representative sample of 5,675 inmates in 424 jails, updating data from a similar survey conducted in 1983.[125] These data provide this profile of incarcerated women: In 1989, more than one in three female inmates were in jail for a drug offense, an increase from one in eight in 1983. Among all convicted female inmates, nearly 40 percent reported that they had committed their offense under the influence of drugs. More than half of convicted female inmates had used drugs in the month prior to the current offense, and approximately 40 percent had used drugs daily. These drugs included heroin, cocaine, or crack cocaine, LSD, PCP, and methadone. The percentage of women in jail who had used cocaine or crack cocaine in the month before their current offense more than doubled, from 15 percent in 1983 to 39 percent in 1989. The survey also found that about one in every three convicted women in jail reported they had committed their current offense for money to buy drugs. About one-fifth of all convicted women reported being under the influence of alcohol at the time of the offense, compared to more than 44 percent of convicted men.

Nearly two-thirds of the women in this study had grown up in a household with no parents or only one parent present: 40 percent in a single-parent household and 17 percent in a household without either parent. Almost one-third of all women in jail had a parent or guardian who had abused alcohol or other drugs. About 44 percent of the women reported that they had been either physically or sexually abused at some time in their lives before their current imprisonment.

In a 1992 study of major cities, the Sentencing Project showed that women's drug use is escalating, the severity of women's criminal activity is rising, and their recidivism rates are increasing. Women are being arrested at a much higher rate, and urinalysis testing indicates that their use of chemicals is increasing rapidly. Yet a very limited number of resources and comprehensive treatment efforts within the criminal justice system focus on women, most of whom are mothers, and their children.[126]

2.4.4 Homeless Women

Homeless women represent a highly vulnerable group who engage in at-risk behaviors and develop health-related disorders at a rate greater than that of women in the general population.

Homeless women represent a highly vulnerable group who engage in at-risk behaviors and develop health-related disorders at a rate greater than that of women in the general population. Their children often suffer from a wide range of medical problems, do poorly in school, manifest delays in cognitive and other development, and display behavioral or emotional problems.[127]

Markers of the lifetime prevalence rates of alcohol abuse-related disorders among homeless women have ranged from 10 to 37 percent, with the most recent research indicating a 30 percent lifetime prevalence rate, compared with 5 percent for women in the general population. While alcohol problems are more common among homeless men than homeless women, this gender difference is far less than among men and women who are not homeless.[128]

In contrast to homeless women who are not mothers, homeless mothers are much less likely to suffer from alcohol disorders (40 percent of homeless women without children versus 23 percent of homeless mothers). Homeless mothers are also less likely to be told that they have a drinking problem (31 percent versus 5 percent) than homeless women without children. Three studies have documented an approximate 8 to 10 percent lifetime prevalence rate of alcohol problems in homeless mothers, but the numbers are likely underestimated as are any estimates of health and other problems of the homeless.[129] Reports of lifetime prevalence of problems with drugs other than alcohol among homeless women have varied from 9 to 32 percent as compared to the lifetime rate of 5 percent in the general female population. By contrast, homeless mothers have an estimated lifetime 9 to 12 percent prevalence rate of substance abuse. Anecdotal reports from service providers suggest that growing numbers of homeless mothers are abusing not only alcohol but crack cocaine.[130]

Adverse pregnancy outcomes (miscarriages, low birthweight, and infant mortality) are more likely in homeless women with substance abuse problems because they are usually poorly nourished and have limited access to prenatal health care and substance abuse treatment services. In one comparative study of homeless women in New York City, 39 percent of pregnant homeless women were found to have received no prenatal care, compared to only 14 percent of low-income women living in public housing communities, and 9 percent of the general population.[131]

While women who abuse alcohol and other drugs frequently experience depression and anxiety, homeless women are likely to exhibit more profound levels of these disorders. Unfortunately there are no recent data available on this subject.

2.4.5   Lesbian Women

According to Underhill's review of the limited research data available, an estimated 25 to 35 percent of lesbians have "serious problems with alcohol."[132] A 1987 national survey of lesbians found that 16 percent of lesbians believed that they had a problem with alcohol, 14 percent used marijuana several times a week (33 percent used it several times a month), and 8 percent used stimulants in the past year.[133] These rates are much higher than for women as a whole. The results of the 1988 NIDA Household Survey found that 2 percent of female respondents used marijuana once a week or more, and 2.2 percent of female respondents engaged in nonmedical use of stimulants in the past year.[134] Lesbians also engage in polydrug use at high rates. Although the data are relatively old, a 1978 study found that 60 percent of lesbians used alcohol in combination with marijuana or amphetamines, hallucinogens, and barbiturates.[135] In spite of these relatively high rates of substance abuse, few treatment programs target lesbians or even have services that address their particular needs.

Lesbians experience most risk factors common to other women but also must cope with the effects of stigma, denial, alienation, self-doubt, guilt, and discrimination. These factors can take a heavy toll on the self-esteem of lesbians and make it difficult for them to meet their needs for affiliation.[136] The relative lack of treatment services responsive to the needs of lesbians and women in general is also a factor in the relatively high rates of alcoholism in this population. Not only are there few programs that conduct outreach to lesbians, few hold meetings or therapy sessions designed to meet their needs, and few have staff trained to address the needs of lesbians.[137]

Although epidemiologic data are not available regarding substance abuse by adolescent lesbians, the recent report of the Department of Health and Human Services Secretary's Task Force on Youth Suicide indicates that lesbian adolescents begin to use drugs to reduce anxiety and pain when they become aware of their sexual orientation. Therefore, outreach, early intervention, and treatment are critical.[138]

2.4.6 Women with Disabilities

The Americans with Disabilities Act (ADA), the landmark civil rights act for people with disabilities, notes that 43 million Americans have some type of disability.[139] These include persons with physical health, sensory, learning, intellectual, or mental disabilities.

While data on the prevalence of alcohol and other drug problems among women with disabilities are lacking, the small body of research on disability and substance abuse suggests that people with disabilities use substances at the same or higher rates than those without disabilities.[140] Women with disabilities face a similar set of risk factors as non-disabled women, including issues regarding body image, self-esteem, dependence, and sexual abuse, which in some instances are exacerbated by their disability status.[141] Another risk factor for women with disabilities is easy access to substances prescribed for pain or other aspects of the disability, as well as the compounding, often dangerous effects of prescription medication used in combination with alcohol and other drugs.[142]

2.4.7 African American Women

African American women suffer disproportionately from the health consequences of alcoholism, including cancer, obstructive pulmonary disease, severe malnutrition, hypertension, and birth defects.

In 1991, there were 15.8 million African American women in the United States: 6 percent of the total population.[143] As with other populations, alcohol is the most commonly abused substance among African American women and represents a health problem of significant proportions. According to a 1987 NIAAA report, African American women suffer disproportionately from the health consequences of alcoholism, including cancer, obstructive pulmonary disease, severe malnutrition, hypertension, and birth defects.[144]

Alcoholism was cited as a factor in the declining health status of African Americans in the 1991 report on the Health Status of Minority and Low Income Populations.[145] Death rates from chronic liver disease and cirrhosis are twice as high for African Americans of both sexes as for Caucasians. Among women aged 15 to 34, cirrhosis rates for African American women are six times higher than those for Caucasian women,[146] and the risk of FAS is seven times higher for African American infants than for Caucasian infants.[147]

The available data suggest that, while alcohol use begins later among African Americans than among Caucasians, the onset of alcohol-related problems appears earlier among African Americans.[148] However, there are few differences in reported heavy alcohol use by African American and Caucasian women. In 1985, both groups of women were equally likely to be heavy drinkers (9 percent of respondents). In 1988, 7 percent of Caucasian women and 6 percent of African American women reported being heavy drinkers.[149]

Patterns of drug use (other than alcohol) among African American women, as reflected in studies of women in treatment, indicate that they are more likely than other women in treatment to use opiates. A survey of treatment program data in 1980 showed that 70 percent of African Americans in treatment used opiates compared with 65 percent of Hispanics and 35 percent of Caucasians. African American women who use opiates enter treatment earlier than African American men and are more motivated by specific health problems.[150] In the past, African American women were less likely to engage in nonmedical use of psychotropic drugs than Caucasian or Hispanic women, but in 1992, according to the SAMHSA Survey, they were as likely to do so. African American women's reported use of cocaine in the previous month increased slightly between 1988 and 1992 (.5 percent to .6 percent of respondents), in contrast with Caucasian and Hispanic women whose reported use decreased (see Figure 6).

2.4.8 American Indian Women

According to the 1990 census, there were 992,000 American Indian women in the United States.[151] Alcoholism is the predominant health problem for American Indian women in what has been described as a "triad" that includes violence and depression. The rates of these problems have increased significantly for this population since 1970.[152] Fleming has reported that American Indian youth (including girls) "become involved with alcohol at an earlier age, consume alcohol more frequently and in greater quantities, and suffer greater negative consequences" than Caucasian women.[153] Fleming also noted that, as of 1985, alcoholism was the fifth most frequent cause of death among American Indian women.[154]

In all age groups, the alcohol-related mortality rates were significantly higher for American Indian women than for other women; for example, for the age group 45 to 54, the rate for American Indian women was 48.3/1,000,000, while for women of all other races it was 8.4, and for all other races other than Caucasian it was 14.9.[155] The FAS rate among American Indian populations is reportedly as high as 1 in 50, significantly higher than that of the general population of women.[156] As with Asian

In all age groups, the alcohol-related mortality rates were significantly higher for American Indian women than for other women.

American women, data concerning use and abuse of other drugs are scarce, in part because the SAMHSA Survey and the NIDA-sponsored High School Survey do not present disaggregated data for this population. There is minimal data available on Alaskan Native women.

2.4.9   Asian and Pacific Islander Women

The term "Asian and Pacific Islanders" is often misunderstood as describing a homogeneous ethnic group. In reality, this label represents more than 60 different Asian and Pacific Islander groups, each with distinct cultural, language, and ethnic identities. Asian Americans have emigrated from countries and cultures as diverse as Japan, China, Vietnam, Cambodia, Thailand, Korea, India, and the Philippines. As of 1990, 3.7 million American women of Asian or Pacific Island origin—a 108 percent increase over the 1980 census—were American citizens.[157]

There have been only a few studies of alcohol and other drug use among Asian Americans and these studies have focused on Asian Americans in California and Hawaii.[158] However, the prevalence of alcohol and drug use among Asian American women is believed to be relatively low,[159] and to vary considerably by acculturation status. For example, the Institute of Medicine study of alcohol use found a strong influence of traditional cultures:

> There is a significantly lower prevalence of alcohol use and abuse by females [among Asian American populations] until they acculturate over several generations. Even then, the prevalence rates may be lower than those found among Caucasian females.[160]

The low prevalence of alcohol and other drug use by Asian American women is related to strong cultural traditions, several of which were described by Sun in 1990:

•   the traditional emphasis on family versus individualism;

•   the more restrictive definition of the female role; and

•   the predominant belief systems—Confucianism and Taoism stress and advocate the concept of moderation.[161]

For example, in a study of 125 female Koreans in Los Angeles, only one woman was classified as a heavy drinker, and 75 percent reported being abstainers.[162] However, as Sun notes, the low prevalence rates "could very well be due to the low reporting of alcohol and drug use or the low utilization of professional mental health and social services among Asian American women."[163] Moreover, the length of time that an individual Asian American has been in the U.S. and that there has been a wave of immigration from the country of origin, (e.g., Chinese vs. Cambodian patterns of immigration) has not been addressed in the research. Neither the NHSDA nor the NIDA-sponsored High School Survey—the two most important sources of national population data on alcohol and other drug use—present data for Asian American populations because the sample size was insufficient to do so.

2.4.10 Hispanic/Latina Women

Because most of the data regarding this ethnic group refers to "Hispanics" rather than Latinas, the former term is used in this chapter, which presents primarily epidemiological data. In the remainder of the manual, the term Hispanics/Latina is used to account for the full range of populations of Hispanic and Latin origin. As with other populations (including female Caucasians), it is important to note that:

> ...the population is not a unitary ethnic group. On the contrary, this group is quite heterogeneous, composed of "subgroups that vary by Latin American national origin, [race], generational status in the United States, and socio-

economic level." The second is that, "although there are commonalities that have been well summarized in the literature ... many of these cultural attributes are continually undergoing modification as a result of acculturation."[164]

Hispanic Americans are among the fastest growing ethnic groups in the United States. From 1980 to 1990, their numbers increased 53 percent, compared to an increase of 9.8 percent for the rest of the population.[165] In 1990, just under 11 million Hispanic/Latina women lived in the United States, 4.4 percent of the total population.[166] The largest defined subgroup of Americans is Mexican American (54 percent), and the second largest subgroup is Puerto Rican (35 percent).[167] The total population of Hispanics/Latinas was 22 million or 9 percent of the total population. Importantly, the Hispanic/Latina population is one of the United States' youngest: 38.7 percent of this ethnic group were age 19 or under in 1990, compared with 26.7 percent of Caucasians and 32.2 percent of Asian Americans. Only American Indians in general were a younger population, with 39.3 percent 19 or younger.[168]

According to data derived from the NHSDA, Hispanic Americans were slightly more likely to have reported the use of illicit drugs in the month before the survey than were Caucasian women (5.0 percent versus 4.7 percent). They were much more likely to have used cocaine specifically (1.2 percent versus 0.4 percent). However, Hispanic women were less likely to have consumed alcohol once a week or more than were their Caucasian counterparts: 9.2 percent versus 14.4 percent.[169] Reported use of inhalants by Hispanic/Latina women increased from .3 percent of respondents in 1988 to .5 percent in 1992, from an estimated 25,000 to 39,000. The increase for Caucasian women was smaller (.2 percent to .3 percent).[170]

Although Hispanic women do not have the same disproportionately high rates of infant mortality or low birthweight babies as African American and American Indian women, they do have high rates of diabetes. This condition, which is also a complicating factor with alcohol abuse, contributes to infant morbidity, including developmental disabilities.

According to the Center for Substance Abuse Prevention (CSAP), there are important differences among Hispanic American adolescents by subgroup. Although these data are not disaggregated by gender, they are important to consider in the treatment of adolescent Hispanic girls. "In the NHSDA [National Household Survey on Drug Abuse] data, Hispanics/Latinos in this [12 - 17] age bracket had rates of lifetime use of cocaine higher than those for white or Blacks; these rates were highest among Puerto Ricans and Cubans, while Mexican Americans' use rate was lower than all other groups. Regarding marijuana use, Mexican Americans had higher rates than Puerto Ricans; in comparing Hispanic-subHANES (Health and Nutrition Examination Survey) to NHSDA data specifically on marijuana use, it appears that the rate for Mexican Americans surpasses that for non-whites."[171]

Although Hispanic women do not have the same disproportionately high rates of infant mortality or low birthweight babies as African American and American Indian women, they do have high rates of diabetes.

References

1.   Substance Abuse and Mental Health Services Administration. (1993).
        National Household Survey on Drug Abuse: Population Estimates 1992.
        Rockville, MD, 10.

2.   Substance Abuse and Mental Health Services Administration. (1993).
        National Household Survey on Drug Abuse: Preliminary Estimates
        1992. Rockville, MD, 19.

3.   National Household Survey on Drug Abuse: Population Estimates 1992,
        55.

4.   National Household Survey on Drug Abuse: Population Estimates 1992,
        31.

5.   National Household Survey on Drug Abuse: Population Estimates 1992,
        37.

6.   National Center for Health Statistics. (1993). Health United States:
        1992. Hyattsville, Maryland: Department of Health and Human Ser-
        vices, Public Health Service, 46.

7.   Health United States: 1992, 50-51.

8.   Calculated based on data derived from: Health United States: 1992, 21
        and 314.

9.   Health United States: 1992, 92.

10.   Substance Abuse and Mental Health Services Administration. (1993).
        Estimates from the Drug Abuse Warning Network (DAWN): 1992
        Estimates of Drug-related Emergency Room Episodes; Advanced Report
        # 4. Rockville, MD.

11.   ibid.

12.   National Household Survey on Drug Abuse: Preliminary Estimates
        1992, 9.

13.   National Institute on Alcohol Abuse and Alcoholism. (1993). Eighth
        Special Report to the U.S. Congress on Alcohol and Health. Rockville,
        MD: U.S. Department of Health and Human Services Public Health
        Service, 9.

14.   Calculated based on Eighth Special Report to the U.S. Congress on
       Alcohol and Health, 9 and population data derived from: U.S. Depart-
       ment of Commerce, Economics and Statistics Administration, Bureau of
       the Census. (1991) Statistical Abstract of the United States 1992, 18.

15.   National Institute on Alcohol Abuse and Alcoholism. (1993). Eighth
       Special Report to the U.S. Congress on Alcohol and Health. Rockville,
       MD: U.S. Department of Health and Human Services Public Health
       Service, 17.

16.   U.S. Department of Health and Human Services, Public Health Service.
       (1990). Seventh Special Report to the U.S. Congress on Alcohol and
       Health from the Secretary of Health and Human Services, January,
       1990. Rockville, MD: Alcohol, Drug Abuse and Mental Health Admin-
       istration, xxi.

17.   ibid.

18.   Calculated based on data derived from National Household Survey on
       Drug Abuse: Preliminary Estimates 1992, 10, and National Household
       Survey: Population Estimates 1992, 13.

19.   National Household Survey on Drug Abuse: Population Estimates
       1992, 121.

20.   National Household Survey on Drug Abuse: Population Estimates
       1992, 19.

21.   National Household Survey on Drug Abuse: Population Estimates
       1992, 122-123.

22.   See for example Ross, H. E. (1989). Alcohol and Drug Abuse in
       Treated Alcoholics: A Comparison of Men and Women. Alcoholism:
       Clinical and Experimental Research 13 (6), 815.

23.   National Household Survey on Drug Abuse: Population Estimates
       1992, 19.

24.   National Household Survey on Drug Abuse: Population Estimates
       1992, 25.

25.   National Household Survey on Drug Abuse: Population Estimates
       1992, 31.

26.   National Household Survey on Drug Abuse: Population Estimates
       1992, 37.

27.   Estimates from the Drug Abuse Warning Network (DAWN): 1992 Estimates of Drug-related Emergency Room Episodes.

28.   National Household Survey on Drug Abuse: Population Estimates 1992, 104.

29.   National Household Survey on Drug Abuse: Population Estimates 1992, 104.

30.   National Household Survey on Drug Abuse: Population Estimates 1992, 55.

31.   National Institute on Drug Abuse. (1989). National Household Survey on Drug Abuse: Population Estimates 1988. Rockville, MD: Substance Abuse and Mental Health Services Administration, 53.

32.   National Household Survey on Drug Abuse: Population Estimates 1992, 55.

33.   Matteo, S. (1988). The Risk of Multiple Addictions: Guidelines for Assessing a Woman's Alcohol and Drug Use. The Western Journal of Medicine (149), 742.

34.   Roth, P., Ed. (1991). The Model Program Guide. Alcohol and Drugs are Women's Issues, Volumes I and II. Metuchen: NJ: The Scarecrow Press, ix.

35.   Substance Abuse and Mental Health Services Administration. (1992). National Household Survey on Drug Abuse: Main Findings 1990. Rockville, MD, 129.

36.   Ross, H.E., 814.

37.   Office of National Drug Control Policy. (1992). National Drug Control Strategy: A Nation Responds to Drug Use. Washington, DC: The Government Printing Office, 58.

38.   Institute of Medicine. (1990). The Treatment of Special Populations: Overview and Definitions. In Broadening the Base of Treatment for Alcohol Problems. Washington, DC: National Academy of Sciences Press, 352.

39.   Institute of Medicine. (1990). Populations Defined by Structural Characteristics. In Broadening the Base of Treatment for Alcohol Problems, 356.

40.   U.S. Department of Health and Human Services. (1992). State
       Resources and Services Related to Alcohol and Other Drug Abuse
       Problems. Rockville, MD: National Institute on Drug Abuse and
       National Institute on Alcohol Abuse and Alcoholism, 31-32.

41.   ibid.

42.   Bigel Institute for Health Policy. (1992). Drug Services Research
       Survey: Phase II, Final Report. Waltham, MA: Brandeis University,
       Table 20.

43.   Substance Abuse and Mental Health Services Administration. (1992).
       National Household Survey on Drug Abuse: Population Estimates
       1991. Rockville, MD, 104.

44.   National Household Survey on Drug Abuse: Population Estimates
       1991, 55.

45.   The MayaTech Corporation. (1990). Evaluation of the Health Care
       Financing Administration's Alcohol Services Demonstration: The
       Medicare Experience. Silver Spring, MD: The MayaTech Corporation,
       52.

46.   General Services Branch of Alcoholics Anonymous. (1993). 1992
       Membership Survey. New York: Alcoholics Anonymous, Inc.

47.   National Household Survey on Drug Abuse: Population Estimates
       1992, 19.

48.   National Household Survey on Drug Abuse: Population Estimates
       1992, 55.

49.   National Household Survey on Drug Abuse: Preliminary Estimates
       1992, 10.

50.   National Household Survey on Drug Abuse: Population Estimates
       1992, 19.

51.   Migram, G.G. (1990). Adolescent Women. In Engs, R. C., Ed.
       Women: Alcohol and Other Drugs. Dubuque, IA: Kendall/Hunt.

52.   Health United States: 1991, 207.

53.   Department of Health and Human Services. (1993). National Survey
       Results on Drug Use from the Monitoring the Future Study, 1975-1992.
       Rockville, MD: National Institute on Drug Abuse, 12.

54.   Galbraith, S. (1991). Women and Legal Drugs. In Roth, P., Ed. Alcohol and Drugs are Women's Issues; Volume 1: A Review of the Issues. Metuchen, N. J.: Scarecrow Press, 150.

55.   Matteo, S., 742.

56.   Moise, R., Kovach, J., Reed, B., and Bellows, N. (1982). A Comparison of Black and White Women Entering Drug Abuse Treatment Programs. The International Journal of Addictions, 17(1), 46-47.

57.   Matteo, S., 742.

58.   Health United States: 1992, 56.

59.   Seventh Special Report to the U.S. Congress on Alcohol and Health from the Secretary of Health and Human Services.

60.   Seventh Special Report to the U.S. Congress, 114.

61.   Seventh Special Report to the U.S. Congress, 116.

62.   Seventh Special Report to the U.S. Congress, 117.

63.   Seventh Special Report to the U.S. Congress, 121.

64.   Seventh Special Report to the U.S. Congress, 124.

65.   Seventh Special Report to the U.S. Congress, 116.

66.   Seventh Special Report to the U.S. Congress, 117.

67.   Seventh Special Report to the U.S. Congress, 123.

68.   Center for Substance Abuse Treatment. Screening for Infectious Diseases Among Substance Abusers. U.S. Department of Health and Human Services, Public Health Service. Rockville, MD, 2.

69.   ibid.

70.   Centers for Disease Control. (1993). Sexually Transmitted Disease Surveillance 1992. Atlanta, GA: U.S. Department of Health and Human Services Public Health Service, 140.

71.   Centers for Disease Control. (1993). Sexually Transmitted Disease Surveillance 1992. Atlanta, GA: U.S. Department of Health and Human Services, Public Health Service, 146.

72. Centers for Disease Control. (1993). Sexually Transmitted Disease Surveillance 1992. Atlanta, GA: U.S. Department of Health and Human Services, Public Health Service, 166-167.

73. Centers for Disease Control. (1993). Sexually Transmitted Disease Surveillance 1992. Atlanta, GA: U.S. Department of Health and Human Services, Public Health Service, 178.

74. Centers for Disease Control. (1993). Sexually Transmitted Disease Surveillance 1992. Atlanta, GA: U.S. Department of Health and Human Services, Public Health Service, 178.

75. Centers for Disease Control. (1993). Sexually Transmitted Disease Surveillance 1992. Atlanta, GA: U.S. Department of Health and Human Services, Public Health Service, 178.

76. Centers for Disease Control. (1993). Sexually Transmitted Disease Surveillance 1992. Atlanta, GA: U.S. Department of Health and Human Services, Public Health Service, 178.

77. Schultz, S., Zweis, M., Sing, T., and Hgoos, M. (1990). Congenital Syphilis: New York City 1968-1988. American Journal of Diseases of Children (144), 279.

78. Centers for Disease Control. Morbidity and Mortality Weekly Report. Nov 19, 1993, 42(45), 870.

79. Centers for Disease Control and Prevention. (1993). HIV/AIDS Surveillance Report. Atlanta, GA: Public Health Service. March, 1993, 9.

80. ibid.

81. ibid.

82. McArthur, L. (1991). Women and AIDS. In Roth, P., Ed., Alcohol and Drugs Are Women's Issues, Volume 1: A Review of the Issues. Metuchen, NJ: Scarecrow Press, 114-119.

83. HIV/AIDS Surveillance Report 1993, 9.

84. Trapido, E., Lewis, N., and Comeford, M. (1990). HIV-1 and AIDS in Belle Glade, Florida: A Re-examination of the Issues. American Behavioral Scientist (33), 451-64.

85. Inciardi, J., Lockwood, D., and Pottieger, A. (1991). Crack Dependent Women and Sexuality: Implications for STD Acquisition and Transmission. Addiction and Recovery (11) 4, 25-28.

86.   Sterk, C. and Elifson, K. (1990). Drug-related Violence and Street Prostitution. In De La Rosa, M., Lambert, E., and Gropper, B., Eds., Drugs and Violence: Causes, Correlates, and Consequences: NIDA Research Monograph (103). Rockville, MD: U.S. Department of Health and Human Services, Public Health Service, 1721.

87.   Center for Disease Control. (1994). Unpublished Data. Atlanta, GA.

88.   Centers for Disease Control. (1994). Morbidity and Mortality Weekly Report. Atlanta, GA: Public Health Service. May 27, 1994, 43(20).

89.   Mondanaro, J. (1989). Chemically Dependent Women: Assessment and Treatment. Lexington, MA: Lexington Books, 114.

90.   Institute of Medicine. (1990). Populations Defined by Functional Characteristics. In Broadening the Base of Treatment for Alcohol Problems, 385.

91.   Institute of Medicine, 386.

92.   Daley, D.C., Moss, H.B., and Campbell, F. (1993). Dual Disorders: Counseling Clients with Chemical Dependency and Mental Illness. Center City, MN: Hazelden Foundation, 1-4.

93.   ibid.

94.   Blume, S. (1990). Alcohol and Drug Problems in Women: Old Attitudes, New Knowledge. In Mikman, H.B. and L.I. Sederer, Eds., Treatment Choices for Alcoholism and Substance Abuse. New York: Lexington Books, 191. (81).

95.   ibid.

96.   ibid.

97.   Bernstein, L., Folkman, S., and Lazarus, R. (1989). Characterization of the Use and Misuse of Medications by the Elderly Ambulatory Population. Medical Care 27(6), 654-663.

98.   Among the consequences of psychotherapeutic drug abuse are suicide, compulsive use, overdose, affective and sleep disturbances, depression, and cognitive and motor impairment. See The Risk of Multiple Addictions: Guidelines for Assessing a Woman's Alcohol and Drug Use, 741-745.

99.   Abrams, R., and Alexsopoulues, G. (1987). Substance Abuse in The Elderly: Alcohol and Prescription Drugs. Hospital and Community Psychiatry (38)12, 1286.

100.   Morse, R. (1988). Substance Abuse Among the Elderly. Bulletin of
        the Menniger Clinic (52), 259-68.

101.   The Risk of Multiple Addictions: Guidelines for Assessing a Woman's
        Alcohol and Drug Use, 741-745.

102.   Select Committee on Aging, House of Representatives. (1992). Alco-
        hol Abuse and Misuse Among the Elderly. Washington, DC: Govern-
        ment Printing Office.

103.   National Institute on Alcohol Abuse and Alcoholism. (1993). Eighth
        Special Report to the U.S. Congress on Alcohol and Health from the
        Secretary of Health and Human Services. Rockville, MD: U.S.
        Department of Health and Human Services, Public Health Services. 20.

104.   Serdula, M., Williamson, D.F., Kendrick, J.S., Anda, R.F., and Byers, T.
        (1991). Trends in Alcohol Consumption by Pregnant Women: 1985
        through 1988. Journal of the American Medical Association 265(7):
        876-879.

105.   Gomby, D.S., and Shino, P.H. (1991). Estimating the number of
        substance-exposed infants. In Behreman R.E., Ed., The Future of
        Children: Drug Exposed Infant, 1(1), 36-49.

106.   Clarren, S.K. (1981). Recognition of Fetal Alcohol Syndrome.   Jour-
        nal of the American Medical Association 245 (23), 2436-2439.

107.   Streissguth, A.P., et al. (1991). Fetal Alcohol Syndrome in Adolescents
        and Adults. Journal of the American Medical Association. (265)15,
        1961-1967.

108.   ibid.

109.   LaDue, R.A., Streissguth, A.P., and Randels, S.P. (1992). Clinical
        Considerations Pertaining to Adolescents and Adults with Fetal Alcohol
        Syndrome. In Sonderegger, T., Ed., Perinatal Substance Abuse:
        Research Findings and Clinical Implications., Baltimore, MD: The
        John Hopkins University Press, 116.

110.   Clark, H.W., and Weinstein, M. (1993). Chemical Dependency. In
        Paul, M., Ed., Occupational and Environmental Hazards: A Guide for
        Clinicians. Baltimore, MD: Williams and Wikins, 350.

111.   National Household Survey on Drug Abuse: Population Estimates
        1992, 31, 37.

112.   Chasnoff, I.J. (1989). Drug Use and Women: Establishing a Standard
        of Care. New York Academy of Science (562), 208-210.

113. National Association of Perinatal Addiction Research and Education. News release. 8 Aug., 1988, Chicago, IL.

114. Zuckerman, B. (1985). Developmental Consequences of Maternal Drug Use During Pregnancy. In Pinkert T.M., Ed., and Hutchings, D.E. (1985). Prenatal Opioid Exposure and the Problem of Causal Inference. Current Research on Consequences of Maternal Drug Abuse: NIDA Research Monograph (59). Rockville, MD: Substance Abuse and Mental Health Services Administration.

115. Householder, J., et al. (1982). "Infants Born to Narcotic-Addicted Mothers." Psychology Bulletin (2)2, 453-68, and Hutchings, D.E. Prenatal Opioid Exposure and the Problem of Causal Reference. In Pinkert, T.M., Eds., Current Research on the Consequences of Maternal Drug Abuse: NIDA Research Monograph (59).

116. Chasnoff, C., MacGregor S., and Chisum, G. (1988). Cocaine Use During Pregnancy: Adverse Perinatal Outcome. In Harris, L.S., Ed., Problems of Drug Dependence 1987; NIDA Research Monograph Series (81). Rockville, MD: U.S. Department of Health and Human Services.

117. Chouteau, M., Namerow, P., and Leppert, P. (1988). The Effect of Cocaine on Birth Weight and Gestational Age. Obstetrics and Gynecology 72(3), 352-354.

118. Cherukuri, R., et al., (1988). A Cohort Study of Alkaloid Cocaine ("crack") in Pregnancy. Obstetrics and Gynecology 72(2), 147-151.

119. Abramowitz, M. (1989). Sharp Increase in D.C. Infant Deaths Attributed to Drug Abuse. Washington Post. July 21.

120. Snell, T.L., and Morton, D.C. (1992). "D.C. Prisoners in 1991." Bureau of Justice Statistics. Washington, DC: Government Printing Office.

121. ibid.

122. Greenfield, L.A. and Minor-Harper, S. (1991). "Women in Prison." Bureau of Justice Statistics Special Report, Washington, DC: Government Printing Office, 1.

123. The Bureau of Justice Statistics. (1990). Drugs and Crime Facts. Washington, DC: Government Printing Office, 1.

124. ibid.

125.   Snell, T.L. (1992). "Women in Jail." Bureau of Justice Statistics Special Report. Washington, DC, 1.

126.   Shine, C. and Mauer, M. (1993). Does the Punishment Fit the Crime? Drug Users and Drunk Drivers, Questions of Race and Class. Washington, DC: The Sentencing Project.

127.   Weinreb, L. and Rossi, P. (1991). Programs and Evaluation. Homeless Families with Children: Research Perspectives. Rockville: MD: National Institute on Alcohol Abuse and Alcoholism, 53-57.

128.   Smith, E. and North E. (1991). Substance Abuse. Homeless Families with Children: Research Perspectives. Rockville: MD: National Institute on Alcohol Abuse and Alcoholism and National Institutes of Mental Health, 43-45.

129.   ibid.

130.   ibid.

131.   Tessler, R.C. and Dennis, D.L. (1989). A Synthesis of NIMH-Funded Research Concerning Persons Who Are Homeless and Mentally Ill. Rockville, MD: National Institutes of Mental Health.

132.   Underhill, B. (1991). Recovery Needs of Lesbian Alcoholics in Treatment. In VandenBerg, N., Ed., Feminist Perspectives on Addiction. New York: Speinger Publishing, 73-84.

133.   National Gay and Lesbian Task Force. (1993). Lesbian Health Issues and Recommendations. Washington, DC: Policy Institute.

134.   National Household Survey on Drug Abuse: Population Estimates 1988, 59, 105.

135.   Glaus, K. O'H. (1988). Alcoholism, Chemical Dependency, and the Lesbian Client. Women and Therapy, A Feminist Quarterly 8(1 & 2).

136.   Finnegan, D. and McNally, E. (1990). Lesbian Women. Dubuque, IA: Kendall/Hunt.

137.   Underhill, B., 73-86.

138.   Gibson, P. (1989). Gay Male and Lesbian Youth Suicide. In Feinlab, M., Ed., Report of the Secretary's Task Force on Youth Suicide. Washington, DC: U.S. Department of Health and Human Services, 3/110-3/142.

139.   The Americans with Disabilities Act broadly defines individuals with disabilities to include 1) people with physical or mental impairments that substantially limit one or more major life activities; 2) people with histories of disability; or 3) people who are regarded by the law as having a disability. The definition excludes people who continue to abuse drugs, but includes former users as well as alcoholics. The law prohibits discrimination against people with disabilities in employment, state and local government, public accommodations, transportation, and telecommunications. Substance abuse treatment centers are covered under the law as service providers and, depending on size, as employers. Free publications such as the ADA Handbook, as well as Questions and Answers on the ADA, both published jointly by the Equal Employment Opportunity Commission and the Department of Justice, are available by writing to the Public Access Section, Civil Rights Division, P.O. Box 66738, Washington, DC 20035, or by calling (202) 514-0301.

140.   Finklestein, N., Duncan, S., Derman, L. and Smeltz, J. (1990). Getting Sober, Getting Well. Cambridge, MA.: The Women's Alcoholism Program of CASPAR, 497.

141.   Finklestein, et al., 495-6.

142.   Resource Center on Substance Abuse Prevention. (1991). An Overview of Alcohol and Other Drug Abuse Prevention and Disability. Washington, DC.

143.   U.S. Department of Commerce, Economics and Statistics Administration, Bureau of the Census. Statistical Abstract of the United States 1992, 18.

144.   Taha-Cisse, A.H. (1991). Issues for African American Women. In Roth, P., Ed., Alcohol and Drugs are Women's Issues, Volume I. Metuchen, NJ: The Scarecrow Press, 55.

145.   Health Resources and Services Administration. (1991). Health Status of Minority and Low Income Populations. Rockville, MD: U.S. Government Printing Office.

146.   ibid.

147.   ibid.

148.   Leland, J. (1984). Alcohol Use and Abuse in Ethnic Minority Women. In Wilsnak, S.C., and Beckman, L.J. Alcohol Problems in Women, Volume I. New York: Guilford Press.

149.   National Household Survey on Drug Abuse: Population Estimates 1985 and 1988.

150. Marsh, K.L. and Simpson, D.D. (1986). "Sex Differences in Opioid Addiction Careers." American Journal of Drug and Alcohol Abuse 12(4), 309-29.

151. Statistical Abstract of the United States: 1992, 18.

152. LaDue, R.A. (1990). Coyote Returns: Survival for Native American Women. In Roth, P., Ed., Alcohol and Drugs are Women's Issues, Volume I, 26.

153. Fleming, C.M. and Manson, S.M. (1990). Native American Women. In Eng, R.C., Ed., Women: Alcohol and Other Drugs. Dubuque, IA: Kendall/Hunt.

154. ibid.

155. LaDue, 26.

156. LaDue, 27.

157. Statistical Abstract of the United States 1992, 17.

158. Institute of Medicine, 368.

159. Lubben, J.E., Chi, I., and Kitano, H. (1989). The Relative Influence of Social Factors in Korean Drinking Behavior in Los Angeles. Advances in Alcohol and Substance Abuse 8(1), 1-17.

160. Institute of Medicine, 369.

161. Sun, A. (1991). Issues for Asian American Women. In Roth, P., Ed., Alcohol and Drugs are Women's Issues, Volume I, 125.

162. Lubben, et al., 18.

163. Sun, 126.

164. Casas, J.M. (1992). A Culturally Sensitive Model for Evaluating Alcohol and Other Drug Abuse Prevention Programs: An Hispanic Perspective. In Orlandi, M., Ed., Cultural Competence for Evaluators: A Guide for Alcohol and Other Drug Abuse Prevention Practitioners Working with Ethnic/Racial Communities. Rockville, MD: Office of Substance Abuse Prevention, 77.

165. Statistical Abstract of the United States 1992, 18.

166. Statistical Abstract of the United States 1992, 17.

167.   Statistical Abstract of the United States 1992, 18.

168.   Statistical Abstract of the United States 1992, 18.

169.   National Household Survey on Drug Abuse: Population Estimates 1992, 20, 32, 122.

170.   Office of Substance Abuse Prevention. Communication About Alcohol and Other Drugs: Strategies for Reaching Populations at Risk. Rockville, MD: 182.

171.   National Household Survey on Drug Abuse: Population Estimates 1992, 49.

Treatment of Alcohol and Other Drug Abuse: An Introduction

Photo by Robin Sachs

*Caring for women
with substance
abuse problems
must be part of
a broad public
health and social
services response.*

Chapter 3

Treatment of Alcohol and Other Drug Abuse: An Introduction

In its 1990 report on the treatment of alcohol problems, the Institute of Medicine provided a definition of treatment that applies to treatment of other substance abuse as well and that takes into account the continuum of care, from outreach (identification) to continuing care:

> Treatment refers to a broad range of services, including identification, brief intervention, assessment, diagnosis, counseling, medical services, psychiatric services, psychological services, social services, and follow-up, for persons with alcohol problems.[1]

The need for an array of comprehensive services much more extensive than one that merely focuses on alcohol and other drug use has been also underscored in CSAT's Comprehensive Treatment Model for Alcohol and Other Drug Abusing Women and their Children, which describes the types of medical, psychological, and social services that should constitute the full range of treatment for women and their children (presented in appendix A; the categories of services recommended in the comprehensive model are described in section 3.4.1). As the model states, "Treatment that addresses alcohol and other drug abuse only may well fail and contribute to a higher potential for relapse."[2]

Treatment programs must not only offer a continuum of services—both internal and external, from outreach through follow-up and continuing care—they must integrate these services within the larger community. Because many factors affect a woman's substance abuse problem, the purpose of comprehensive treatment, according to the CSAT model, is to "address a woman's substance abuse in the context of her health and her relationship with her children and other family members, the community, and society."[3] An understanding of the interrelationships among the woman/client, the treatment program, and the community is critical to the success of the comprehensive treatment approach. The intent is to consider the holistic needs of women—an adaptation of the World Health

Organization's definition of health as well-being rather than an absence of disease. As CSAT notes in its statement of mission, goals, and programs:

> The general consensus among those foremost in the field of addiction is that, for most individuals, treatment and recovery services work best in the context of a community-centered, coordinated system of comprehensive services designed to assure a continuum of support for recovery.[4]

Caring for women with substance abuse problems must be part of a broad public health and social services response.

Thus, the comprehensive treatment model makes clear that caring for women with substance abuse problems must be part of a broad public health and social services response. The interrelationships between a treatment program offering comprehensive services for women and the community are depicted in Figure 1 (see page 70). This model depicts the various aspects of the community which impact on the client and with which she may interact in the process of initiating alcohol or other drug use, continuing its use, and engaging in and continuing the recovery process. These include, for example, the availability of illicit drugs in her community, local laws and practices that govern distribution of alcohol, the local economy and related unemployment rates (which impact on her ability to obtain gainful employment), and the availability of health and social services prior to, during, and following treatment. Within the context of the treatment program are the various phases of care with which the client interacts and which are related in turn to the myriad of community variables. For example, the degree to which the treatment program can provide comprehensive services is in part dependent on the availability of social and other support services in the community (e.g., primary health care, low-income housing) as well as on the ability of the program to formulate and maintain community linkages. This model thus describes the interdependence of the client, the treatment program, and the broader community in which they exist.

3.1   CSAT's Vision of Treatment

From CSAT's perspective—and from the perspective of many in the field of addiction treatment—the goals of treatment service and recovery programs should be the following:

- attract and retain individuals in treatment and recovery;

- reduce alcohol and other drug use by these individuals;

- reduce rates of relapse by these individuals;

- improve the individual's physical health and psychological wellness; and

- improve family, social, and economic functioning.

In addition, CSAT believes that the reduction of crime, unemployment, and other socioeconomic costs of addiction are important goals of treatment programs.

3.2   Treatment Methods and Modalities

This section presents an overview of methods and modalities for substance abuse treatment. Because it is assumed that the reader has received training in substance abuse treatment and/or has experience in the field, this section will not present the different philosophies of treatment or describe treatment methods and modalities in detail. Rather, it will provide a framework for considering the issues and strategies addressed in the next three chapters that relate to the primary stages of care: outreach, comprehensive treatment, and continuing care. Research has demonstrated that no single modality of care is effective for all individuals and that clients may experience varying degrees of success with different modalities (or combinations of modalities) at different times. The combination of comprehen-

Figure 1

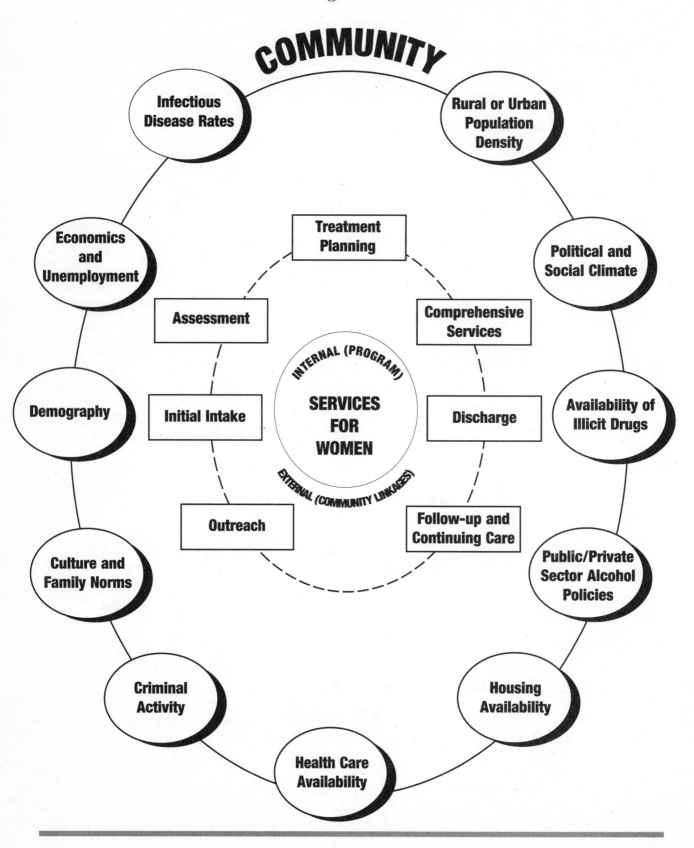

sive services required can vary according to the gender, race, ethnicity, socioeconomic status, age, and physiological and neurophysiological condition of the client. This chapter also presents a condensed discussion of key issues related to women in recovery, as well as issues that apply to all stages of care.

3.2.1   Treatment Methods

Generally, treatment of substance abuse includes the following methods:

- pharmacological treatment, including, for example:

    - the use of antabuse in the treatment of alcoholism. Antabuse is an alcohol-sensitizing drug used primarily during the initial course of treatment and rehabilitation; and

    - the use of methadone in the treatment of heroin addiction. Although originally developed for use in detoxification of heroin addicts, methadone is now used primarily as a maintenance drug for indefinite periods;

        (Please note: Although it is not commonly used, naltrexone has been an adjunct in the treatment of opioid addiction. Data does not support its effectiveness.)

- psychosocial treatment, including biofeedback and role playing; psychological counseling that involves the client and her family/ significant others;

- nontraditional healing (e.g., acupuncture); and

- social learning, which usually requires becoming and remaining drug-free and which focuses on the social service needs of the client.

These methods of care are not mutually exclusive. In fact, they are often used in combination or sequentially at different stages in the treatment process. For example, many programs combine psychosocial treatment with social learning and/or nontraditional healing methods. Methadone treatment usually includes rehabilitative counseling, psychotherapeutic services, and comprehensive medical services.

Increasingly, as treatment of substance abuse is linked with programs that provide services to persons with AIDS or who are HIV-positive, persons in the field are struggling to determine the most appropriate combination of care modalities to serve these clients. The CSAT Comprehensive Treatment Model suggests that, at a minimum, the [treatment] program must provide for pre- and post-test counseling for clients seeking to be tested for HIV. Individual counseling and support groups should be provided for clients diagnosed with HIV or AIDS. Staff should be properly trained to intervene on[5] behalf of those who are HIV-seropositive, whether symptomatic or asymptomatic.

3.2.2   Modalities of Care

Modalities of substance abuse treatment can be classified in many ways. Among these are: by setting (e.g., inpatient/medical facility-based, residential, or outpatient); by length of care (e.g., short-term or long-term); and by philosophical approach (e.g., medical model or social services model).

The remainder of this chapter summarizes the services provided in the most frequently used types of modalities based on the setting of care: inpatient detoxification, residential treatment and rehabilitation, outpatient detoxification, and outpatient treatment. Generally, these classifications apply for treatment programs that address problems of substance abuse or a combination of alcohol and other drug use. In reality, treatment is not usually static, but often occurs in different settings and with the use of different treatment modalities. Most commonly, there is a continuum of services from the following:

- inpatient detoxification, referral to residential treatment and rehabilitation, referral to outpatient or intensive day treatment, and continuing care and follow-up, or

- residential treatment and rehabilitation referral to outpatient rehabilitation, and continuing care and follow-up.

Inpatient or residential detoxification, whatever the setting or approach, is designed to facilitate the client's safe physiological withdrawal from drugs. Services usually include intensive client counseling to encourage further treatment and referral of detoxified persons to appropriate treatment programs for continuing care. Detoxification programs can last from one to seven days. However, they may be longer for women withdrawing from addictive prescription drugs, for pregnant women, for women who present with medical risks, or for those who have co-occurring disorders, including for example, mental health disorders, eating disorders, and other health problems.

Inpatient detoxification services can include the following: nursing care; individual, group, and family counseling; physical examinations (including laboratory tests); psychiatric evaluations; the provision of medications (for social setting programs, these would be limited to medications for other health problems); education concerning alcohol and other drugs; and referral for longer term treatment. Inpatient detoxification, which focuses on medical stabilization, is provided in two types of settings:

- short-term inpatient services provided in a medical facility (e.g., a hospital) or in a non-hospital residential facility that has medical services available. In these settings, the goal is to reduce systematically the amount of alcohol or other drugs in the body through medications given by medical personnel under a physician's supervision.

• short-term services provided in a residential setting by trained personnel, with physician services available when required. Such facilities (which are often considered to provide "social detoxifica-tion") can include freestanding inpatient treatment centers, quarterway houses, and halfway houses.

Residential treatment and rehabilitation are provided to individuals who need treatment services in a controlled and structured environment over a longer period of time.

Many clients are referred to residential treatment programs because they are experiencing withdrawal symptoms, psychotic manifestations, or severe illness related to substance abuse. In the latter case, they are usually stabilized in a medical facility before entering the residential program for treatment. Others are referred (or refer themselves) because the counselor or the client believe that the structured setting will benefit the client. Sometimes hospital-based residential programs are the only treatment resource available or the only one that is covered by the client's third-party payer (public or private). As with inpatient detoxification, two types of settings predominate:

• services provided in a medical facility or in a non-hospital residential program that, if affiliated with a medical facility, have medical services available and that may use medication as a means of treatment (e.g., methadone for treatment of heroin addiction), and

• services provided in a residential setting by trained personnel, with physician services available when required.

Residential treatment and rehabilitation services can be short-term (seven to 60 days, depending on the type of facility) and longer term (30 days to six months or longer). Freestanding residential programs usually have treatment methods lasting 30 days to six months; quarterway houses (usually seven to 21 days long), and halfway houses (usually 14 to 60 days long, but which can last up to six months). It should be noted that these "typical" duration periods are frequently—if not primarily—driven by coverage decisions by third party payers (including Medicaid, Medicare, and private health insurance companies), rather than by standards of care set by the treatment community.

In its grant programs, CSAT tries to ensure that programs seek the optimum length of treatment necessary to meet the primary goal of recovery. Programs funded by CSAT—particularly programs serving pregnant and postpartum women and infants, and parenting women and their children—have longer terms of stay (six to 18 months). CSAT funds up to 12 months of residential treatment.

As with detoxification programs, residential treatment and rehabilitation services can include nursing care; individual, group, and family counseling; physical examinations (including laboratory tests); psychiatric evaluations; and provision of medications. For social service programs, medications are limited to clients with other health problems. These programs may include more comprehensive services such as employment counseling, referral for primary health care and social services, and referral of pregnant women for prenatal care. Therapeutic communities that are freestanding residential treatment programs use the social setting, drug-free treatment modality.

Outpatient detoxification services are less common than inpatient detoxification services. They are usually provided under the observation and supervision of trained treatment personnel to a client whose condition requires monitoring and observation for a period of time but does not require admission to an inpatient treatment facility. The services, which usually last seven to 14 days, can include nursing and related care; individual, group, and family counseling; physical examinations (including laboratory tests); psychiatric evaluations; drug testing; and provision of medications (for detoxification and/or other health problems). During this period, the program may also arrange for outpatient follow-up care, either in the same facility or in another facility that offers outpatient treatment services. Outpatient detoxification services are provided through the following:

- medical facilities (not limited to hospitals), or

- freestanding programs that may or may not be independent of residential treatment programs.

Outpatient treatment services are programs in which clients may participate for widely varying periods (from 30 days to a year or more). More intensive outpatient programs may require visits totalling eight to 10 or more hours per week. Some hospital-based programs require hospitalization five days a week during daytime hours, or even daily, including weekends. Less intensive programs may require visits two or more times per week for individual counseling and participation in program-sponsored group counseling or 12-step meetings. Services usually include individual, group, and family counseling; employment counseling; and referral for health (medical and mental) and social (e.g., housing and Aid to Families with Dependent Children [AFDC]) services if not available in the treatment program itself. These programs are often affiliated with inpatient services and provide continuing care and follow-up services.

Self-Help/Support Groups. Mutual help or facilitated support groups such as Alcoholics Anonymous (AA) and Narcotics Anonymous (NA) are increasingly used by women recovering from alcoholism or other drug dependence. For example, women now comprise more than one-third of AA participants. The involvement of women in self-help groups may be related in part to their convenience, which is an important attribute when the woman's motivation and possible roles as primary caregiver need to be considered.

As Covington notes:[6]

> mutual help groups...are free and, in most urban communities, readily available throughout most of every day...[they] are often found in women's centers or other places in communities that provide other types of help to women...[who] are permitted to come and go freely without records being kept or contracts drawn. Meetings occur as scheduled through cooperative efforts; they are dependable and consistent in their format.

Covington also notes that women "can use meetings for a variety of different purposes as well as staying sober. As a woman's needs shift in recovery, the meetings she attends may change to reflect this."[7] A particularly useful advantage of mutual self-help groups for the woman in continuing care is the fact that the meetings provide an opportunity for social activities that are alcohol-and drug-free.[8] Covington has also cautioned, however, that the 12-Step Model has limitations of which programs should be aware. These include, for example, the fact that "the ideology does not [necessarily] encourage attention to the relational, cultural, or sociopolitical factors that foster substance abuse in women... [and that] much of the AA literature was written 20-50 years ago and is overtly sexist in its content and connotations."[9] It should be pointed out that there is an increasing number of women's 12-step groups that are addressing the specific needs and circumstances of women.

Several of the CSAT Treatment Improvement Protocol (TIP) documents describe the use of support groups such as AA, NA, Women for Sobriety, and Rational Recovery in the treatment process. For example, the TIP Assessment and Treatment of Patients with Coexisting Mental Illness and Alcohol and Other Drug Abuse[10] describes the use of support groups in sequential, parallel, and integrated approaches to addressing dual disorders. The TIP Pregnant, Substance Abusing Women,[11] describes the use of support groups in the context of comprehensive service delivery.

3.2.3   Treatment of Multiple Drug Use/Abuse

Since many individuals in substance abuse programs use more than one drug, programs are increasingly combining treatment for alcohol problems with treatment for other drug problems. For example, in 1990, of 7,743 treatment programs that received federal funds administered by the state alcohol and drug agency, 67.1 percent were combined alcohol and other drug treatment programs, 18.1 percent were programs exclusively for the treatment of alcoholism, and 14.9 percent were programs for the treatment of other drugs.[12] No gender disaggregated data were available.

3.3   Knowledge About Effective Treatment for Women

Gender-disaggregated data for treatment outcome continue to be relatively scarce, in spite of an expanded interest and a federal mandate to make such data available. Some descriptive data are available (e.g., proportion of clients who are women), and relatively more data are available for women in treatment for alcoholism. Outcome data from several federal data bases are forthcoming, and other studies that are specifically designed to determine treatment outcomes for women or that will provide gender-disaggregated data are currently underway.

The lack of gender-specific treatment outcome data hinders the valid design or adaptation of treatment methods specifically for women. Nonetheless, at least with respect to the treatment of alcoholism, the Institute of Medicine's earlier (1980s) research on treatment outcomes remains valid.

Quoting Braiker, the Institute notes that such research either failed "to distinguish between outcome rates for women and men or excluded [women] from the study sample altogether."[13] Although the data are minimal, those that exist, according to Blume and Roman, suggest the following:

> In general, in treatment for alcohol problems, males and females with comparable sociodemographic characteristics (marital status, employment, social stability, etc.) and at the same levels of problem severity appear to do equally well in the same treatment settings.[14]

Notably, however, Blume states that "what is not known are the components of treatment that would improve treatment outcome for both males and females."[15] In fact, few research studies have demonstrated the effectiveness of specific attributes of substance abuse treatment for any client, irrespective of gender. The experience of those who have provided treatment services for women in a variety of settings suggests that women have more successful outcomes when they receive gender-specific treatment for at least several months.[16]

The relative appropriateness of a particular method of treatment for women has not been determined. In fact, there has been little research on which to base any determination. The use of methadone is an established pharmacotherapy for the treatment of opioid addiction. However, its use as a treatment form has led to some degree of controversy. Examples of those who disagree with its use in the treatment of pregnant women are those who see methadone as only a replacement for heroin with another highly addictive substance. The CSAT Treatment Model states that:

> pharmacotherapy intervention (e.g., methadone) should be provided on an as-needed basis and should include provision of, or established referral linkages, for concomitant assessment and monitoring by qualified medical or psychiatric staff.[17]

The use of methadone is an established pharmacotherapy for the treatment of opioid addiction.

There is, however, no consensus in the field on the use of methadone in the treatment of pregnant women. CSAT's TIP document, Pregnant, Substance-Using Women, recommends methadone maintenance combined with psychosocial counseling and medical services for pregnant opioid-addicted women. The primary reason for this recommendation is that the fetus is also dependent on the opioid and could be spontaneously aborted if the woman is no longer taking the opioid and the fetus has withdrawal symptoms in utero. The physician prescribes as small a methadone dosage as possible to help ensure that the fetus can be born. After the birth, the physician provides medical assistance to help the mother and child withdraw from the drug(s).

In the treatment of pregnant heroin-addicted women, according to CSAT's 1992 report, State Methadone Maintenance Treatment Guidelines, "methadone maintenance by itself is not necessarily sufficient to reduce perinatal complications."[18] In its 1993 update of that document, CSAT suggested that for pregnant women who are enrolled in programs that use methadone to treat heroin addiction, methadone "must be offered in conjunction with prenatal care reinforced by psychosocial counseling and other medical services."[19] Importantly, CSAT notes that pregnant women who received methadone prior to pregnancy can initially be maintained on their prepregnancy dose, but those who did not receive methadone prior to pregnancy should receive inpatient care for a general and obstetrical assessment, a determination of their physiologic dependence on heroin and other drugs, and to initiate their methadone treatment.[20]

Treatment of pregnant women at the point of withdrawal from crack or cocaine is a particular problem, and, as CSAT has noted, "The evidence is extremely limited for all methods of medical withdrawal." Although inpatient or residential treatment is "the ideal whenever possible... these facilities may not always be available."[21]

The lack of adequate data and information in the field of women and substance abuse treatment underscores the need for more research on the effectiveness of various treatment approaches for women. For example, in a 1993 study of the accessibility, relevancy, and validity of published literature concerning minority women and substance abuse, a thorough search of the literature revealed only 200 relevant articles, of which only 92 were research-based.[22] Thus, in spite of longstanding purported interest on the part of the public health community and widespread media attention to such problems as babies born to crack cocaine-using women, only limited funds have been made available for research to design an effective program specifically for substance abusing women.

3.3.1   Critical Components of Treatment for Women

In its Comprehensive Treatment Model, CSAT recommends that the following services, among others, be provided either on-site or through referral as part of the treatment process:[23]

Medical Interventions

- testing and treatment for infectious diseases, including hepatitis, TB, HIV, and STDs.

- screening and treatment of general health problems, including anemia and poor nutrition, hypertension, diabetes, cancer, liver disorders, eating disorders, dental and vision problems, and poor hygiene.

- obstetrical and gynecological services, including family planning, breast cancer screening, periodic gynecological screening (e.g., pap smears), and general gynecological services.

- infant and child health services, including primary and acute health care for infants and children, immunizations, nutrition services (including assessment for Women, Infants, and Children (WIC)

The lack of adequate data and information in the field of women and substance abuse treatment under-scores the need for more research on the effectiveness of various treatment approaches for women.

program eligibility), and developmental assessments performed by qualified personnel.

Substance Abuse Counseling and Psychological Counseling

- counseling regarding the use and abuse of substances directly, as well as other issues which may include low self-esteem, race and ethnicity issues, gender-specific issues, disability-related issues, family relationships, unhealthy interpersonal relationships, violence, including incest, rape, and other abuse, eating disorders, sexuality, grief related to loss of children, family, or partners, sexual orientation, and responsibility for one's feelings including shame, guilt, and anger.

- parenting counseling, including information on child development, child safety, injury prevention, and child abuse prevention.

- relapse prevention, which should be a discrete component or phase of each woman's recovery plan.

Health Education and Prevention Activities

- health education and prevention activities should cover the following subjects: HIV/AIDS, the physiology and transmission of STDs, reproductive health, preconception care, prenatal care, childbirth, female sexuality, childhood safety and injury prevention, physical and sexual abuse prevention, nutrition, smoking cessation, and general health.

Life Skills

- education should include practical life skills, vocational evaluation, financial management, negotiating access to services, stress management and coping skills, and personal image building.

- parenting, including infant/child nutrition, child development, and child/parent relationships.

- educational training and remedial services should be provided with access to local education/GED programs and other educational services as identified at intake.

- English language competency and literacy assessment programs should be facilitated.

- job counseling, training, and referral should be provided, if possible, via case managed/coordinated referrals to community programs.

Other Social Services

- transportation for clients to gain access to substance abuse treatment services and related community services.

- child care.

- legal services.

- housing.

It is important that all treatment components be accessible to all women. This may entail making accommodations for women with disabilities and for older women. Chapters 4, 5, and 6 detail strategies related to these types of services in the outreach/identification, comprehensive treatment, and continuing care/follow-up phases of treatment, respectively.

3.4   Case Management

Case management is a critical component of any substance abuse treatment program. For programs that provide comprehensive treatment services which require accessing and coordinating numerous sources of such services and which involve multiple disciplines of different care providers, it is imperative. The International Certification Reciprocity Consortium/Alcohol and Other Drug Abuse, Inc. (ICRC/AODA) has defined case management to include the following:

...activities which bring services, agencies, resources, or people together within a planned framework of action toward the achievement of established goals. It may involve liaison activities and collateral contacts."[24]

Case management should be an integral part of the treatment process, from the point of intake through continuing care. In describing practical aspects of case management in the treatment of alcohol and other drug disorders, Kulewicz suggests that:

> In the treatment process, either inpatient or outpatient, the basic concepts remain the same. Effective treatment is contingent upon a cooperative effort of the client and the treatment staff. The treatment staff usually consists of the primary counselor, counselor, clinical supervisor, staff psychologist, and consulting psychiatrist. It is not unusual to include the staff physician and/or nursing staff member in those cases where it is appropriate to meet the individual client's needs. The interacting and consulting efforts on the part of the team enable the treatment process to be continually monitored and updated on an ongoing, regular basis.[25]

Effective treatment is contingent upon a cooperative effort of the client and the treatment staff.

In treatment programs serving women, especially those offering comprehensive services, the client's records—including for example the treatment plan, the counselor's notes and those of other treatment providers, and follow-up forms from programs to which the client has been referred—form the basis for case management. These records must be current and complete, reflecting the full range of services provided to the client and the full range of her needs. Additional information regarding the client should be discussed during periodic case management conferences (usually held weekly), and any determinations made on the basis of this conference should be recorded in the client's file.

Examples of the application of case management techniques are provided in Chapters 4, 5, and 6.

3.5   Issues Related to Treatment of Alcohol and Other Drug Use in Women

This section describes a number of issues related to the treatment of substance abuse in women. It is not intended to address all issues specifically related to women, but rather to highlight those that are generally perceived as the most critical in implementing substance abuse treatment. The strategies that are recommended for addressing these issues are described throughout the remaining chapters of the manual. To the extent that epidemiologic data are available, they have been presented in Chapter 2.

3.5.1   Relationships and Other Gender Issues

A number of experts in the field of women and addiction have noted that women who abuse alcohol and other drugs tend to have relationships that are characterized by unhealthy dependencies and poor communication skills.[26] Because many recovering women have had few positive relationships, they have few models for developing healthy relationships.

Covington and Surrey have described a useful model for understanding the importance of relationships in women's lives and in the process of substance abuse and recovery. Termed the "relational model," it emphasizes the centrality of relationships for women, considers their role as caretakers, addresses the issue of co-dependency, and focuses on strengths in women's relationships as a means of recovery. Covington and others have found the model to be helpful in "conceptualizing the contexts and meanings of substance abuse in women's lives and particularly helpful in suggesting new treatment models."[27]

Following are examples of unresolved relationship issues and strategies to address these issues; most have been derived from Advances in

Women who abuse alcohol and other drugs tend to have relationships that are characterized by unhealthy dependencies and poor communication skills.

Alcoholism Treatment Services for Women:[28]

- Issues between mother and children

  — Invite mothers and children to participate in educational activities.

  — Involve mothers and children in individual, group, and family therapy sessions.

- Issues of intimacy and friendship (often confused with issues of sexuality)

  — Hold therapy groups and workshop sessions in which educational material and experiential exercises are used to help clients understand the difference between intimacy and sexuality.

  — Encourage nonsexual friendships between women and men.

  — Review patterns of relationships through individual and group therapy.

  — Explore personal needs and wants in the following areas: economic, sensual/sexual, emotional, social, intellectual, and spiritual.

  — In some circumstances, recommend periods of celibacy.

- Issues of mistrust and competitiveness with other women

  — Involve the clients in women-only therapy groups and include discussions designed to empower women to trust themselves first, as a basis for developing trust in others.

  — Educate clients about women's history, including socialization of women's relationships with one another.

- Issues of self-development, independence, and interdependence.

— Use group living situations to refocus attention on individual needs.

— Use visual aids to enable the client to see and analyze various aspects of her life's activities (the "circle overlap").

The concept of "codependency" was developed to describe the complex interrelationships that can occur with the underresponsibility/overresponsibility dynamics that develop in many relationships marked by alcohol and other drug use.[29] Until recently, most substance abuse treatment programs have addressed primarily the needs of men. Therefore, to the extent that codependency issues have been confronted, this has been done primarily with male clients vis-a-vis their female partners.

There is a significant lack of clarity in the definition of the terms "enabling" and "codependency," with viewpoints expressed in the literature deriving from the particular author's vantage point. Sociopolitical issues concerning gender relationships and relative positions in society are often not addressed in the substance abuse treatment literature. Rather, there seems to be a focus on the "pathology" of codependency, which implies (and can encourage) guilt on the part of the woman.[30] As Beattie has described in her books on codependency, the client needs to learn that she can continue to care about people, but that she has choices. She is responsible for her behavior and the consequences of that behavior, including unhealthy codependency.[31] Identifying her codependent behaviors and those with whom she is involved in these behaviors is an important step in recovery from codependent relationships. These behaviors include, for example, controlling relationships, repressing feelings, self-neglect, and not setting boundaries.[32]

Treatment program staff, clients, and their partners need to address the imbalances of responsibility and gender patterns found in families and personal relationships that are so often destructive to both women and men.

When a woman has gained a degree of stability in treatment, it is often helpful for her to participate in both women-only and mixed gender codependency groups for support in recovering from unhealthy codependent behavior characterized by past relationships. Treatment programs should ensure that clients who are codependent have access to groups (either on-site or through referral) that address issues of codependency, including, for example, Codependents Anonymous (CoDA) and Families Anonymous.

An example of a client who has relationship problems along with treatment strategies to address them is shown on the following page.

Example of Presenting Problem

Relationships

After several months in an outpatient program in which she is being treated for heroin addiction, a 35-year-old woman with a history of relapse expresses to a counselor discomfort with both physical and emotional aspects of sexual relationships. After some discussion during the counseling session, it is revealed that the woman's parents were both alcoholics. Her father also used heroin for several years and had sexually abused her. Although the woman had several brothers, she was invariably the child who cared for the parents. Her father died when she was 18, but she cared for her mother until she died, at which time the client was 33.

Alternative Strategies

While treating the woman's substance abuse problem itself, staff should consider the following to address the relationship issues she faces:

- Assess treatment history, particularly her experience in methadone programs (as with heroin, methadone can reduce libido; given the woman's personal sexual history, this is important information).

- During individual counseling, the woman should be assisted in understanding unresolved issues with her parents and with her brothers, whom she feels did not share responsibility for care of their parents.

- Arrange for group counseling with other women in recovery who are adult children of alcoholics and/or heroin addicts.

- During individual and group counseling, explore issues of intimacy and friendship and those of self-development, independence, and interdependence. Encourage nonsexual friendships with women and men.

- Arrange for assertiveness training conducted by trained staff or through referral to appropriate services in the community.

- In discharge planning, either conduct directly or arrange for post-treatment psychological assessment and evaluation of client outcome in terms of psychosocial measures and for continuing psychological counseling, as necessary.

3.5.2   Issues of Sexuality

Women in treatment for substance abuse problems often must not only address issues of sexuality faced by other women, but a myriad of other issues as well. As noted in Chapter 2, women who have abused alcohol and other drugs have many physiological repercussions that may affect their sexual functioning (e.g., hormonal changes, liver damage). Covington has found that women recovering from alcohol abuse were much less likely to report satisfaction with their sexual functioning than were nonalcoholic women (55 percent versus 85 percent, respectively).[33] She also has identified related psychological repercussions, including diminished self-worth, an avoidance of relationships, and possible depression related to sexual functioning.[34] Comparable data relating sexual functioning to the use of other drugs is not readily available.

Many women go through treatment without addressing their sexuality and intimacy issues, in part because few counselors are prepared to deal effectively with women's sexual concerns. Because alcohol and other drug use and sexuality can be entwined, staff members must be knowledgeable about and comfortable with discussing sexuality and intimacy issues with women in individual and women-only group sessions. If staff members are unable or unwilling to talk openly about these issues, a woman's fears and concerns will only be exacerbated, and the possibility of a healthy recovery may be limited. Staff members also must be comfortable talking with women about incest, rape, or sexual abuse issues since these are often the core problems underlying sexual dysfunction in women who abuse substances.

An additional issue to be addressed is the fact that, as a recently published CSAT report, State Methadone Maintenance Guidelines, states: "because addicted women rarely have highly paid roles in the drug-dealing network, prostitution is common and also negatively influences intimate

Staff members must be knowledgeable about and comfortable with discussing sexuality and intimacy issues with women.

relationships."[35] Sexual relationships with injecting drug users also place the woman at-risk for AIDS/HIV, as is discussed in Chapter 2. Both of these are issues that can be addressed through individual and group counseling focusing on intimate relationships; however, the issue of prostitution is one related to economic status and self-sufficiency as well.

The following types of strategies are useful to address sexuality issues:

- Conduct workshops and use educational materials on the relationship between substance abuse and sexuality, sexual functioning, and incest and other sexual abuse to show women that their experience is not unique and that it is possible to heal and develop a more satisfying life.

- Offer group counseling for women only, so that sexual problems and sexuality (including sexual communication styles and the dynamics of sex and power) may be comfortably and openly discussed in language familiar to clients.

- Encourage women to discuss their sexual problems, and let them know that some sexual problems (for example, physical problems related to drug use such as lack of sexual desire among heroin-addicted women) may resolve themselves over time with continued abstinence from drugs. Other problems that result from underlying experiences such as incest or suppressing sexual feelings as a result of prostitution, will require clients to explore and work out their feelings about those experiences.

- Refer women who are sexually dysfunctional for medical and psychological assessment to determine the organic and or psychological bases for the dysfunction. Treatment should follow this assessment. For example, the client who has been sexually abused should be referred for psychological counseling or sex therapy to a therapist who can address her needs. Ensure that such counseling is culturally sensitive and that it addresses a women's spiritual needs.

- Provide specific supportive treatment for the client who has been a prostitute and/or who has exchanged sex for drugs. Help her explore her lifestyle and, through internal and external community resources, give her the tools to change her lifestyle.

- Hold discussions to inform women of their legal rights, and educate female clients about what constitutes violence and abuse against women including physical battering, forms of verbal abuse, violation of physical space boundaries, forced sex, unwanted touching, or a partner's flaunting of affairs. Raise consciousness about what constitutes abuse, so that women become empowered to stand up for their rights and educate their children about their rights.

3.5.3   Women, Violence, and Substance Abuse

The prevalence of violence against women in the general population, while of startling proportions, is overshadowed by the reported prevalence among women who enter substance abuse treatment programs.

The first comprehensive national survey of the health of American women, conducted in 1993, found that thirty percent of women (an estimated 30 million women) suffered some type of abuse as a child. Ten percent reported having been sexually abused, 13 percent reported having been physically abused, 27 percent reported having been emotionally or verbally abused.[36] This same study found that in the year prior to the survey, seven percent of women reported being physically abused and 37 percent reported being emotionally or verbally abused by their partner.[37] Two percent of respondents —an estimated 1.9 million women —reported having been raped in the previous five years.[38]

The prevalence of violence against women in the general population, while of startling proportions, is overshadowed by the reported prevalence among women who enter substance abuse treatment programs. In her review of published research on sexuality and drinking behavior, Wilsnack found that between 41 percent and 74 percent of women in treatment for alcohol and other drugs reported being childhood or adult victims of sexual abuse, including incest.[39] A number of researchers (e.g, Bergman, et al[40] and Covington[41]) have found significantly higher proportions of a history of sexual and/or physical abuse among women in treatment than among comparison groups of women. In some cases, at least half of the women entering treatment have been battered or raped and most have been emotionally abused. There is little data available on women's exposure to violence in their environment (e.g., murder, armed robbery, or assault), which has also been linked with post-traumatic stress disorder (PTSD) and which can contribute to the woman's vulnerability to seeking drug-induced means of removing herself from her unsafe and insecure environment.

The wide range of findings with respect to history of sexual abuse among women in treatment is in part due to the difference in definitions of abuse used by the researchers. For example, in describing a range of 30-80 percent in reported incest among women in treatment for heroin addiction in studies published over several decades, Worth[42] noted the inconsistent definitions of incest used by the authors of the published studies.

Most women who are victims of partner violence do not discuss the incidents with anyone and most who are victims of any type of crime and who required medical treatment are not referred to any type of support service by a treatment provider.[43] Both as a result of the violence itself and the inadequacy of support systems, the victim endures physical and psychological impacts that are well documented. It is also important to acknowledge that racial, ethical, and cultural differences do exist in patterns, interrelationships, and outcomes associated with violence. These factors have not been systematically examined.

The psychological impact of violence includes mood disorders (e.g., depression), anxiety disorders (e.g., PTSD), and low self-esteem. A recently-published CSAT TIP entitled "Assessment and Treatment of Patients with Coexisting Mental Illness and Alcohol and Other Drug Abuse," specifically addressed the relationship between sexual abuse (including incest) and alcohol and other drug use:

For many women who have been victims of personal violence, use of alcohol and other drugs can become a coping mechanism.

Clinicians note that long-term responses to childhood and adult sexual abuse often include symptoms associated with PTSD and other psychiatric problems, including an increased risk for [alcohol and other drug] AOD disorders.[44]

Paone and others have noted that, for many women who have been victims of personal violence, use of alcohol and other drugs can become a coping mechanism, whereby they self-medicate to alleviate feelings of anxiety, guilt, fear, and anger that result from the violence.[45]

It is important to note that alcohol abuse by lesbians has been identified as both a cause and effect factor related to violence among partners.

Because the partner of the woman in treatment is often a user of alcohol or other drugs, the link between such use and violence is also an important consideration for treatment programs, particularly those which have as an objective family reunification. It is important to note that alcohol abuse by lesbians has been identified as both a cause and effect factor related to violence among partners.[46] Alcohol consumption has been linked to fight-related homicide, assault, rape, and spouse and child abuse, all of which the woman may have experienced just prior to entering treatment and to which she may be vulnerable following treatment. For example, in a national study of homicide perpetrators, 36% were under the influence of alcohol alone at the time of the crime and an additional 13% were under the influence of alcohol in combination with another drug.[47] A subsidiary issue is the fact that, increasingly, use of alcohol by the victim is seen as related to increased vulnerability to victimization. However, this should in no way be interpreted as suggesting that, for example in the case of spouse abuse, this vulnerability is "an excuse for [or] a direct cause of" the crime.[48] Use of crack cocaine has also been associated with violent behavior, but minimal data are available specifically with regard to its impact on personal violence directed at women, or conversely, personal violence committed by crack cocaine-addicted women.

Chapters 4, 5, and 6 address issues related to outreach, treatment, and follow-up of women in treatment who have experienced personal violence. These issues include assessing the woman to identify dual diagnoses (including, for example, PTSD), individualizing treatment to ensure that the woman's abuse history is addressed, and prevention relapse.

An example of a woman client presenting with sexual abuse issues and strategies to address them is presented on the following page.

Example of Presenting Problem

Sexual Abuse

A 23-year-old woman with a history of multiple drug abuse (heavy alcohol use since age 13, occasional crack use since age 15, and nonmedical use of tranquilizers since age 18) is having difficulty adjusting to the outpatient program's schedule and is reluctant to discuss the underlying causes of her substance abuse. She is the mother of two children and has recently left an abusive relationship with her husband.

Alternative Strategies

In addition to addressing substance abuse, staff should consider the following to address the issue of sexual abuse:

- Have a trained female staff person, or a consulting female psychologist meet with the client to determine if there is a history of sexual abuse and to carry out a complete psychological assessment of the client. Because disclosure at intake may be difficult, periodic assessment is necessary.

- If it is found that the client has a history of sexual abuse, arrange for individual and group counseling to address this issue specifically. Therapy could be provided by trained staff in the program or by referral to a rape crisis center or to a mental health professional specializing in sexual abuse problems.

- Arrange for counseling to address the spouse abuse problem, including individual counseling for the woman, therapy for the spouse, and family therapy.

- Arrange for legal and other assistance, as necessary, to address the spouse abuse issue. Arrange for temporary care of children, if appropriate, and, at a minimum, for child care while the client is in treatment.

- The treatment team should ensure that comprehensive services are being provided.

- In discharge planning, either conduct directly or arrange for post-treatment psychological assessment and evaluation of client outcome in terms of psychosocial measures and for counseling. Also arrange for housing and other social service needs as necessary. (This will depend on the client's relationship with her spouse at discharge.)

3.5.4   Children

Women are the primary caretakers of children in the United States (as in most countries) even when a spouse or partner is present in the home. The proportion of female-headed family households (no spouse present) is significant: in 1992, nearly one-third of families with children under 18 fell into this category.[49] Low-income women who are single heads of households have particular problems, with diminished economic and/or geographic access to treatment, health, social, and other support services.

Substance abuse treatment programs need to address the issues of women with children. In terms of outreach and identification, many women report that concern for their children is a major motivation in their decision to enter treatment for substance abuse problems.[50] For example, in a recent study of cocaine or crack-addicted mothers in New York City, 75 percent of respondents indicated that "concern for their children would be their major motivation for entering treatment."[51] However, lack of access to treatment programs that can meet their needs impedes the ability of women to obtain care. As Coletti et al noted:

> Mothers without access to child care may have to forego treatment, leave treatment early, or face the frustrations of bringing young children with them - if children are allowed on the premises."[52]

The lack of adequate treatment programs for women with children was identified by the General Accounting Office in 1992; that agency found that, in 1991, 105,000 cocaine or crack-addicted women were in need of treatment.[53] Note that this does not include women addicted to any other type of drug, including alcohol. (The CSAT Women and Children's Branch is currently funding 65 programs designed to serve women and their children. This is part of CSAT's effort to expand services to meet the needs of women with children.) In addition to inadequate availability of

Many women report that concern for their children is a major motivation in their decision to enter treatment for substance abuse problems.

treatment programs, the lack of regular affordable child care (and health care services) and the fear of interference by the Department of Social Services in the family may be important barriers to treatment. These factors need to be considered in designing outreach and treatment services for women with children.

An important consideration for treatment is the fact that the mother's abuse of alcohol and other drugs has been demonstrated to impair mother and infant bonding and development of nurturing relationships.[54] Thus, even if the mother is motivated to care for her child (see above discussion), it may be psychologically (and practically) difficult for her to do so while she is still abusing alcohol or other drugs. Treatment program staff need to ensure that in all phases of care the woman's positive motivation and nurturing instincts are encouraged and that she is given access to the social support systems that promote and sustain her role as mother.

For these reasons, and to help ensure retention in treatment and continued recovery in follow-up, child care and attention to parenting issues must be major components of treatment for women. Specific strategies to address these issues are discussed in the remaining chapters of the manual.

3.5.5   Dual Disorders

The recently-published CSAT TIP report, "Assessment and Treatment of Patients with Coexisting Mental Illness and Alcohol and other Drug Abuse," points out that:

> "The term dual diagnosis is a common, broad term that indicates the simultaneous presence of two independent medical disorders....The equivalent phrase dual disorders also denotes the coexistence of two independent (but invariably interactive) disorders.[55]

That same report identifies common examples of dual disorders: major depression with cocaine addiction, alcohol addiction with panic disorder, alcoholism and polydrug addiction with schizophrenia, and borderline personality disorder with episodic polydrug abuse. The report also suggests that the term "mentally ill chemically affected people" is the preferred designation for those who have an alcohol or other drug disorder and "a markedly severe and persistent mental disorder such as schizophrenia or bipolar disorder."[56] Using the broad definition of dual disorders, they can include eating disorders and others that interfere with full well-being and functioning.

Accurate diagnosis and appropriate treatment of clients who have dual disorders is difficult, particularly in the early treatment for substance abuse. In fact, according to Dackis and Gold, there are three diagnostic possibilities in dually diagnosed clients:[57]

- The psychiatric symptoms may result from the addiction and/or withdrawal from the drug (e.g., depression that comes with cocaine crash, hallucinations with cocaine intoxication).

- Drugs may be used as self-medication (e.g., alcohol overuse in panic disorders or tranquilizers used for pain, which may become entrenched into an addiction).

- Addiction and psychiatric illness may coexist (e.g., the alcoholic with bipolar disorder).

It is important that staff members of treatment programs serving women are aware of the general classification of mental health disorders (e.g., mood disorders, anxiety disorders, personality disorders, and psychotic disorders) and that they are aware of gender differences in presentation of these conditions among women. For example, given the high proportion of women clients who are adult or childhood victims of sexual or physical abuse (see 3.4.3 above), and the relationship between post-traumatic stress disorder (PTSD) and history of sexual abuse, staff members should be aware of treatment approaches related to PTSD and be aware of similar symptomatology (e.g., blackout phenomena) associated with alcohol or amnesia related to the PTSD.

Increasing attention is being paid to the need for treatment program staff to detect and screen for dual disorders (and make referrals for identified problems) or to immediately arrange for screening by medical or mental health professionals early in the outreach or treatment process. Strategies related to addressing dual disorders should be an integral part of the treatment plan, as should continued attention to any identified dual disorders, because progress in treating these disorders affects the outcome of the substance abuse treatment process. Addressing dual disorders may also be a key factor in relapse prevention. Maintaining contact with the agency where the client was sent for medical or mental health treatment, or with the provider on the program staff, is an important part of the treatment process.

It is also important that health care providers identify substance abuse as a disorder that often co-occurs with other medical and mental problems. They must try to avoid the tendency to project negative attitudes about people who have substance abuse problems. These problems should be seen as part of a complex set of physical and psychological actions and reactions that will continue if not directly addressed. The lack of early detection by health care providers has been exacerbated by the tendency of many physicians to prescribe sedatives/hypnotics or tranquilizers to those already experiencing substance abuse.[58]

Concurrent treatment for clients with dual disorders is also crucial. This does not mean that addiction specialists treat the addiction and mental health professionals (psychologists, psychiatrists, etc.) treat the psychiatric disorder. Concurrent treatment involves all treatment professionals in case management to identify the impact the diagnoses have on one another and to determine the most appropriate and effective course of treatment. Given the complex interaction between substance abuse and mental health disorders, and the many issues that need to be considered in outreach, treatment, and continuing care, treatment program staff serving women are encouraged to review the CSAT TIP report on dual disorders (referenced above).

References

1.   Institute of Medicine. (1990). Broadening the Base of Treatment for Alcohol Problems. Washington, DC: National Academy of Sciences Press, 84.

2.   Center for Substance Abuse Treatment. (1993). CSAT Comprehensive Treatment Model for Alcohol and Other Drug Abusing Women and Their Children. Rockville, MD: U.S. Department of Health and Human Services, Public Health Service.

3.   ibid.

4.   Center for Substance Abuse Treatment. (1993). Providing National Leadership in Treatment Services: Mission, Goals, and Programs. Rockville, MD: U.S. Department of Health and Human Services. Substance Abuse and Mental Health Services Administration, 3.

5.   State Methadone Maintenance Treatment Guidelines, 69.

6.   Covington, S. (1991). Sororities of Helping and Healing: Women and Mutual Help Groups. In Roth, P., Ed. Alcohol and Drugs are Women's Issues, Vol. I. Metuchen, NJ: Scarecrow Press, 91.

7.   ibid.

8.   ibid.

9.   Covington, S. (1994). Spirituality. A Paper Prepared for Policy Research Incorporated. Bethesda, MD: Policy Research Incorporated, 2.

10. Center for Substance Abuse Treatment. (1994). Assessment and Treatment of Patients with Coexisting Mental Illness and Alcohol and Other Drug Abuse. Rockville, MD: U.S. Department of Health and Human Services, Public Health Service; pp. 13-14.

11. Center for Substance Abuse Treatment. (1993). Pregnant, Substance-Using Women. Rockville, MD: U.S. Department of Health and Human Services. Public Health Service, 10.

12. U.S. Department of Health and Human Services. (1992). State Resources and Services Related to Alcohol and Other Drug Abuse Problems. Rockville, MD: National Institute on Drug Abuse and National Institute on Alcohol Abuse and Alcoholism, 14.

13. Institute of Medicine. (1990). The Diagnosis and Treatment of Alcoholism in Women. In Broadening the Base of Treatment for Alcohol Problems, 351.

14. Institute of Medicine. (1990). Populations Defined by Structural Characteristics. In Broadening the Base of Treatment for Alcohol Problems, 356.

15. ibid.

16. ibid.

17. CSAT Comprehensive Treatment Model for Alcohol and Other Drug Abusing Women and Their Children, 4.

18. Center for Substance Abuse Treatment. (1992). State Methadone Maintenance Treatment Guidelines. Rockville, MD: U.S. Department of Health and Human Services, Public Health Service, 174.

19. Center for Substance Abuse Treatment. (1993). State Methadone Treatment Guidelines. Rockville, MD: U.S. Department of Health and Human Services, Public Health Service, 90.

20. State Methadone Maintenance Treatment Guidelines, 177.

21. Center for Substance Abuse Treatment. (1993). Pregnant, Substance-Using Women. Rockville, MD: U.S. Department of Health and Human Services. Public Health Service, 22.

22. Policy Research Incorporated. (1993). Substance Abuse Among Women From Ethnic/Racial Population Cohorts: Review of the Relevance, Accessibility and Validity of the Literature. Clarksville, MD.

23. CSAT Comprehensive Treatment Model for Alcohol and Other Drug Abusing Women and Their Children, 4.

24. Kulewicz, S.F. (1992). The Twelve Core Functions of a Counselor. Somerville, MA: David & Goliath Creative, 57.

25. Kulewicz, S.F. (1992). The Twelve Core Functions of a Counselor. Somerville, MA: David & Goliath Creative, 57.

26. Bepko, C. The Responsibility Trap. (1985). New York: The Free Press, 198-232.

27. Covington, S.S. and Surrey, J.L. (undated). The Relational Model of Women's Psychological Development: Implications for Substance Abuse, (unpublished document), 2.

28. U.S. Department of Health and Human Services. (1985). Advances in Alcoholism Treatment Services for Women. Rockville, MD: National Institute on Alcohol Abuse and Alcoholism, 15.

29. See National Coalition on Domestic Violence. (1988). Chemical Dependency, Codependency, and Battered Women. In NCADV Voice (Special Issue) and in Wetzel, J.W. (1991). Working with Pregnant Women at High Risk for HIV Infection: Outreach and Intervention. Bulletin of the New York Academy of Medicine, 67(3), 291-300.

30. ibid.

31. Beattie, M. (1989). Beyond Codependency and Getting Better All the Time. San Francisco, CA: Harper & Row, Publishers, p. 15.

32. Beattie, M. (1990). Codependents' Guide to the Twelve Steps. New York, N.Y.: Prentice Hall Press, 65.

33. Covington, S.S., Ph.D. (1991). Awakening Your Sexuality: A Guide for Recovering Women. San Francisco: Harper, 232.

34. ibid.

35. State Methadone Treatment Guidelines, 69.

36. The Commonwealth Fund. (1993) Survey of Women's Health. New York, NY: The Commonwealth Fund, 9.

37. Survey of Women's Health, 8.

38. Survey of Women's Health, 9.

39. Alcohol Problems in Women: Antecedents, Consequences, and Intervention, New 204-205.

40. Bergman, G., Larsson, G., Brismar, B., et al, (1989). Battered Wives and Female Alcoholics: A Comparative Social and Psychiatric Study. J. of Advanced Nursing; 14:727-734.

41. Covington, S.S. and Kohen, J. (1984). Women, Alcohol & Sexuality. Advances in Alcohol & Substance Abuse, 4(1).

42. Worth, D. (1994). Good Girls, Bad Girls. New York, NY: Unpublished Paper, 3.

43. Survey of Women's Health, 9.

44. Center for Substance Abuse Treatment. (1994). Assessment and Treatment of Patients with Coexisting Mental Illness and Alcohol and Other Drug Abuse. Rockville, MD: Substance Abuse and Mental Health Services Administration, 44.

45. Paone, D., et al, (1992). The Impact of Sexual Abuse: Implications for Drug Treatment. Journal of Women's Health, 1(2): 149-153.

46. Diamond, D., & Wilsnack, S.C. (1978). Alcohol Abuse Among Lesbians: A Descriptive Study. Journal of Homosexuality, 4: 123-142.

47. Wieczorek et al, (1990). Cited in: U.S. Department of Health and Human Services (1993). Eighth Special Report to the U.S. Congress on Alcohol and Health. Rockville, Md.: National Institute on Alcohol Abuse and Alcoholism, 246.

48. Eighth Special Report to the U.S. Congress on Alcohol and Health, 247.

49. U.S. Department of Commerce, Bureau of the Census. (1993). Statistical Abstract of the United States: 1992. Washington, DC: U.S. Government Printing Office, 55.

50. Wilsnack, R.W., Wilsnack, S.C., and Klassen, A.D. (1984). Women's Drinking and Drinking Problems: Patterns from a 1981 Survey. American Journal of Public Health (74), 1231-1238.

51. Chavkin, W. and Paone, D. (1993). Treatment for Crack-Using Mothers: A Study and Guidelines for Program Design. New York: Beth Israel Medical Center Chemical Dependency Institute, 4.

52. Coletti, S.D., et al, (1992). PAR Village: Specialized Intervention for Cocaine Abusing Women and Their Children. J. Florida Medical Association. 79(10): 701-705.

53. U.S. General Accounting Office. (1991). Drug Abuse - The Crack Cocaine Epidemic: Health Consequences and Treatment.

54. DeLeon, G. and Jainchill, N. (1991). Residential Therapeutic Communities for Female Substance Abusers. Bul. of N.Y. Acad. Med.; 67(3): 277-289.

55. Assessment and Treatment of Patients with Coexisting Mental Illness and Alcohol and Other Drug Abuse, 4.

56. ibid.

57. Dackis, C.A., and Gold, M.S. "Psychiatric Hospitals for Treatment of Dual Diagnosis." (1992). In Lowinson, J., Ruiz, P., et al, Eds. Substance Abuse: A Comprehensive Textbook. Baltimore: Williams and Wilkins, 467-485.

58. Mondanara, J., M.D. (1989). Chemically Dependent Women: Assessment and Treatment. D.C. Lexington, MA: Heath and Company, 114.

Chapter 4

Outreach To and Identification of Women

Photo courtesy of the Office of Minority Health

Program directors and administrators must understand and accept the importance of customized outreach that uses gender-specific strategies.

Chapter 4

Outreach to and Identification of Women

Although there is growing awareness, understanding, and acceptance among health professionals and the public that alcoholism and other drug addictions are major public health issues, negative attitudes and misconceptions concerning women and substance abuse still abound. These attitudes and misconceptions often pose silent barriers to treatment for women. Women with substance abuse problems are often reluctant to admit their need for treatment. They may fear social rejection or loss of their children or they may have internalized the prevailing social attitudes toward addiction. Furthermore, for many women, poverty and related socioeconomic conditions, often compounded by discrimination based on race, psychiatric disorders, ethnicity, disability, sexual orientation, and/or age, create additional problems that may further inhibit them from seeking treatment.

A woman who needs treatment for a substance abuse problem may be deterred by the relative lack of treatment services designed specifically for women. Women with children may be discouraged by the shortage of treatment services that include provisions for child care if they must leave their children in unreliable hands to enter treatment. A successful outreach program must recognize these factors as barriers to treatment and ensure that the treatment program addresses them.

To develop an outreach program for women with substance abuse problems, it is important to acknowledge that substance abusing women are represented in all ages, races, cultures, ethnic groups, educational levels, and socioeconomic status, as described in Chapter 2. To be successful, outreach efforts must recognize these differences and target specific populations.

A woman who needs treatment for a substance abuse problem may be deterred by the relative lack of treatment services designed specifically for women.

This chapter addresses these issues by:

- describing barriers to outreach and treatment;

- describing barriers to outreach and treatment for specific population groups; and

- presenting general approaches to outreach.

4.1   Barriers to Outreach and Treatment

Women often confront barriers to finding, entering, and completing substance abuse treatment programs. Society imposes some of the barriers. Others are internal within the woman herself. Some barriers are unique to special populations, but many are relevant to women of different ages, races, and socioeconomic status. There are generally three types of barriers:

- Generic, systemic barriers that are not gender-specific (e.g., racism, classism, aversion to behavior perceived as "deviant," lack of community-based social support services);

- Gender-specific barriers (e.g., lack of geographically accessible treatment services for women; lack of child care); and

- Internalized reaction to either the generic or gender-specific barriers, or other individual experiences or issues faced by an individual woman (e.g., the client's belief that she is indispensable and cannot leave home to seek treatment).

In practice, specific barriers often cross these general types. Barriers that cut across different populations are in this section; those that are unique to special populations are presented in Section 4.3.

Economic inequality. Women earn $0.70 for every $1.00 earned by men, are much more likely to be single heads of households, and are much more likely to live in poverty. The cost of treatment may be a significant obstacle for uninsured and low income women who need treatment for substance abuse and its related problems.

By the end of 1993, nearly 40 million Americans had no health insurance. In 1989, the most recent year for which gender breakdowns of uninsured Americans are available, 15 percent of American women had no health insurance coverage (compared with 16 percent of men) and 7.6 percent of women were covered by Medicaid (compared with 5.2 percent of men).[1] Women who are insured by programs such as Medicaid often find it difficult to locate a program that will accept this type of payment.

Furthermore, even if a woman has insurance, it may not cover alcohol or other drug treatment, or there may be limits to either the setting of care or the number and types of services (e.g., detoxification days or therapy sessions that may be covered in a lifetime). The coverage or entitlement program may also require a co-payment that the woman cannot afford. Because of the lower incomes of women in comparison to men, health insurance factors significantly affect financial access to care.

Social Stigmatization. Women who have substance abuse problems are often perceived as less "socially acceptable" than their male counterparts. They are, therefore, less likely to disclose their need for treatment and more likely to have sustained periods during which substance abuse is not diagnosed or is misdiagnosed. In our society a substance-abusing woman is often considered a second-class citizen. She may also be seen as sexually promiscuous and weak-willed because of her alcohol and other drug abuse.[2] Social stigma exacerbates denial, a primary barrier to outreach. Outreach workers need to engage women in discussions that will overcome the psychological and emotional results of social stigma.

Women who are insured by programs such as Medicaid often find it difficult to locate a program that will accept this type of payment.

Women who have substance abuse problems are often perceived as less "socially acceptable" than their male counterparts.

In certain cultures, the fear of social stigmatization may be particularly strong. For example:

> Women of color [who abuse alcohol] share a double stigma as alcoholics and as minority women. For a woman of color who is also lesbian, the stigma and isolation is further compounded. Women of color are usually alone or in a small minority in either minority programs dominated by men or women's programs dominated by Caucasian women.[3]

Thus, women of color experience many layers of stigmatization: gender, race/ethnicity, culture, and substance abuse.

Lack of Social and Emotional Support. Women generally encourage men who have substance abuse problems to enter treatment. However, women's partners, family members, and friends often enable women to continue their substance abuse by denying the existence of the problem or its seriousness rather than encouraging them to seek treatment. Women are more likely to bear the primary responsibility for care of their family members, in part because they are four times as likely as men to be the head of a single parent household with children. Therefore, women face practical considerations surrounding a decision to enter treatment, especially inpatient or residential care, that men do not confront as frequently.

Lack of Institutional Mechanisms to Help the Substance-Abusing Woman. Institutional mechanisms that identify and sometimes help men with substance abuse problems are not as readily available as outreach vehicles to women. For example, women who need treatment are less likely than are men to be identified in the workplace because proportionally fewer are employed (63 percent of women were employed in 1990 in comparison to 75 percent of men).[4] Although the number of adolescent girls and adult women in the criminal justice system is increasing (there has

Prisons for men are more likely to have medical services, substance abuse treatment, and other support services than are those for women.

been a 200 percent increase in the women's prison population in the past 8 years), prisons for men are more likely to have medical services, substance abuse treatment, and other support services than are those for women. However, women have more contact with staff from social services (welfare), Head Start, shelters, hospitals (when giving birth), and emergency rooms (when battered). The personnel employed by these institutions need to be trained to identify substance-abusing women.

Cultural Values and Norms. Until fairly recently, cultural differences have been largely ignored in addressing treatment issues. Today, it is understood that to treat women with substance abuse problems successfully a program must have a certain level of "cultural competency."

Culture, as defined in *Cultural Competence for Evaluators*, is the shared values, norms, traditions, customs, arts, history, folklore, and institutions of a group of people. Within this perspective and from this definition, cultural competence is a set of academic and interpersonal skills that allow individuals to increase their understanding and appreciation of cultural differences and similarities within, among, and between groups. This requires a willingness and ability to draw on community-based values, traditions, and customs, and to work with knowledgeable persons of and from the community to develop focused interventions and other supports.[5]

As Orlandi has noted,

> Cultures do not remain the same indefinitely. Cultural subgroups exert an influence over and are influenced by individuals who are members of those groups as well as other cultural groups with whom these subgroups come into contact.[6]

It is important to note that cultural competency is a key issue in attracting women of color into treatment programs.

It is important to note that cultural competency is a key issue in attracting women of color into treatment programs:

> Women of color fear not only outright racism but a treatment system insensitive to their cultural and ethnic values which may also have little sensitivity to the special needs of women...[7] The culturally liberated caregiver acknowledges the reality of racism without allowing it to be an excuse for the client's self-destructive behavior.[8]

This can apply to other populations as well, including lesbians, women with disabilities, and women who have been or are prostitutes.

Family Responsibilities. Many women will not enroll in outpatient treatment programs unless they can arrange adequate supervision for their children. Women entering inpatient treatment who leave their children in someone else's care may fear losing custody of their children. This is particularly true for the following women:

- women already in the criminal justice system who believe disclosure of a substance abuse problem will be the "last straw" as far as custody is concerned;

- pregnant women who fear being called "unfit mothers" or facing legal sanctions for using drugs while pregnant;

- women subjected to domestic violence who fear that no one will protect their children;

- homeless women who fear that Child Protective Services will remove their children from their custody;

- lesbians who are concerned that disclosure of their lifestyle will result in losing custody of their children;

- women with disabilities who, even without the stigma of substance abuse, are often perceived as unable to fulfill the parenting role; and

- any woman with children who does not have a family or support system to care for her children while she is in treatment.

The treatment program staff should be aware that the degree of fear experienced by these women (expressed or not) may depend on the cultural "value" placed on children and the role of children in the family.

Thus if a program does not provide child care, neither inpatient nor outpatient treatment is truly available to women with children, who are the majority of substance abusing women. To attract women with children, the treatment program should do at least one of the following:

- investigate and evaluate the possibility of providing full or partial child care on the premises during the mother's treatment process and meet the necessary licensing require- ments for providing such care;

- recruit volunteers among program staff, women in the final stages of treatment, family members, retired persons or senior citizens, interns from local schools and places of worship, and members of self-help groups to staff the child care program; and

- compile and distribute a directory of free or low-cost licensed day care service providers in the community and explore financial subsidies to improve access.

Denial. Denial is a primary characteristic of addiction. Outreach programs may, in fact, be the first step in helping a woman break through denial. Reaching out to a woman and engaging her in a process of acknowledging a need for help is a prerequisite for effective treatment. A

If a program does not provide child care, neither inpatient nor outpatient treat- ment is truly available to women with children.

woman who acknowledges that she needs help is much more empowered to accept and remain in treatment.

Women's Fears. Substance-abusing women have many fears that must be addressed in designing and implementing outreach strategies. These include the following:

Many women live in great fear of being rejected and abandoned.

Fear of Rejection. Many women live in great fear of being rejected and abandoned by loved ones, friends, and by others, for example co-workers. They believe their loved ones may reject them if they learn that their mother, spouse, daughter, partner, friend, or sibling is addicted to alcohol and/or other drugs. Some adolescent girls and adult women also believe that a treatment program or its staff will reject them. They may fear rejection because they are "too bad," they engage in life styles not approved of by society.

Fear of rejection may be particularly pronounced among adolescents, especially those in the criminal justice system, whose families may have already rejected them. Also, women with AIDS or women who are HIV-positive may fear rejection if they have already felt rejected by health care providers, employers, family, and friends once they revealed their medical status.

Fear of Becoming Abstinent or Getting Well. For women who have developed few if any coping skills (e.g., assertiveness skills, stress management techniques), the idea of facing life without the temporary relief and/or escape that alcohol and other drugs offer at least in the early stages of use may be overwhelming. During the outreach phase, these women need assurance that it is possible not only to face life but to enjoy it without the "help" of mood-altering or mind-altering chemicals. Using recovering women as role models in the outreach program can provide this assurance, as will involvement in recreational programs related to stress management.

Fear of Dealing with Authority Figures. This fear may be particularly pronounced for these types of women:

- women from economically or racially disadvantaged populations;

- women who have had negative experiences in trying to obtain social services (housing, medical care, food stamps, job training, etc.);

- women in the criminal justice system who see the system as punitive rather than rehabilitative, women with criminal records and/or outstanding warrants, and women who have engaged in illegal activities to support their addiction;

- female adolescents who have had behavioral problems;

- illegal aliens who fear deportation (and fear that registering anywhere will mean that the government will find them, whether a program is government-funded or not); and

- women who have been victims of incest or sexual abuse.

To address these concerns, outreach programs should develop relationships with departments of education, local legal aid offices, law offices, and other relevant agencies to identify individuals who are sensitive to the needs of women who abuse alcohol and/or other substances. These individuals could then be "gatekeepers" for referrals to that agency and could also visit the program periodically to meet with women in treatment. By conducting training sessions for the staffs of these agencies, the outreach program would sensitize them to the needs of women in treatment. The program could then advertise the availability of these services in its outreach materials.

Substance-abusing women may be involved in family and/or significant-other relationships with individuals who do not support their interest in treatment.

Fear of Retaliation. Substance-abusing women may be involved in family and/or significant-other relationships with individuals who do not support their interest in treatment, and who often threaten to retaliate if they decide to enter treatment. Retaliation may take many forms, including "cutting the purse strings," threatening to report them as unfit mothers, abandoning them, putting them out of their homes, telling other people (such as employers and/or children) "all about them," and committing acts of physical violence against them, including the threat of death.

Fear of Exposure. Women may fear being publicly "branded" as alcoholics and/or addicts if they enter treatment. In addition, concerns about confidentiality may be particularly acute for women fearing revelation of their status as pregnant and/or HIV-positive. Outreach materials should include statements that all client information is kept confidential (noting specifically what exceptions apply).

Fear of Failure or Hopelessness. If women have already been in a treatment program and have relapsed or have had an unpleasant experience in a previous treatment program, they may feel hopeless about their ability to recover. Other factors may contribute to this sense of hopelessness:

•   HIV-positive women/women with AIDS who believe that since they are going to die anyway, it is hopeless (or irrelevant) to become alcohol and drug free;

•   women who feel trapped in abusive relationships, who see no hope of getting out of them, who believe that only alcohol or other drugs make the situation tolerable; and

•   young women who believe they have no future.

4.2   Barriers to Outreach Unique to Population Groups

This section briefly describes barriers to outreach that are unique to specific groups of women, including the following:

- age groups (adolescents and older women);

- pregnant and postpartum women;

- ethnic and racial minority populations; and

- other specific groups of women.

4.2.1   Age Groups

This section summarizes information about outreach strategies targeting adolescent girls (aged 12-18) and older women (65 and older).

Adolescent Girls

The outreach information in this section addresses the concerns of both male and female adolescents because most of the available literature does not specifically address outreach to adolescent girls. It is important to note that this information may also apply to adolescents residing in programs with their mothers.

Some obstacles to reaching high-risk teenagers, which apply to both boys and girls, include the following:[9]

- a false sense of bravado and willingness to take risks, coupled with a fear of being branded as "sick." This can lead to a normalizing of substance abuse;

- feelings of ambivalence and confusion about alcohol because of conflicting messages about alcohol use in the home, in society and within peer groups;

- skepticism, distrust and fear of continued rejection based on the individual's history of treatment and of poor family relationships;

- hopelessness among young people in inner cities regarding the possibility of ever having a worthwhile future with a decent job; and

- the presence in some inner-city neighborhoods of an open, accessible drug culture without apparent social sanctions, and the easy way in which large sums of money can be obtained by those who deal in drugs.

Many high-risk youth have had lifelong difficulties trying to "fit in" and to find a sense of belonging with their families, at school, and with peers.

Many high-risk youth have had lifelong difficulties trying to "fit in" and to find a sense of belonging with their families, at school, and with peers. These youth may be harder to reach because they resist traditional authority. Some may have a low literacy level. If so, materials targeting this population are most effective if written on a third or fourth grade level.

Before designing and implementing outreach programs for adolescent girls, it is important to assess the community and learn as much as possible about the particular environment in which the girls live. According to Resnick and Wojcicki:

> understanding key adolescent issues is critical in planning intervention activities. Effective outreach programs make contact with high-risk youth in settings where they are most comfortable. Youth at high risk for use of alcohol and other drugs tend to be alienated from traditional institutions and, thus, difficult to reach through conventional approaches.[10]

Outreach to adolescents is often conducted through existing community youth organizations, such as places of worship, parent organizations, and schools. However, some adolescents at risk for or already involved in the use or abuse of alcohol and other drugs have dropped out of school or are not involved with community groups. In such cases, an effective outreach approach is to "hang out" and distribute literature in locations in which adolescents congregate, including fast food restaurants, street corners, and shopping malls. Outreach activities should focus on places where adolescent girls may seek services, such as family planning and STD clinics, general health care clinics, and welfare and other social agency offices. Networking with probation, parole, and correctional officers and with youth workers or community activists involved in outreach to gangs can help identify adolescent girls who need substance abuse treatment services.

Beyond distribution of literature, more creative, youth-oriented strategies should be implemented. These strategies may include involvement in the following activities:

- street theater performed at locations frequented by youth;

- rap videos and music;

- distributing colorful, eye catching T-shirts; and

- special events at recreation centers or juvenile detention centers.

Activities and services need to be appealing to young people to encourage their participation. The National Council on Alcoholism and Drug Dependence, the AIDS Clearinghouse, and other agencies have produced many informative brochures, posters, and other material for youth. These materials can be distributed with information from the treatment program.

Physicians and other primary health care practitioners often do not diagnose substance abuse problems within the older female population.

Outreach workers need to be specifically trained to identify youth at risk and to speak with them using their vocabulary; peer outreach can be utilized where feasible and appropriate. By knowing how to communicate with adolescents, outreach workers can encourage potential clients to seek help.

Older Women

In general, neither the early- nor late-onset cases of alcohol and/or other drug abuse among older people come to the attention of the substance abuse treatment professional through the usual referral networks (courts, employers, spouses, families). Older women may be isolated from their community and family because they may no longer drive, may have retired from their jobs, and may be living alone because of separation or death. Widows may be a particularly vulnerable population for alcohol and prescription drug abuse.

Therefore, the primary route of intervention may be through the health care system, including the health care provider(s) and the acute care setting where older women seek treatment for age-related health problems. However, physicians and other primary health care practitioners often do not diagnose substance abuse problems within the older female population, in part because of insufficient specialized training in addictions. Many physicians do not fully understand the potential consequences of alcohol and other drug interactions in this age group. Even when problems are recognized, many physicians, other health care workers, and family members are reluctant to intervene because of the mistaken notion that the woman's age precludes change or that withdrawal from the substance would cause her undue stress. Some family members even believe that the older woman is easier to deal with when she is numbed by alcohol and other drugs. Finally, family members and friends may have little knowledge about how alcohol, prescription drugs, and over-the-counter (OTC) preparations may affect their loved one's mood and physical condition.

Many substance abuse treatment professionals are unfamiliar with the senior services network (and vice versa); thus, the network of senior services is underutilized in outreach and program development. Specific programming for older women has not, for the most part, become standard in substance abuse treatment programs. This is true partly because the proportion of substance-abusing women in older age groups is significantly lower than that of younger age groups. Also, because alcohol and other drug use patterns, lifestyles, and environments of older women are often different from those of many younger women, they may not readily fit into programs designed to treat younger substance-abusing women.

Because alcohol and other drug use patterns, lifestyles, and environments of older women are often different from those of many younger women, they may not readily fit into programs designed to treat younger substance-abusing women.

Outreach and identification must be modified to attract the older woman with a substance abuse problem. Many women in this age range are socialized to believe that you do not "air your dirty laundry in public," and you do not to talk about problems. This makes outreach, access, treatment, and coordinating care more difficult. It also should be emphasized that women 65 and older have significantly varying physical and mental health states. Some "older" women of 75 or 80 may be in better health than women who are younger, although this is less likely to be true for women who abused alcohol or other drugs for long periods. As with other issues and populations, culture may play a role in outreach to this population.

Specific outreach strategies for older women include the following:

- establish relationships with social service agencies and community organizations to work with older women. Arrange to distribute flyers through these agencies and conduct seminars about substance abuse among older women for their staff;

- arrange workshops and special events at adult day care centers and at meetings or activities sponsored by groups such as the American Association of Retired Persons, Gray Panthers, and the Older Women's League;

- meet with physicians who primarily serve older women to discuss substance abuse problems in this age group and to discuss drug interactions;

- train health aides who work with older women about alcohol and substance abuse;

- conduct seminars or workshops through state and local medical and nursing associations on substance abuse problems among older women;

- develop a list of signs and symptoms that are consistent with substance abuse in older women. The list of indicators should include the following: combined use of alcohol/prescription/OTC medications; broken bones associated with falls or accidents; gaps in memory; cognitive impairment; trembling; weight loss; fatigue; insomnia; malnutrition; incontinence; aggression; depression; general debility; inadequate self-care/poor hygiene; lack of physical exercise; social isolation; and difficulty controlling such diseases as diabetes, gout, or angina. The list should be designed for use by primary care providers and should describe the possible array of indicators that may warrant further investigation of substance abuse or misuse; and

- maintain a list of older women in recovery who are willing to share their stories with other women in the program.

4.2.2   Pregnant and Postpartum Women

It is important to reach out and enroll substance abusing women in treatment when they are pregnant. However, it is often difficult to do so because of complex societal and medical problems. Frequently, pregnant and postpartum women who use and abuse alcohol and other drugs are

much more severely stigmatized than women who are not pregnant. Therefore, they may deny their drug use, its possible effects and their need for
help. Pregnant and postpartum women, particularly young poor women,
are often afraid of the medical and social welfare system and/or personnel
within these systems because they have had negative experiences with
them. A recent report by experts in the field and issued with support from
CSAT, the Treatment Improvement Protocol (TIP) for pregnant substance
abusing women, provides information about these issues.[11]

Pregnant and postpartum women, particularly young poor women, are often afraid of the medical and social welfare system.

Government agencies and the public are increasingly concerned
about the use of both legal and illegal drugs by pregnant women. Some
groups have taken or proposed punitive actions (including jail sentences)
against substance-abusing women who are pregnant and women of
childbearing age who are using cocaine and/or crack cocaine. Many states
require hospitals to report pregnant women suspected of heavy alcohol and
other drug use to local public health authorities or the criminal justice
system when the women present for delivery. This reporting may cause
women to be even more wary of acknowledging that they have a problem.
In fact, it may result in some women avoiding prenatal care and hospital
delivery, particularly if they have other children who are in the custody of
Child Protective Services (CPS) or who are living with relatives. The
women then fear the loss of their children. In many states, CPS, foster care
placements, and review boards base their decisions on whether to return a
child to his/her mother on the length of time the child is away from the
mother. This serves as a deterrent to women seeking effective long-term
substance abuse treatment if child care is not available in such treatment
programs.

Strategies to encourage pregnant and postpartum women and
adolescent girls to enter treatment include the following:

- develop and advertise specific services for pregnant and postpartum women. Materials should include information about the program's social services and child care provisions offered at or through the treatment program;

- conduct outreach activities in places such as WIC programs, ob/gyn clinics, family planning centers, well-baby clinics, departments of social services, Head Start offices, and Le Leche League chapters;

- develop and show videotaped stories of other pregnant women who have successfully completed substance abuse treatment;

- provide education on the relevance of seeking treatment before delivery; and

- educate physicians, midwives, and other health professionals about treatment resources and the importance of identifying substance-abusing women within their patient populations.

The possibility of having their children reunited with them is often an incentive for mothers to enter treatment.

Many women who seek treatment for substance abuse problems were teenagers when giving birth to their first children. Outreach to this population of mothers needs to co-occur with the development of specific programs for them. Intervening with the woman and the child(ren) she has at present, rather than waiting until subsequent children are born, is critical.

The possibility of having their children reunited with them is often an incentive for mothers to enter treatment. Under supervision, mothers can learn effective parenting skills, become drug-free and experience improved relationships with their children. This not only provides further incentive for the mothers to enter treatment, it unburdens foster care systems by assuring the safety of the child in a therapeutic milieu. This reunification model is often not emphasized.

4.2.3 Ethnic and Racial Populations

Successful identification and outreach to women with substance abuse problems requires racial, ethnic, and cultural knowledge, competency, and sensitivity. When staff members engage in outreach to women, they should understand the issues confronted by diverse ethnic and racial minority populations and recognize that there is diversity within racial and ethnic groups. For example, the culture and experience of an African American woman whose family has lived in an urban area in the Midwest for generations may be significantly different from an African American woman who lives in a rural community in the South. Their experiences will be different from a woman of primarily African descent who recently immigrated from Jamaica. The culture and experience of a Laotian woman who recently immigrated to the United States will differ significantly from a third generation woman of Japanese descent. Cultural values and norms vary across ethnic groups of Caucasian women as well, particularly among those who are recent immigrants or first-generation Americans.

African American Women. Having survived a historical experience that demanded extraordinary courage and inner strength, traditionally African American women are seen as strong and as not needing anyone or anything to cope with life and its challenges. This perception is perpetuated by continuing socioeconomic conditions that require African American women to maintain a predominant role in caring for their families. If an African American woman believes she should be strong, regardless of her circumstances, she might feel that admitting she needs help is a sign of personal failure and that she has failed her family. This can result in low self-esteem and feelings of shame that could keep her from admitting to herself or others that she has a substance abuse problem.

African American women are most likely to rely on other African American women or their place of worship for assistance with crises. For

When staff members engage in outreach to women, they should understand the issues confronted by diverse ethnic and racial minority populations.

African American women are most likely to rely on other African American women or their place of worship for assistance with crises.

example, African American women often establish sisterhood relationships to help each other with proactive listening, counseling, and emotional support. Informal neighborhood groups (card playing groups), formal clubs (social and charity), church groups and to a lesser degree, sororities have been important sources of networking for African American women. Recently three of the largest sororities (Zeta Phi Beta, Delta Sigma Theta, and Alpha Kappa Alpha) have developed substance abuse prevention programs. These sororities differ from the mainstream sororities in that their dominant focus is on community action and social service.

To facilitate the African American woman's acceptance of treatment, it is important for a program to establish relationships with respected African American individuals and organizations in the community. Religious institutions and community organizations that serve African American women can be vital resources for a successful outreach program.

American Indian Women. American Indian populations consist of approximately 450 different tribes with varying customs and some 250 languages. For American Indian women, barriers to treatment include the following:

- the disproportionate number of unemployed American Indian women, which hinders early detection and referral in the workplace;

- the lack of education in cross-cultural issues among physicians, nurses, social workers, and other health care providers may result in a lack of sensitivity to the values, beliefs, and practices of American Indian women; the use of stereotypes, although unconsciously by health care providers, can be a basis for assessment and diagnosis;

- geographic isolation, which limits access to substance abuse treatment; the lack of funding in the Indian Health Service for needed programs; and the disproportionate poverty among American Indian women, further limiting financial access to treatment; and

- cultural differences among American Indian women in the relative value placed on the use of different substances (some of which they do not consider addictive), may preclude the women from accepting or seeking help for their abuse of other substances.

Because of a long history of a lack of trust in the United States federal government (because of broken treaties, outlawing of American Indian languages and religious practices, and inadequate services provided through the government), American Indians often mistrust health care programs run by government agencies, including substance abuse programs. Developing a relationship of trust with American Indian women is, therefore, critical in the outreach phase.

A simple, cost-effective strategy to identify high-risk American Indian women is for treatment programs to establish relationships with existing American Indian programs, such as cultural centers, Indian Health Boards, and Indian healers.

However, it should be noted that a little less than half of all American Indians live in rural and/or reservation communities. The remaining population lives in urban locations scattered among other racial/cultural groups rather than in cohesive communities. This poses another barrier in identifying American Indian women who are at risk.

Asian and Pacific Islander Women. To design an outreach program for Asian/Pacific Islander women, it is important to understand the complexity of the historical, social, economic, political, and cultural factors that underscore the Asian/Pacific Islander experience in the United States and the diversity of the population itself. Sue has suggested that for Asian

Developing a relationship of trust with American Indian women is critical in the outreach phase.

Asian/Pacific Islander women who are immigrants and refugees confront many stressors that exacerbate already severe challenges in their daily ability to cope and function.

American populations (as would be true for other recent immigrant populations), it is important to consider the specific ethnic group, place of birth, generational status, and degree of acculturation.[12]

Asian/Pacific Islander women who are immigrants and refugees confront many stressors that exacerbate already severe challenges in their daily ability to cope and function. These challenges may include language barriers (which can make it difficult to obtain basic resources such as health care), racism, social isolation, changes in traditional family roles, economic distress, and family disintegration. Mainstream services are often underutilized by Asian/Pacific Islander women because the services are inaccessible, too expensive, culturally irrelevant, and/or unavailable in their native language.

Sun has suggested the following as useful strategies to intervene with Asian American women:[13]

- have bilingual and bicultural professionals available who can engage and be involved in the treatment process for newly arrived immigrants - the program might gain access to volunteer professionals through Asian American organizations in their community;

- eliminate terms such as "mental illness" or "psychiatric dysfunction," which Asian Americans tend to be more sensitive to than Westerners; and

- include information that reflects cultural sensitivity, including recognition of the Asian woman's traditional role, ethnic, and cultural identity(ies) and the importance of intergenerational relationships in outreach material.

Hispanic/Latina Women. The Hispanic population in the United States is heterogenous, representing different cultures and ethnic groups.

Many communities are inhabited by multiple Hispanic groups where generational differences exist within each group. Treatment programs conducting outreach to Hispanic women should become familiar with the diversity, origins, dynamics, cultures, and problems of the different Hispanic groups living in the community. Treatment providers should not assume that one approach will work for all Hispanic groups or that all Hispanic women exhibit the same pattern or type of substance abuse problem.

Many substance abuse treatment programs do not have staff who can communicate in Spanish. Hispanic women, therefore, tend to view these programs as less than "user-friendly." If possible, programs serving Spanish-speaking women should have treatment staff who can speak Spanish. Also, educational materials on substance abuse and treatment often assume high levels of reading ability. This presents an obstacle for those who are not proficient in the English language. Thus, materials should be available in Spanish.

Outreach to Hispanic women requires a genuine respect for the women and their family culture.

Outreach to Hispanic women requires a genuine respect for the women and their family culture. The families of Hispanic women can be important resources to help these women get treatment for substance abuse problems. However, if family members feel that a woman's participation in treatment threatens the status quo or legal standing of the family, they can work against a woman who is responding to outreach efforts. Disclosure may be a particular problem for undocumented Hispanic women who fear that this may result in their deportation; they may also fear that undocumented family members (and friends) will be discovered and deported if they enter the "system" in any way.

4.2.4   Other Specific Groups of Women

Many women are not aware of their HIV status until they are symptomatic with AIDS and/or have been diagnosed through the health care system, often through prenatal testing.

Women with HIV/AIDS. During the second decade of the AIDS epidemic, the number of women with HIV/AIDS has increased dramatically. In recognition of the differences in disease progression and types of opportunistic infections of HIV/AIDS in women, the CDC recently revised the diagnostic categories used to define an individual as having AIDS. (Chapter 2 presented more detailed epidemiologic data on women and HIV/AIDS.) The increase in the number of reported AIDS cases may, in part, be because of this expanded definition.

Outreach and identification of HIV-infected women often occurs at their point of need, such as through primary or acute health care, public assistance, or other social service agencies. However, it is important to note that many women are not aware of their HIV status until they are symptomatic with AIDS and/or have been diagnosed through the health care system, often through prenatal testing.

HIV-positive women from lower socioeconomic groups often lack the resources to meet their most basic needs for food, housing, and transportation. As a result, they may delay seeking care for their substance abuse problems or for their HIV status until they become symptomatic or until their basic needs, or those of their children, have been met. HIV-positive women who are addicted to illicit drugs may fear interacting with the health care system, for fear of being placed in the criminal justice system. They may choose not to seek treatment until they have established a trusting relationship with a case worker or health care professional or until there is a medical crisis.

Specific outreach strategies include the following:

- work with local AIDS prevention and advocacy groups, including street outreach programs, to promote the program's services for women at high risk for or with HIV/AIDS; and

- encourage staff members to appear on local radio and television talk shows to discuss the needs of substance using women with HIV/AIDS and how the treatment program tries to address those needs.

Women Residing in Rural Areas. A shortage of primary care physicians exists in poor urban neighborhoods and in rural areas. Families who must travel from rural areas to urban clinics for health care may have no place to stay in the city. Few have the energy to make multiple visits to different institutions at different times (often waiting for a long time to receive services) to obtain care for themselves and their families. Because it may be difficult to find lodging when traveling long distances for services, many women delay seeking treatment until a crisis develops. Helping women from rural areas to use health and social services is important. This may require providing or helping the women to access transportation. Also important are methods of "getting the word out" about women-specific services across large, often sparsely-populated geographic areas.

Specific outreach strategies include the following:

- work with staff of rural hospitals and health clinics to identify women who need services and make home visits, where appropriate, with health care or social services personnel; and

- advertise program services on local radio stations and in local county newspapers.

Many homeless women are substance-abusing, psychiatrically impaired, and physically ill individuals.

Homeless Women.   Homeless women are vulnerable to a variety of risky behaviors, diseases, and disorders.   Many homeless women are substance-abusing, psychiatrically impaired, and physically ill individuals. The stigma attached to being "homeless" impedes many women from seeking assistance.   Some homeless women who have children fear that they will lose their children and/or their places in homeless shelters if they admit to having substance abuse problems.   Homeless women may be frightened, distrustful, and/or unfamiliar with systems of care and treatment.   Some women who are homeless and who have few dependents will move from one shelter to another.   It is critical to note here that all homeless women are not in shelters: some may be in living arrangements with family or friends.   Also, some women may be in a battering relationship and may be abusing alcohol or other drugs as a result of the stressors caused by this relationship.   Such women may live temporarily with relatives or friends, and their residential status may be difficult to discern.

Because homeless women are outside the mainstream networks of referrals and intervention, those who require acute medical attention or who are being detained for alleged civil or criminal violations often come to the attention of police and emergency room personnel more frequently than they do to substance abuse treatment professionals.   The primary routes of intervention, therefore, must be through street outreach, medical clinics, law enforcement, emergency rooms, public housing communities (for those women still in housing), and jails or detention centers.

Lesbians.   Lesbians, unlike many other minority groups, cannot be readily identified based on appearance, language, or socioeconomic criteria. The lesbian category embraces women of all ages (including adolescents and older women), races, ethnicities, religions, socioeconomic groups, and physical abilities.   Since determining the percentage of lesbians in our society depends on self-reporting, and knowing that many lesbians will not identify themselves because of society's stigmatization of homosexuality,

the number of lesbians in any community is likely to be grossly underestimated. Adolescent lesbians (an extremely high-risk group with a very high
suicide rate) and lesbians who are parents (approximately one-third of
lesbians) are underserved by substance abuse treatment providers.
Treatment programs may not have staff who are sensitive to the needs of
lesbians, and in fact, the staff may even be hostile. These factors create barriers
to outreach, treatment, and continuing care because a lesbian would not want to
enter a program with an insensitive or hostile environment.

Women of color who are lesbians face an even greater potential for
discrimination than Caucasian women. Many of these women may be
more difficult to identify and serve effectively than their Caucasian counterparts. Very few programs are designed for lesbians of color. Outreach
strategies developed for this population must be detailed, consistent, and
use appropriate language and events. Above all, the outreach strategies
must be safe. As noted by Kanuha, lesbians of color face a variety of
challenges because of the prejudices inherent in both the heterosexual and
lesbian communities. Racism in the lesbian community is reinforced by the
relative lack of presence of women of color in the mainstream lesbian
culture. For lesbians of color to benefit from therapy, clinicians must
understand the dynamics of being both a woman of color and a lesbian.[14]

The overriding emotion that drives almost all of the individual barriers to outreach for lesbians is fear.

The overriding emotion that drives almost all of the individual
barriers to outreach for lesbians is fear. Lesbians fear losing anonymity or
acknowledging homosexuality in a setting outside the lesbian community
or an immediate circle of friends. A lesbian may fear that revealing her
sexual orientation could result in losing a job or being separated from
valuable relationships.

Lesbians are cautious about obtaining help if they feel that their
partners or significant others will not be treated with respect. Very often,
programs are not willing or prepared to integrate same-sex partners into

groups of couples or family therapy sessions. In addition, many lesbians who are mothers hesitate to seek services because they fear they will lose custody of their children.

Outreach to lesbians must be specific to the population, must be community-based, and safe. Resources for lesbians in rural settings will, as a rule, be more difficult to develop because lesbians may be more difficult to reach (i.e., be less open about their sexual orientation) than those living in urban areas. Programs that seek to serve lesbians must be prepared to advocate on their behalf for health and social services, to anticipate the possibility of receiving criticism from the heterosexual population, and to invest time developing credibility within the lesbian community.

Specific outreach strategies include the following:

- develop relationships with gay/lesbian bookstores, offering them, for example, space to sell books at program events in return for their distributing program materials at gay/lesbian bookstores;

- support lesbian-specific community events, and provide staff and/or assistance with advertising and distributing announcements;

- advertise programs and activities in publications created specifically for the lesbian community;

- have an information booth at lesbian and gay events;

- use language in program materials to indicate that services are available for partners of women, rather than for husbands or spouses only; and

- sponsor alcohol and drug-free social and sports events for lesbians.

Women with Disabilities. Women with physical and mental health disabilities, who often face double discrimination based on disability and gender[15] and who have limited socially sanctioned roles,[16] are under-represented in treatment programs for a variety of reasons. Barriers to women with disabilities receiving needed substance abuse treatment services include the following:

- social isolation because of transportation, architecture, and communication barriers as well as negative social attitudes toward people with disabilities;

- enabling behavior by physicians, family, and friends who feel frustrated by their inability to "fix" the woman's disability and unwittingly encourage the use of alcohol and other drugs;[17]

- failure to identify substance abuse problems since abuse-related behaviors are mistakenly attributed to the disability;[18] and

- lack of access to treatment services. Historic patterns of segregation have deprived women and men with disabilities access to the same range of substance abuse treatment services and programs available to their nondisabled peers.[19]

To reach women with disabilities, treatment programs must engage in an active, highly visible outreach campaign.

To reach women with disabilities, treatment programs must engage in an active, highly visible outreach campaign. One idea is to include women with disabilities or representatives from advocacy groups on the program's advisory board. Another idea is to work with representatives from local independent living centers, which are advocacy organizations governed and staffed by people with disabilities and located throughout the country. These representatives can help treatment programs become a presence in the disability community by serving as spokespersons at meetings and events, by serving as liaisons between programs and disability agencies, and by referring clients to the program.

Advisory board members can also help design outreach materials in a range of formats that will be accessible to women with diverse disabilities. For example, brochures should be made available in braille, large print, and on audiotape to reach women with visual disabilities. They should also be available in simplified language to reach women with intellectual or learning disabilities. Public service announcements (PSAs) on television should be available with open or closed captions to reach women who are deaf. All materials should provide information on the accessibility of the facility and program to people with disabilities. Using images of women with disabilities in program publicity also sends a strong message of inclusion.

Disability awareness training for all staff members is critical.

Networking with disability and rehabilitation organizations is another useful outreach strategy. Such organizations often have limited awareness of the signs and symptoms of substance abuse and may benefit from training in the identification of substance abuse problems and referral strategies. Their staff, in turn, may serve as a resource to the organization on disability issues.

Disability awareness training for all staff members is critical, not only to develop effective outreach strategies, but also to ensure that women with disabilities remain in treatment past the intake stage. Training should include an opportunity for staff to explore their own attitudes toward disability, since stereotypes and negative assumptions can be a major barrier to effective treatment.

Staff members need to learn how disability relates to gender and the relationship of both disability and gender bias to substance abuse. Information on substance abuse issues for different types of disability groups is also useful.[20] Ideally, the trainers should include women with disabilities. This is particularly important when staff members have had limited exposure to people with disabilities.

Finally, programs should become familiar with the requirements of the Americans with Disabilities Act (ADA) which prohibits discrimination against people with disabilities. The ADA applies to all substance abuse treatment programs regardless of size as service providers.[21] Privately-run treatment programs are covered under the public accommodations section of the law (Title III), and government-run programs are covered under state and local government provisions (Title II). Knowledge of the law is essential to ensure compliance as well as effective outreach. The law mandates that people with disabilities be served in the most integrated settings possible. To ensure nondiscrimination, the law establishes a series of specific requirements covering such areas as 1) eligibility criteria; 2) policies, practices, and procedures; 3) auxiliary aides and services for people with communication disabilities; and 4) architectural access. To obtain a full description of the law and its requirements, program administrators are advised to consult the growing body of available resources.[22] Local disability advocacy groups are additional sources of information.

Women and Adolescent Girls in the Criminal Justice System. Data show that most women in the criminal justice system are involved or have been involved in substance abuse. However, reaching these women for treatment requires overcoming many barriers, including their fear of self-disclosure, legal sanctions, and losing custody of their children. While many young women in particular fear self-disclosure (especially to adults, who may be judgmental about their behaviors), women in the criminal justice system generally fear that disclosing their need for substance abuse treatment will result in additional sanctions, including increased time on probation or parole, incarceration, a transfer to higher security or longer term facilities, or severance of their parental rights. Commonly, women who have lost or are in danger of losing custody of their children as a result of incarceration are cut off from the most potent motivation for them to enter treatment. Also, the laws on child abuse in many states require outreach workers to report women suspected of criminal negligence to

Women in the criminal justice system generally fear that disclosing their need for substance abuse treatment will result in additional sanctions.

local public health and/or criminal justice system authorities. When this occurs, the outreach worker becomes an adversary rather than an advocate for the woman, defeating the purpose of outreach. Moreover, a number of systemic factors in the criminal justice system impede the treatment process for women and should be considered as part of outreach. These include the fact that women are often given "flat time" in local jails, which frequently lack substance abuse treatment services (and general health and mental health services). The local jails also may not have adequate systems of referral for women to substance abuse treatment (and other support systems) following release.

Often, by the time women are in the criminal justice system, traditional sources that might have supported their entry into substance abuse treatment have failed repeatedly. Treatment may also have failed, and these women are likely to believe that no other way of life is possible. The combination of fear and cynicism make it unlikely that they will voluntarily seek treatment. Criminal justice system personnel often view incarcerated women more negatively than incarcerated men. This further stigmatizes women, creates resistance among women to seek treatment, and creates resistance among treatment staff and the criminal justice system staff to provide women-specific services.

Many of the criminal justice system personnel have little knowledge or training in the identification of substance abuse problems in women. Furthermore, they may not be aware of the daily realities of a substance-abusing woman's life and therefore may not be sensitive to her needs. They may also be unaware of the scope of women's issues as related to substance abuse and criminal behavior. These issues may include prostitution and rape, incest, or other sexual abuse.

Although some level of treatment services is available either directly or indirectly through referrals in many jails and prisons, the services are generally considered inadequate. Referral to treatment as an alternative to incarceration is increasingly used in communities throughout the country, but these arrangements frequently do not have sufficient contact with other health and social service providers. In fact, there is a general lack of coordination among social service, substance abuse treatment, medical, and criminal justice agencies. This fragmentation and lack of coordination deters women with substance abuse problems from seeking treatment and has made it difficult to establish "user-friendly" support networks for women and adolescent girls in the system.

Strategies to engage women in the criminal justice system include the following:

- establish relationships with parole, probation, third-party custody, advocacy, and other agencies and organizations from which clients can be referred; and

- hold meetings in detention centers for women of all ages. Provide them with written and audio visual materials.

CSAT currently funds a few demonstration projects involving the treatment of women in the criminal justice system. The evaluation of these projects will provide valuable information to plan and implement both outreach and treatment services.

4.3   General Approaches to Effective Outreach Programs

Designing and implementing effective outreach programs for women requires an understanding of the basic principles of marketing social programs. These include defining the product, creating an effective message, and delivering the message to the target audiences. Trained outreach workers and strong community contacts are essential. Most importantly, comprehensive services that meet women's needs must be

Asking a woman seeking treatment to come back "tomorrow" or "next week" is dismissing an opportunity, and/or may actually place her in danger.

developed and made available. Finally, it is important to note that many alcoholic and drug-addicted individuals have brief moments when they show a willingness to acknowledge their problem and seek treatment for it. Outreach professionals must take advantage of these opportunities whenever they occur. For example, asking a woman seeking treatment to come back "tomorrow" or "next week" is dismissing an opportunity, and/or may actually place her in danger.

4.3.1   Staffing the Outreach Program

Outreach workers who go into the community play a critical role in the success of the treatment program's outreach. Therefore, they need to be familiar with the community in which they work, both geographically and culturally. They must understand and be sensitive to the reality of women's lives and the many "pretreatment" issues women must face. In addition, they must understand the process of addiction and agree with their program's philosophy. Outreach workers must also convey respect and demonstrate support for women. They need to be able to describe to potential clients the problem of substance abuse and the opportunities offered by the treatment program in concise and understandable terms. Moreover, all program staff members should receive communication skills and outreach training because, in a sense, every contact outside the treatment program is a form of outreach.

Treatment programs have several options in staffing the outreach program:

- train existing program staff in outreach techniques;

- hire a former client or community resident who is a trained outreach worker with experience in or knowledge of substance abuse;

- contract with a community-based organization that has trained outreach workers in the community; or

- a combination of the above.

Because different skills are needed for clinical work than for outreach, the latter three options may be preferable.

4.3.2 The Product: Designing a Program that Actually Meets the Needs of the Women in the Target Population

To develop effective outreach strategies and identify women who need treatment, program directors and administrators must understand and accept the importance of customized outreach that uses gender-specific strategies based on existing knowledge and techniques. They must be willing to examine critically whether the current structure of the program helps or hinders outreach and to allocate the necessary staff and other resources to achieve outreach goals.

Program directors and administrators must understand and accept the importance of customized outreach that uses gender-specific strategies.

Before initiating outreach activities, the program staff and outreach workers must:

- identify the women to be reached within the community and understand their perspectives; and

- set specific program goals and objectives for treating women.

Outreach may be conducted in many different ways. Each program should assess its own resources, both human and financial, before deciding which outreach strategies to employ. The strategies suggested below vary in terms of cost and complexity, but they can be applied or adapted for women of different ages, ethnic groups, and other specific populations.

Specifically, experts recommend that outreach personnel do the following:

- collect and analyze available demographic data to form an accurate and comprehensive picture of the extent and nature of substance abuse problems among population groups in the community;

- examine whether the structure of the program's advisory board, board of directors, and staff is appropriate for the client population, and whether those individuals understand the impact of substance abuse on women. Add women of color, older women, women in rural areas, women with disabilities, and women who are bilingual, bicultural, or lesbians as appropriate to ensure that the board and staff represent a cross-section of women in the community;

- solicit ideas from health, mental health, disability/rehabilitation, legal, and social service personnel in the community who are in contact with the target population. Also, solicit ideas from women in recovery who can share their own experiences and concerns about treatment, and from the program staff;

- form teams from these groups and have them develop common goals, shared values, and agreements on how to approach treatment for women and adolescent girls who have abused alcohol and other drugs; ensure that directions and guidelines are consistent and that they foster trust and interest in treatment; and

- examine the language that the program uses to ensure that it: helps women understand addiction as a health issue; does not reinforce low self-esteem or powerlessness; does not further stigmatize women by insinuating that addiction is a moral failing; and helps them to understand their anger and express it in healthy ways.

Beyond recognizing the obstacles to treatment that women face, the program must be architecturally, economically, geographically, and culturally accessible. Strategies to accomplish this goal include the following:

- have a sliding-fee scale based on the woman's own ability to pay, if a fee is charged;

- arrange for safe, reliable, and low cost transportation to and from the facility. Provide bus or subway tokens for adolescents and low-income clients and, if necessary, request an extra bus stop by the facility or an extension of hours for bus service. If possible, have a donated vehicle available on-site or make arrangements to use a vehicle maintained by a local community organization or place of worship.

- for older women, work with the appropriate senior services agency to add bus routes that deliver passengers to the treatment facility; then schedule activities for seniors accordingly. Ensure that women with disabilities have accessible transportation. Explore a car-pool or other transportation for women who do not have access to public transportation;

- ensure that the individual program and facilities comply with the ADA requirements and that the staff is responsive to disability-related issues;

- ensure that the substance abuse services offered (or for which it makes referrals) are indeed available and responsive to the clients. A treatment program must develop a reputation for "keeping promises" in the community and to the women in its target population. It is important to ensure that this reputation is one that will attract women into treatment and that the program's success in this area is described in outreach efforts;

- recognize that providing treatment services to women is an evolutionary process that can be adapted based on the information gained from the program itself and from outside

The program must be architecturally, economically, geographically, and culturally accessible.

sources. In this regard, evaluation and feedback are extremely important aspects of treatment, but they have not been readily integrated into the treatment process or specifically into outreach. Part of the difficulty may be in misunderstanding these processes, which can be defined in two ways:

1.   evaluate the degree to which the program is meeting its goals and objectives. The process usually involves a variety of methods, including review of client records and follow-up of clients after treatment;

2.   obtain feedback as part of the formal or informal process of collecting subjective and objective information from clients and staff, and use these opinions in the treatment process and in program management.

To ensure that evaluation and feedback support the outreach process, the program should hold regular staff discussions on perceptions of the program's strengths and weaknesses and solicit feedback from clients, community, and others. These discussions should include staff commentary on the program structure and various components of the program, including outreach. The program also should establish a policy that encourages women in the treatment program to provide input into the outreach program to learn what works and to build their self-esteem. Evaluation is further discussed in Chapter 7.

4.3.3   The Message: Make it Compelling and Appealing to the Targeted Women

Substance abuse should be described as a health care issue, focusing, for example, on how substance abuse affects women's bodies. The message can also create an awareness that, for many women, the emotional and/or spiritual consequences of substance abuse led them to seek out or be receptive to treatment. Publications and media and community presentations should present a balanced message that does not blame women for their addiction problems, but instead recognizes the need for personal responsibility. To do otherwise only supports the woman's denial.

Materials should communicate an understanding of the stress that many women face in their everyday lives (e.g., poverty, discrimination, violence, unemployment, sexual or emotional abuse, problems with children) and acknowledge cultural or gender roles that contribute to or help lessen such stresses. Women often use alcohol or other drugs to "self-medicate" to deal with the effects of these stress factors. However, the lifestyle of substance abuse, particularly the use of illegal drugs, is itself a stressor. Outreach materials should inform women that there are ways to reduce and cope with stress, including understanding the factors over which they have no control.

All written materials about the program, such as pamphlets, brochures, and posters, should be culturally sensitive, easy to read, and relevant to women targeted for services. Because some substance-abusing women may have learning deficits or reading difficulties, the language should be simple and illustrations should be frequently used. Large print should be used in materials directed at older women. Materials should be published in Spanish and in other languages as appropriate for the target populations. Describe the services and activities offered by the program, or through referral, that meet women's needs. These may include the following:

All written materials about the program should be culturally sensitive, easy to read, and relevant to women targeted for services.

- information on the substance abuse treatment modalities used in the program. Be specific about whether the program is inpatient or outpatient, the duration of the program, and what child care services are available;

- a description of comprehensive health care and social services provided for women and children and special services for pregnant and postpartum women, such as assistance in obtaining entitlements for themselves and their children, infant care and developmental education, parenting training, pre- and postnatal health care for pregnant women, and nutrition education during pregnancy;

• counseling and support group options for women, by women;

• referral and resource information, including telephone numbers that women can call for food, shelter, medical care, and other forms of help in addition to treatment; and

• information on facility accessibility and referral resources to wheelchair users and women with other disabilities. Many programs have purchased telecommunication devices (TDDs) so that women who are deaf can contact the program.

In addition to basic print materials, programs may develop and market public service announcements (PSAs) for radio and television. Collaborating with a local high school, community college, university, radio/television/cable station, or other businesses with a media center to produce professional quality audio and video PSAs that focus on substance abuse has been a highly successful approach. Success stories need to convey to women that they can confront addiction problems and begin their recovery process. If resources are available, develop a PSA targeted to women and adolescent girls in the criminal justice system that informs them about their rights and the services available. Produce a brochure and a PSA about the effects of alcohol and other drugs on an unborn child for distribution to pregnant women, mothers, and women of childbearing age. Advisory board members, advocacy groups (organized around the issues of women and substance abuse), alumnae association members, staff, and female clients can help develop and critique outreach materials.

Programs can employ or request voluntary services from artists in the community to help design posters and flyers for the program. Many programs use art created by alumnae. Often, public relations and advertising firms may be willing to provide services to nonprofit organizations as a way of contributing to the community and reaping a tax benefit. The program can also conduct focus groups, formal or informal, with women who reflect the demographics of the target community to pretest the concepts and information developed for PSAs and print materials. This helps to ensure their relevance and effectiveness and create a sense of "ownership" among women in the community.

Often, public relations and advertising firms may be willing to provide services to nonprofit organizations as a way of contributing to the community and reaping a tax benefit.

4.3.4 Delivering the Message: The Message Must Reach the Women Targeted for Services

In most cases, one-on-one personal contact will be the most effective way to encourage substance-abusing women to enter treatment. These personal contacts may be formal (e.g., making a presentation at a club meeting or at a community-based women's health service organization) or informal (e.g., striking up conversations with women in the places where they gather in the community). Examples of strategies for delivering the message include the following:

Print Materials

- distribute materials in locations such as schools, grocery stores, malls, college campuses, places of worship, homeless shelters, food banks, runaway houses, battered women's shelters, senior citizen centers, day care facilities, welfare and public aid offices, detention centers, youth and recreation centers, major employers, the YWCA, health clubs, local police stations, probation and parole offices, soup kitchens, laundromats, beauty parlors, restaurants, bars, and gas stations;

- have local supermarkets print messages on grocery bags or insert flyers in the bags;

- display posters describing the program's services with phone numbers on telephone poles throughout the community, in compliance with local regulations regarding posters;

- post brochures and posters on bulletin boards in convenience stores;

- encourage local businesses to include flyers in salary envelopes;

- leave materials for distribution in doctors' offices (especially ob/gyn clinics, family practitioners and pediatricians), public health clinics, physical rehabilitation hospitals, emergency rooms, WIC offices, and other locations providing health care and social services for women;

- print buttons and t-shirts with the program's logo on them to advertise the program. Distribute them to women and girls involved in other programs and institutions through a social event arranged with the institutions, such as a movie and a discussion session with refreshments; and

- distribute materials at meetings of clubs, churches, and schools (e.g., Junior Leagues, Parent Teacher Associations).

Media

- write articles for the local newspaper on women, addiction, and health issues. Submit them to mainstream newspapers and periodicals as well as to publications for special population groups. Include information about the signs and symptoms of substance abuse and ways to get help;

- encourage local newspapers and radio and television (TV) stations to advertise the program free of charge. Using local media in rural areas can be a particularly effective outreach strategy because local newspapers and radio and TV stations reach women across large rural counties. Some newspapers may even provide free space;

- hand deliver the program's PSAs to TV and radio stations and try to meet with the person responsible for scheduling PSAs. Work with the station programmers to place the PSAs during programs that are most frequently viewed or listened to by the target populations;

- schedule the program's medical director or other staff members who are sensitive to women's issues as guests on local radio and television talk shows or call-in programs. This can be particularly effective in reaching older women, many of whom are devotees of talk shows; and

- use media outlets with specific target populations. For example, have program personnel fluent in Spanish speak on Spanish language radio and television programs to describe services for Hispanic women. Advertise program services in appropriate language on local radio stations that reach American Indian reservations.

Events

- hold information/education sessions in community settings, such as places of worship, community centers, schools, senior citizen centers, and other safe, familiar environments for potential clients;

- have a stand or booth at local health fairs, church gatherings, street fairs, and other community events. Answer questions and distribute information on women with substance abuse problems and the services that are available for them and their families;

- hold a potluck supper or an open house at a neighborhood center or public housing community and invite neighborhood women to attend. Arrange to have a recovering woman talk about her experience with substance abuse problems; and

- be sure events are held in locations that are accessible to persons in wheelchairs. Offer to provide sign language interpreters and other accommodations.

4.3.5   Professional and Community Contacts

The success of program outreach efforts will depend in large part on the strength of relationships with community-based groups and local, state, and federal service agencies. These groups and agencies will serve as major referral and support sources for the treatment program. The types of agencies to be contacted include: 1) public health and social services; 2) community-based programs for women; 3) the criminal justice system (e.g. the local probation and parole agency, public defenders, detention centers, and jails); 4) major employers; 5) charitable institutions (e.g. the Salvation Army, YWCA, Girl Scouts); and 6) places of worship. To develop liaisons with these organizations it would be appropriate to: 1) send a letter requesting a meeting and enclosing program materials; 2) meet with the appropriate personnel and explain the services provided by the program; 3) arrange to give a presentation or hold an event at the organization; and 4) maintain contact with the organization.

Other specific strategies include the following:

- invite health care providers working in the community to agency functions, community events, outdoor bazaars, and block parties;

- establish a relationship with child protection agencies to help identify women who need substance abuse treatment services and assist recovering women with family reintegration, if appropriate; and

- educate the housing authority about the importance of not evicting women with substance abuse problems, and promote the alternative of having women seek treatment and continuing care services.

4.3.6 Reaching Women's Support Groups

The message must also reach and educate the substance-abusing woman's support group (family, significant others, friends, coworkers) and social systems (spiritual leaders, shelter personnel, law enforcement officials, physicians, pharmacists, visiting nurses, teachers, home health care aides, probation, and correctional officers, etc.). Specifically, an outreach program can reach support groups in the following ways:

- arrange for, facilitate, and/or recommend educational programs for physicians and other health care providers. Topics may include how to diagnose substance abuse and how to refrain from prescribing minor tranquilizers, benzodiazopines or sedative hypnotics for women who abuse alcohol and other drugs;

- encourage families, friends, and coworkers of substance-abusing women to contact the treatment program even if the women deny having a problem or resist help. These individuals may need counseling or other support for themselves. If the program does not have support available for the client's family or friends, the program can refer them to a support group for help (e.g. Al-Anon);

- develop a clear and specific list of symptoms of mental illness evidenced in women who abuse substances for physicians, psychiatrists, and psychologists. Delineate possible substance abuse connections in commonly misdiagnosed ailments such as depression, anxiety, and confusion. Share the list with other health care and treatment providers so they can refer women with dual disorders to substance abuse treatment programs;

- compile a roster of women program graduates and/or family members who can be organized into a community support network that will encourage women who need substance abuse treatment to enter a program; and

- collaborate with local hospitals and other service providers, including other treatment providers, and agencies to co-sponsor events related to women's health, economic issues, parenting responsibilities, family health, and empowerment.

References

1. National Center for Health Statistics. (1993). Health United States: 1992. Rockville, MD: Department of Health and Human Services, Public Health Service, 291.

2. Finklestein, N., PhD, MSW, Duncan, S.A., MSW, Derman, L., MPH, MSW, and Smeltz, J., MEd, CAC. (1990). Getting Sober, Getting Well. Cambridge, MA.: The Women's Alcoholism Program of CASPAR.

3. ibid.

4. U.S. Department of Commerce, Bureau of the Census. (1992). Statistical Abstract of the United States: 1992. Washington, DC: Government Printing Office, 381.

5. Office of Substance Abuse Prevention Cultural Competence Series. (1992). Cultural Competence for Evaluators: A Guide for Alcohol and Other Drug Abuse Prevention Practitioners Working with Ethnic/Racial Communities. Orlandi, M., PhD, MPH, Ed. Rockville, MD: U.S. Department of Health and Human Service, Public Health Service.

6. ibid.

7. Getting Sober, Getting Well, 440.

8. Getting Sober, Getting Well, 441.

9. Arkin, E.B., and Funkhouser, J.E., Eds. (1990). Addendum to Chapter I: High Risk Teenagers. Office of Substance Abuse Prevention Monograph (5): Communicating About Alcohol and Other Drugs; Strategies for Reaching Populations at Risk. U.S. Department of Health and Human Services, Public Health Service, 89.

10. Gopelrud, E.N., PhD, Ed. (1991). Office of Substance Abuse Prevention Monograph (8): Preventing Adolescent Drug Use; From Theory to Practice. Rockville, MD: U.S. Department of Health and Human Services, Public Health Service, 92-94.

11. The Center for Substance Abuse Treatment. (1992). Treatment Improvement Protocol (TIP) for Pregnant, Substance-Using Women. Rockville, MD: U.S. Department of Health and Human Services, Public Health Service.

12. Sue, D. (1987). Use and Abuse of Alcohol by Asian Americans. J. Psychoactive Drugs 19(1) as cited in U.S. Department of Health and

Human Services, Public Health Service. (1990). Seventh Special Report to the U.S. Congress on Alcohol and Health from the Secretary of Health and Human Services. January, 1990. Rockville, MD.

13.   Sun, A. (1991). Issues for Asian American Women. In Roth, P., Ed., Alcohol and Drugs are Women's Issues, Vol. I. Metuchen, NJ: Scarecrow Press, 127-128.

14.   Kanuha, V. (1990). Compounding the Triple Jeopardy: Battering in Lesbian of Color Relationships. In Brown, Laura S., and Root, Maria P.P., Diversity and Complexity in Feminist Therapy. New York: Harrington Park/Hawthorne Press, 169-184.

15.   Fine, M., and Asch, A. (1988). Introduction: Beyond Pedestals. In Fine, M., and Asch, A., Eds. Women with Disabilities: Essays in Psychology, Culture, and Politics. Philadelphia, PA: Temple University Press.

16.   Fine, M., and Ashe, A. (1981). Disabled Women: Sexism Without the Pedestal. Journal of Sociology and Social Welfare 8(2), 233-48.

17.   Alcohol, Drugs, and Disability Project of the Pacific Research and Training Alliance. (1993). Disabled Women with Alcohol and Other Drug Problems. Berkeley, CA; (Unpublished Paper).

18.   ibid.

19.   Getting Sober, Getting Well, 498.

20.   For example, see Getting Sober, Getting Well, 508 -511.

21.   Depending on the number of employees, treatment programs also may be covered by the employment sections of the Americans with Disabilities Act (Title I for private programs and Title II for public programs).

22.   Eastern Paralyzed Veterans Association. (1993). The Americans with Disabilities Act: Resource Information. Jackson Heights, NY: Author. For additional free information pertaining to the ADA and produced by the U.S. Department of Justice and the Equal Employment Opportunity Commission, write the Public Access Section, Civil Rights Division, U.S. Department of Justice, P.O. Box #66738, Washington, DC 20035, or call (202) 514-0301.

Chapter 5

Comprehensive Treatment for Women

Photo by Doranne Hardt

*All persons who work
in the treatment program
must be knowledgeable about,
supportive of, and sensitive to
what it takes to meet the
treatment needs of women.*

Chapter 5

Comprehensive Treatment for Women

Women who have alcohol and other drug problems have treatment and recovery needs that must be addressed directly in both the design and management of the treatment process, as discussed in Chapter 3. In this chapter strategies related to the treatment process are offered and presented separately for the treatment environment; intake, orientation, and assessment; the treatment process; and cultural sensitivity/competence. For several of the populations, the information provided in Chapter 4, Outreach, is applicable to treatment as well, and is therefore not repeated. Information related to treatment issues that cross stages of treatment (e.g., relationships, sexuality, and dual diagnosis) are addressed in Chapter 3 and mentioned in this chapter only in terms of specific strategies.

5.1 The Treatment Environment

Clients arrive at the treatment program through a variety of mechanisms: self-referral; referral by a family member, significant other or outreach worker; referral by a health or social welfare agency; or referral by the criminal justice system. In the latter case, treatment may be in lieu of incarceration. Regardless of how they arrive, ensuring that they remain in the program for the duration of the treatment experience, whether a three-day detoxification program or a six-month therapeutic community program, is critical. All necessary measures should be taken to ensure that the treatment environment—physical, social, and healing—is safe and conducive to successful outcomes. Program consistency and staff confidence are imperative.

All persons who work in the treatment program - clinical, administrative, and support staff - must be knowledgeable about, supportive of, and sensitive to what it takes to meet the treatment needs of women. Each staff member must treat clients with understanding and respect, convey optimism about positive client outcomes, and impart a nurturing attitude.

All persons who work in the treatment program must be knowledgeable about, supportive of, and sensitive to what it takes to meet the treatment needs of women.

The treatment facility itself must meet all local and state codes for health and safety and federal requirements for accessibility (pursuant to the Americans with Disabilities Act). The facility should be secure and safe; indoor and outdoor areas should be well lit. If necessary and possible, arrangements should be made for part-time security guards to ensure the safety of clients, particularly during evening hours. It is also important that the facility be as clean, well-ventilated, and as pleasantly furnished as possible. Fresh paint, cheerful wallpaper, and plants can inexpensively transform a cold and drab facility into an inviting, friendly place. Often, local donors will supply materials and labor for this effort. Colorful posters can be obtained free of charge from the National Clearinghouse for Alcohol and Drug Information (NCADI).[1] Decorations should reflect the cultural diversity of the community.

5.2   The Intake, Orientation, and Assessment Processes

The overall goal of the intake, orientation, and assessment process is to establish a foundation for a positive, trusting relationship between the client and the counselor. Specifically, the objectives of this process include the following:

- to determine the factors that resulted in the client's seeking treatment and her expectations of the treatment process;

- to identify any existing health or social needs that require immediate attention and to make the necessary arrangements to have these needs addressed;

- to begin to develop a counseling relationship between the client and the counselor, as well as other staff of and participants in the program;

- to gather information about the client's physical and mental health and social history. This information serves as a foundation for the treatment plan and will also support the ongoing counseling relationship;

- to gather information required by the program for administrative purposes (including client contact information and demographic data); and

- to orient the client to the goals, philosophy, and structure of the treatment program.

Throughout this initial treatment engagement process, the program staff must recognize that this is a critical time to build trust in order to ensure successful treatment. However, clients may not disclose sensitive information (e.g., regarding sexual abuse or history of mental disorders) for some time. Because the symptomatology of certain conditions may not present early in the process or be obvious to the treatment staff, assessment data and information have to be collected, recorded, and used to adjust the treatment plan throughout the process.

5.2.1 The Intake Interview

The intake interview usually consists of an initial assessment from which a comprehensive treatment plan, including clearly specified treatment goals within a defined time frame, will be developed. The counselor should ensure that the client understands why this information is needed, and should assure her that confidentiality will be observed. The importance of client confidentiality cannot be overemphasized. In fact, confidentiality regulations must be strictly observed throughout the treatment process. (See appendix B for a sample confidentiality statement and a consent form for release of confidential information.)

Because a client may be fearful, confused (especially if she is in the process of detoxification or suffers from a co-occurring mental disorder), in a state of denial, and may have short-term memory loss and/or difficulty concentrating, it is seldom possible to do a complete assessment at intake. Intake personnel must be patient and supportive, and repeat questions and information until they believe the client understands the information that is needed and that which must be conveyed. In particular, in view of the possibility that the client may have experienced sexual abuse, it is preferable for the first point of contact at intake to be with a female counselor. If this is not possible, male counselors who carry out the intake interviews with female clients should be trained in gender-related issues.

The program staff should ensure that intake procedures are simple and relevant to a woman's living situation. For example, homeless women cannot easily make calls to a treatment program, and intake workers (both on the telephone and in person) must be sensitive to the particular needs of this population. If the woman has been contacted by an outreach worker, that worker should help the woman to move into and through the intake process.

At the time of the intake interview, if appropriate, the woman should be accompanied by one or more family members or a significant other.

At the time of the intake interview, if appropriate, the woman should be accompanied by one or more family members or a significant other. This may increase the likelihood that reliable information will be obtained and it helps to gain the support and understanding of the family member(s) or significant other. However, in the case of abusive relationships, it probably is not appropriate to involve the family or significant other(s) in the intake interview. The family and/or significant other(s) should be involved only when the counselor or case manager believes that such involvement will help the client's healing process. If the family or significant other is present during intake, the counselor or intake worker should interview the client both alone and with a family member present. The counselor or intake worker should also ensure that, if the woman has children, arrangements are made for their care, whether the woman is to be in an inpatient or outpatient treatment program.

A preliminary discussion of the nature of the disease of addiction is critical during the intake interview to educate clients and their families or significant others. Education on this subject should continue throughout treatment. This may help the client forgive herself and, if the family or significant others participate, may help to change those judgmental attitudes that can hinder recovery.

It is essential to obtain as accurate and complete a <u>substance abuse and treatment history</u> as possible during the intake interview. However, depending on a client's physical and emotional condition at the time of the interview, it may be possible only to identify the current symptoms that are related to her alcohol or other drug use. Questions that can help identify a client's current alcohol or other drug-related problems include the following:

- What types of drugs has she used in the last 24 hours, in what amounts and by what method? In the previous month? Three months?

- What is her current symptomatology? Is she currently having alcoholic delirium tremens (DTs), seizures, or symptoms of withdrawal from other drugs (e.g., heroin, methadone, or a prescription medication)?

- Based on her previous withdrawal experiences, is she at risk of developing DTs or seizures?

- Is she in need of detoxification and does her physical status warrant inpatient or outpatient detoxification?

- What specific treatment modalities seem to be indicated for her (e.g., use of medications, traditional healing methods such as acupuncture and/or intensive individual counseling)?

There are a number of standardized instruments that are useful for assessing the nature and extent of alcohol or other drug abuse as well as co-occurring disorders. These include the Diagnostic Interview Schedule, the Addiction Severity Index (ASI), the Michigan Alcoholism Screening Test, and the Beck Depression Inventory. Because these instruments have been viewed as not relevant to or sufficiently useful for women, several organizations have begun to adapt them for use in the assessment of women. For example, the ASI has been adapted by a number of treatment programs, and the College of Nursing at the University of North Carolina has developed and initially validated an instrument used to identify alcohol dependence specifically in women.[2]

In addition to the data concerning her alcohol and other drug use, as complete a medical and psychological history as possible should be obtained from each client, including the following information:

- general medical status;

- medical problems that have been correlated with abuse of alcohol and other drugs; and

- women's health issues (e.g., gynecological and obstetrical information, breast cancer).

The following are examples of medical problems correlated with alcohol and other drug use that may be observed through the physical assessment:

- anemia;
- cancers of the liver, esophagus, mouth, and stomach;
- cardiovascular disease;
- cellulitis from intravenous or intramuscular needle use;
- cirrhosis;
- eating disorders;

- gastrointestinal disorders (including ulcers);
- hepatitis;
- HIV or AIDS;
- hypoglycemia;
- injuries;
- malnutrition;
- sexual dysfunction;
- sexually transmitted diseases (STDs);
- tuberculosis (TB); and
- upper respiratory infections.

Age category and race/ethnicity should also trigger certain questions. For example, a woman who is African American, age 45 with a history of heart disease in her family, is likely to be at risk for hypertension or cardiovascular disease. An Hispanic women who is overweight should be asked probing questions regarding diabetes.

If a physician, nurse or physician's assistant is available, the medical history can be taken by that health professional. If, during the intake process, the counselor determines that further medical assessment is necessary, a referral should be made so that this assessment can be conducted as soon as possible. Because of the significant increase in the rates of TB in the United States over the past five years, and the threat that TB poses to the health of other clients and program staff members, it is particularly important that clients be screened for this infectious disease and that treatment be initiated immediately if the client meets the criteria for treatment or prophylaxis. It is important that intake workers be observant of the characteristics of infectious TB.

Infectious diseases are critical issues for treatment programs, particularly for residential programs. It is imperative that program staff detect infectious diseases and treat them (or refer women for treatment) as soon as possible. In 1993, CSAT issued a comprehensive and detailed

Infectious diseases are critical issues for treatment programs, particularly for residential programs.

In 1993, CSAT issued a comprehensive and detailed Treatment Improvement Protocol (TIP) entitled: "Screening for Infectious Diseases Among Substance Abusers."

Treatment Improvement Protocol (TIP) entitled: "Screening for Infectious Diseases Among Substance Abusers." This is a useful document for all substance abuse treatment programs and should be a reference document in programs serving women.[3]

If the standard form in use at the program does not include questions specifically related to women's health, those questions should be asked and recorded on the counselor's summary of the intake, and the counselor should work with the program director to revise the "standard" form or to design a separate form for recording such information. This will help to ensure that the information is consistently obtained and recorded for all female clients and that this task is not left to the discretion of the individual counselor.

If the woman is of childbearing age, it is important to identify (preferably during the intake interview) whether she could be pregnant and if she is pregnant, her gestation period. Pregnancy will affect the treatment modality used, and the types of health services to which a client should be referred immediately and throughout the treatment process.

The <u>mental health assessment</u>, which should be carried out in collaboration with trained mental health providers if possible, should provide an evaluation of the client that includes co-occurring mental illness, developmental disabilities, cognitive impairment, and biopsychosocial stressors/vulnerabilities. Obviously, a comprehensive assessment for multiple disorders cannot be accomplished at an intake interview, but it is critical to initially make the following determinations:

- What symptoms may indicate a co-occurring mental disorder?

- What symptoms may be an effect of alcohol or other drug abuse?

- What may be a side effect of withdrawal?

- Is there cognitive impairment related or unrelated to substance abuse? For example, is the woman limited in her ability to understand treatment components?

- Has the woman been so physically and/or sexually abused that she will be unable to focus on her substance abuse problem?

It needs to be emphasized again that differential diagnosis of a co-occurring mental or emotional disorder is likely to be difficult at intake. Relevant information needs to be collected, recorded, and used throughout the treatment process.

Many women suffer from depression and/or anxiety when they are admitted to a substance abuse treatment program. In some cases, psychological problems, whether or not clinically diagnosed, can be directly related to substance abuse and, once the substance abuse stops, these problems disappear. However, if the woman has a mental health condition co-occurring with the substance abuse (e.g., depression or PTSD), it should be diagnosed and addressed as early as possible in the treatment process.

If the woman has a mental health condition co-occurring with the substance abuse, it should be diagnosed and addressed as early as possible in the treatment process.

The manner and timing of symptomatology varies with the condition and the individual woman and her substance abuse history. For example, a panic or anxiety disorder can become more pronounced as the substance abuse stops. Cocaine-addicted clients may require more frequent psychiatric assessments because of the paranoia that can accompany heavy crack/cocaine use and the depression that often follows the cocaine euphoria. Symptoms of AIDS dementia in women infected with HIV will occur later in the progression of AIDS, which can be at any point in the substance abuse treatment process. According to many experts, in order to make an appropriate diagnosis, the client should be drug-free for a period of time so that the symptoms of alcohol and other drug use can abate. However, clinicians do not agree on the appropriate length of time between onset of abstinence and diagnosis.[4] The range is two weeks to two months or more. Dual diagnosis is also discussed in Chapters 2 and 3.

In addition to performing the medical and mental health assessment, the counselor should obtain as much information as possible concerning the woman's <u>family and social history</u> and her <u>current life status</u> to ensure that her immediate and long-term needs will be met as completely and as quickly as possible. If possible, the information obtained during the intake process (and used in the initial and on-going assessment of the client's needs) should include the following:

- substance abuse history, including previous treatment experiences;

- family history and current status (in general, and history of substance abuse);

- employment history and status;

- living arrangements;

- legal or criminal justice status;

- financial information;

- educational history;

- longest friendships and relationships;

- current relationship status;

- sexual orientation;

- country of origin, circumstances concerning arrival in this country and citizenship status;

- primary language spoken;

- death or current terminal illness of loved ones (to identify grief issues);

- pregnancies, children, etc.; and

- birth control knowledge.

Information concerning child care, abusive relationships, sexual abuse or harassment, and other issues of particular importance for women are often overlooked by counselors during intake interviews. However, as with the medical and mental health histories, if the standard form used in the program does not request such information, it should be recorded separately and updated during the course of treatment. This information (including results of referrals for services) should be maintained in the woman's treatment record.

At intake, the client may not divulge information about medical problems, psychological problems, or behavioral or familial circumstances of which she is ashamed, about which she feels guilty or is unwilling to accept help, or which she believes would result in further stigma or legal penalties if known to the treatment program. This reluctance to divulge information (or to disclose) is particularly evident early in the intake and assessment process, because some clients may think staff members will reject them if they reveal certain details about their lives. This can be a particular problem in rural areas where almost everyone may "know everyone else."

Women may also fear that what they say will be repeated by another client or staff member (who may know their family or friends in

Information concerning child care, abusive relationships, sexual abuse or harassment, and other issues of particular importance for women are often overlooked by counselors during intake interviews.

the community). This "talking outside," whether real or perceived, may be a major problem in community-based outpatient substance abuse treatment programs and can be a particular problem for women who fear losing custody of their children. Women need to be assured that the information they disclose to treatment program staff will remain confidential for use only in the treatment process or when otherwise approved by the client for release. The client should be helped to feel empowered to disclose sensitive information.

5.2.2   Orientation to Treatment

The orientation process is another crucial step in building trust between the client and the program staff. To the extent that the client can become comfortable in the treatment setting, acquire confidence that staff members will respond to her questions and needs clearly and sensitively, and understand the scope of the treatment program and her role in the treatment process, she is more likely to fully engage in and complete treatment. During orientation, the client should be fully informed about such matters as:

- the nature and goals of the program, the program's philosophy and specific modalities of care and services;

- the physical facility (this should include a tour of the facility);

- client rights and privileges (See appendix B for sample principles of conduct and client rights statements.);

- the rules governing client conduct and infractions that can lead to disciplinary action or discharge from the program;

- the hours during which services are available; and

- treatment costs and payment procedures, if any.

The program should make the intake interview and orientation setting as comfortable and private as possible for the client and her family. They should be informed by the treatment staff about the disease of addiction and its physical and mental health effects. Written and audiovisual information (e.g., booklets, flyers, and videotapes) should be available and include materials that the woman and her family can keep. Many of these resources can be obtained from the National Clearinghouse on Alcohol and Drug Information (NCADI), state and local clearinghouses, libraries, and elsewhere. The counselor should also give to each woman a resource directory of public health and social services available in the community, particularly those with which the program has agreements for provision of services. Information and resources should be available in alternative formats to accommodate women with disabilities and those who are not functionally literate.

Female staff members should be available to meet with the woman during orientation. Otherwise, the counselor should try to refer the client to a local woman's self-help group, taking the client to the meetings, if possible and if appropriate. Having a female staff member as the first contact during orientation to the program can help the client understand how women feel during treatment, how they cope with the realities of daily life during treatment (e.g., child care, relationships, housing), and how barriers to recovery (e.g., emotional obstacles) can be overcome.

Having a female staff member as the first contact during orientation to the program can help the client understand how women feel during treatment.

5.2.3 Comprehensive Assessment

To develop a treatment plan that addresses a woman's specific needs and keeps her engaged in the treatment process, it is essential to prepare a comprehensive assessment. The International Certification Reciprocity Consortium/Alcohol and Other Drug Abuse (ICRC/AODA) has defined the assessment process as including the following:

...those procedures by which a counselor/program identifies and evaluates an individual's strengths, weaknesses, problems, and needs for the development of the treatment plan.[5]

This assessment is based on information obtained during intake (and recorded on intake and standardized assessment forms) and on the counselor's, case manager's, or team's clinical observations. Staff preparing assessments of client's needs should acknowledge that clients may not have disclosed fully information related to their substance abuse, physical and mental health, and social needs. The assessments will, in many cases, be provisional, contingent on the program staff building trust throughout the treatment process. This requires flexibility in both assessment and treatment planning. It necessitates ensuring that relevant information (e.g., regarding history of exposure to violence) is recorded in the client's file, reported to the clinical team, and used in revising her treatment plan and in providing services.

The counselor should negotiate with the client to determine in what format she will deal with issues that she would be uncomfortable discussing in the group.

The counselor should negotiate with the client to determine in what format she will deal with issues that she would be uncomfortable discussing in a group. If a program does not respond appropriately to such concerns, there is a high probability that the client will not remain in treatment or maintain recovery over a long period.

The client assessment is, essentially, a synthesis of information gathered during intake. It should include a summary of the client's strengths and factors that may impede recovery. It should include space to record the basis for the determinations (e.g., program intake forms, standardized assessment instruments, clinical observation). The assessment should include issues related to basic living skills, such as the following:

- developing and maintaining personal health and hygiene;

- finding and retaining a job;

- obtaining housing;

- managing money;

- maintaining a household; and

- parenting.

The assessment is critical to the program's determination of what specific treatment methods will help empower the client to set and achieve her own treatment goals and make necessary changes to achieve those goals. In that regard, clinical staff must recognize that some women may find it difficult to address immediately the broad range of problems associated with substance abuse, co-occurring mental disorders, physical health problems, or life skills areas. For example, some women who have been unemployed for some time may find it difficult to re-enter the work force, become independent from social support systems (e.g., AFDC) and become drug-free at the same time. (Strategies related to providing services in life skills areas are presented in Section 5.3.1: Providing Comprehensive Treatment Services.)

5.2.4 Treatment Plan

The treatment plan serves as the fundamental basis for providing care to the client throughout her treatment process. While most programs have standardized forms for the treatment plan, each plan needs to address the specific needs of each client, based on the assessment described above. The assessment form should clearly delineate the relationship between the findings of the assessment and recommendations to be included in the treatment plan. The counselor or case manager works with the client to determine the following:

- the priority of the full range of problems that need to be addressed (including those directly and indirectly related to substance abuse and other physical and mental health and social service issues related to the woman and her family);

- immediate and long-term treatment goals; and

- the most appropriate treatment methods and resources to be used.

At intake, the treatment plan can address only the immediate problems presented by the client and observed by the clinical staff. In fact, some clinicians think it is inappropriate to set long range goals at this point because the client may be concerned only about the immediate needs of herself and her family. The treatment plan should specify the services to which the woman will be referred, including the agency or agencies to which referrals are made. Throughout the course of treatment, results of all referrals must be recorded, including outcomes, if known.

It is important that the treatment plan be prepared or reviewed by a treatment team with gender-specific and culturally relevant expertise.

It is important that the treatment plan be prepared or reviewed by a treatment team with gender-specific and culturally relevant expertise. This team should be comprised of staff members or consultants knowledgeable about substance abuse; physical and mental health professionals (e.g., the consulting physician or nurse practitioner and psychologist or psychiatric social worker); educational and employment specialists; and a child care specialist. The latter is particularly important if the woman's children are in treatment with her. This team will help to determine how many individual counseling sessions are appropriate, whether or not the woman should participate in group counseling sessions at the facility, and which sessions she should attend. They will also determine when to refer her to self-help groups within or external to the program (e.g., AA, NA). Treatment providers should keep in mind that some women may be more guarded in their communications than others. Some women may resist the process of sharing experiences common to support groups, including 12-Step, Women for Sobriety, Save Our Selves, and Rational Recovery programs. During treatment, clients should be encouraged to build relationships with their peers in the mutual self-help group of their choice. These relationships can easily develop from activities that teach women how to enjoy life without using alcohol or other drugs.

It is important, throughout the course of treatment, that the woman's treatment plan be revised and updated, in consultation with the treatment team and the woman herself.

5.3   The Treatment Process

As discussed in Chapter 3, the length of the treatment process and the types of modalities used in treatment vary significantly from one program to another. The information provided in this section is intended to be general enough to apply across treatment modalities. Where appropriate, information specific to modalities of care (e.g., inpatient detoxification, outpatient drug free treatment) is provided. Because it is assumed that the reader is a trained substance abuse counselor or administrator and/or has experience in substance abuse counseling, general information concerning approaches to individual, group, and family counseling, and use of medications in treatment (e.g., antabuse and methadone) and other general treatment methods are not addressed. Rather, aspects of the treatment process or of specific modalities of care that relate predominantly to women are described. However, while some treatment strategies may appear to be simple, they have been shown to have demonstrable impact on the success of substance abuse treatment programs—for both women and men.

In planning and implementing treatment services, the program staff should try to ensure that there is a coherent link between the treatment philosophy of the program, the treatment modalities that are used, and the specific services offered for women. This apparently obvious consideration can sometimes be overlooked by programs, particularly when there is

It is important, throughout the course of treatment, that the woman's treatment plan be revised and updated, in consultation with the treatment team and the woman herself.

a change in staff leadership and a consequent change in program philosophy, or when funding considerations dictate changes in services. The staff needs to ensure that the weekly schedule of program services — including individual and group counseling, participation in self-help groups on- and off-site, specialized group meetings (e.g., for adolescents, women with a history of sexual or physical abuse, or pregnant women, sessions on spirituality and personal growth), and time for personal activities (e.g., vocational training, GED classes) — not only reflects the program's treatment philosophy but also takes into account the varying needs of the clients and the reality of scheduling comprehensive services outside of the program.

For programs in which children are present with their mothers, the need for personal time between the mother and her child(ren) is critical. Staff should be aware that balancing the substance abuse treatment needs of the woman (with other needs such as addressing mental health disorders) with the needs of her children requires that considerable attention be given to scheduling activities: those that meet collective needs of the clients; the individual needs of the woman; and those of her child(ren). Throughout treatment, the program should ensure that the clients benefit from effective case management.

5.3.1   Providing Comprehensive Treatment Services

Most women enter treatment with many problems. They are frightened by the prospect of change, and lack confidence in their abilities to assert themselves and lead healthy lives.

Most women enter treatment with many problems. They are frightened by the prospect of change, and lack confidence in their abilities to assert themselves and lead healthy lives. Throughout the treatment process, the clinical staff (in particular the counselor or case manager who works most closely with the client) must ensure the following:

- The client is participating in the individual and group counseling sessions as agreed in her treatment plan, including attendance at 12-Step or other self-help group meetings and fulfilling other requirements set by the program;

- The client's alcohol and other drug use is monitored (e.g., through urine testing, observation, and/or self-report);

- The client's record is complete and up-to-date, with the following information:

  — progress notes of all individual and group counseling sessions, including notes from staff or consultant health and mental health providers and notes from meetings of the treatment team;

  — reports of physical and mental health and social assessments (with a summary of the findings of these assessments and their implications for the treatment process);

  — records of referral for services outside the program, including outcome of the referral;

  — changes in the treatment plan based on new information; and

  — complete and up-to-date information on the child(ren) if these records are maintained with the mother's record; and

- The services provided to the client (either directly by the program or through referral) are meeting her needs and helping to ensure her recovery.

To help each client identify her strengths and increase her level of confidence, the treatment services provided should be designed to help clients appropriately and effectively relate to themselves, and their family, friends, and institutions. The treatment process should gradually lead clients to develop higher self-esteem and then to develop healthier and more loving relationships with others. If treatment services are truly comprehensive, they will likely include strategies that will involve not only

The treatment process should gradually lead clients to develop higher self-esteem and then to develop healthier and more loving relationships with others.

services within the treatment program itself, but a community-wide support system to ensure continued care and support for a woman's physical, emotional, financial, psychological, spiritual, legal, and family needs over the treatment continuum. Because few treatment programs can respond to all the identified needs of substance-abusing women, they must develop referral mechanisms, collaborative agreements and tracking systems that allow women, especially those with children, to receive services before, during, and after treatment.

Within the treatment program, counselors should address the following issues:

- the etiology of addiction, especially gender-specific issues related to addiction (including social, physiological, and psychological consequences of addiction and factors related to onset of addiction);

- low self-esteem;

- race, ethnicity, and cultural issues;

- gender discrimination and harassment;

- disability-related issues, where relevant;

- relationships with family and significant others;

- attachments to unhealthy interpersonal relationships;

- interpersonal violence, including incest, rape, battering, and other abuse;

- eating disorders;

- sexuality, including sexual functioning and sexual orientation;

- parenting;

- grief related to the loss of alcohol or other drugs, children, family members, or partners;

- work;

- appearance and overall health and hygiene;

- isolation related to a lack of support systems (which may or may not include family members and/or partners) and other resources;

- life plan development; and

- child care and child custody.

The ability of women to identify their own needs and to address those needs directly is a factor in their seeking treatment for substance abuse, staying in treatment, and continuing recovery. However, the treatment program staff, and in particular the clients' counselors or case managers, must help women identify those needs and disclose information throughout the treatment process. The staff must continuously work with women to revise their treatment plans based on reconsideration of their needs. Women's "issues" are not stagnant; they may and often do change during the treatment process.

Relapse prevention should be a discrete component of the treatment process and should integrate the client's specific issues into the general modality of care. Relapse strategies are described more fully in Chapter 6.

Treatment providers should be careful to acknowledge clients with children in their various roles: as individuals by addressing their personal

The staff must continuously work with women to revise their treatment plans. Women's "issues" are not stagnant; they may and often do change during the treatment process.

needs and enhancing their self esteem, as mothers by addressing their parenting role, and as members of a community by helping them to participate in various organizations and activities. Treatment plans for women with children should include a children's component; one that offers prevention strategies to reduce the children's risks of developing poor physical and mental health problems, including substance abuse. Such a component could include training for parents, health care for the children, family outings, and therapeutic activities designed specifically for the children of clients.

Arrangements for services outside the program should be clearly defined, preferably with ongoing contracts or cooperative agreements with the service provider. A standard referral form should be used to describe the service proposed and record the service provided and the outcome, if any. This form should be returned to the treatment program and be included in the client's treatment record. If arrangements are made for other health or social services, a staff member, or trained volunteer, or, in the case of residential treatment, a "senior resident" or staff member should accompany the woman to the service provider, if possible. Having someone accompany the client to services, at least for the first time, may help her begin to trust and understand how to accept support, even if she is in a confused state.

Substance abuse often leaves women debilitated, confused, fearful, or disorganized; they also may experience short-term memory loss or craving for alcohol and other drugs. Therefore, it may be difficult for them to either contact or interact with representatives of the referral agency independently.

5.3.2 Strategies for Providing Comprehensive Treatment Services

Strategies that can help ensure that the woman's health and social needs are met include the following:

Health Services

- *Provide physical and mental health care services.* For substance abuse treatment to be effective, health services must be available to meet the immediate and long terms needs of women in treatment. If the treatment program is part of a health care facility, these services can be arranged readily through the various specialty centers or through referral to other health facilities, whether or not the treatment program itself is affiliated with any of these facilities. If the program is freestanding, arrangements may either be permanent (i.e., the physician, nurse, physician's assistant, psychologist, or psychiatric social worker is part of the staff, either full time or part time), or contractual. In the latter case, the services can be provided at the treatment program or off-site.

  The program should ensure that a network of physical and mental healthcare providers is established to help address their clients' general problems and those requiring specialty care. The provider(s), whether on staff or consultants, should be knowledgeable about addiction in general, the particular physical and mental addiction problems of women, the socioeconomic and gender factors that relate to women's addiction and general physical and mental health. They should also be sensitive to diversity based on race, ethnicity, age, disability, and sexual orientation.

- *Arrange for health education.* Arrangements should be made for a health care provider or health education specialist to conduct ongoing health education classes on nutrition (and its role in recovery); self-examination for breast cancer; basic gynecological care; HIV risk reduction; the effects of alcohol and other drug use during pregnancy; basic children's health care issues; the physiology and transmission of STDs; reproductive health; female sexuality; preconception care; prenatal education; childbirth education; family planning; childhood safety and injury prevention; physical and sexual abuse education and prevention; and smoking cessation, especially for pregnant women.

- *Provide testing for HIV, STDs, and TB.* Arrangements should be made to have pretest counseling, HIV, STD, and TB testing and post-test counseling available on-site, if possible, or at a location convenient for the clients.

- *Adjust treatment requirements for pregnant women.* Programs should develop a plan of action and a network of resources to provide a comprehensive program for women who are pregnant and their babies after delivery.

- *Arrange for developmental evaluations of children born while their mothers are in the program.* Identify and address problems while the mother is in treatment. Contact state agencies responsible for developmental services, including assessment of developmental status/problems, and identify Title XX day care slots available in the community. Outreach or other staff can seek help from churches and charitable organizations to obtain equipment to establish a nursery for the newborns. A local child care agency might provide staff to supervise a nursery.

Preconception Counseling

CSAT has identified pre-conception counseling, including the full range of reproductive options, as an important aspect of substance abuse treatment.

CSAT has identified preconception counseling, including the full range of reproductive options, as an important aspect of substance abuse treatment. Specifically, the following issues have been recommended by CSAT, in its TIP on Pregnant, Substance-Using Women, to be addressed in such counseling:[6]

- the various methods of contraception and the attitudes of the woman, her significant other, and her community regarding their use;

- the impact on the woman and the fetus of alcohol and other drug use during pregnancy;

- the teratogenic impact of prescribed medications, such as Antabuse and various anticonvulsants; and

- alternative medications with reduced or no teratogenic potential for such common problems as seizure disorder.

Social and Health Services (basic life skills)

- *Arrange for safe, reliable and low-cost transportation to and from the facility.* Many programs provide bus or subway tokens for female adolescents and adults, especially low-income clients and, if necessary, request an extra bus stop near the facility or an extension of hours for bus service. If possible, have a donated vehicle available on-site, or make arrangements to use vehicles maintained by a local community organization or place of worship. Accessible transportation should be available to women with disabilities.

- *Ensure economic access.* A sliding fee scale based on a client's ability to pay is a significant incentive for women to seek treatment. An assessment of a client's ability to pay should not include her partner's income because she may not have safe access to those finances. The program can help to arrange for "indigent care" at local health facilities at little or no cost. One way to accomplish this is by establishing a relationship with a nearby health service provider who receives McKinney Act funding.

- *Assist with the development of parenting skills.* Counseling, with information on child development, child safety, injury

Parenting education should be integrated with substance abuse counseling to be recovery-oriented.

prevention, and child abuse prevention should be provided. Parenting education should be integrated with substance abuse counseling to be recovery-oriented. Issues that relate to a woman's upbringing and that affect her parenting ability should be addressed in a way that supports rather than compromises her recovery. Specific strategies include asking a local college or university that offers a major in child development to have interested students assist in providing child care and child enrichment classes. It is also important to help a client weigh her options, such as having family, friends, social agencies, or places of worship provide short- or long-term care for children if they are to avoid placement in foster care. Arrange for a network of healthy families to serve as role models for mothers who have never experienced a normal home life, or develop "adopt-a-mother, adopt-a-family" program such as those operated by "100 Black Women" and other groups.

- *Assist with educational services.* Provide a library or reading room, facilitate access to local public libraries and encourage clients to read. Help to arrange for literacy training or GED/high school diploma or other educational or training opportunities.

- *Assist with housing.* Often, a woman entering treatment may need assistance to access housing, either during treatment (if she is in an outpatient program) or after treatment, if she is in a residential program. In these cases, it is critical that the program have on-going arrangements with public or private social service agencies for access to transitional and permanent housing. Affiliations should also be made with organizations such as housing advocacy groups and domestic violence centers (e.g., a local House of Ruth), which may have temporary housing available. If the woman is an AFDC recipient, the program should contact her case worker to determine if there is public or other housing available for the client.

- *Provide recreational and cultural activities.* Arrange for ongoing recreational and cultural activities with an emphasis on activities which will enhance women's self-esteem and improve their general physical and mental well-being. These activities should be culturally specific, and provided through arrangements with such groups as African American, Hispanic/Latina, or lesbian cultural and service organizations. Activities must be made accessible to women with disabilities, pursuant to the Americans with Disabilities Act (ADA).

- *Offer a range of child care options.* These could include child care services located within residential programs or in shared apartments; day care in the community in which the program is located; or program-based day care. Establishing a network of voluntary child care arrangements is highly recommended. Volunteers may include family members, retired senior citizens, interns from local schools (including colleges offering degrees in early childhood education), places of worship, and self-help group members. Local day care nurseries and schools may be willing to provide scholarships for children of mothers in treatment.

- *Arrange for family therapy.* If it is not possible to have full-time or part-time licensed family therapists or psychologists on staff to provide counseling to all clients (including heterosexual and lesbian couples and single women), arrangements should be made for these services on a regular consulting basis. In addition, all counselors should receive training to provide at least minimal family counseling. Counselors should be able to address the specific needs of adolescents, older women, women of color, women in the criminal justice system, low-income women, lesbians, and women with disabilities. The children of clients can be referred to self-help groups specializing in children and youth (e.g., Al Atot, Al Ateen, Al Anon) groups.

- *Provide materials and resources on personal growth and relationships.* Low-cost or free books and pamphlets are widely available on codependency, healthy relationships, families, personality development, and self-help ("personal growth"). They should be obtained for clients to use at the program site, or if possible, for clients to keep. Videotapes should be shown regularly to provide information and encourage discussion of the issues between the client and counselor and among the clients during group sessions and informally.

Staff should be trained to offer support and assistance to help women deal with legal issues.

• *Arrange for legal services when necessary.* Few programs have consulting attorneys on staff, but most have arrangements for referral to legal support systems (e.g., legal aid, law schools, or organizations which specialize in child or spouse abuse). Staff should be trained to offer support and assistance to help women deal with legal issues, such as real or anticipated loss of child custody cases, domestic violence cases, and incest or victimization in their or their child's experience, and to make referrals to the legal system as appropriate. Treatment programs often work with the public defender's office, free or low-cost legal assistance networks, law school facilities, and city or state offices of human rights to conduct workshops on a variety of topics. Many also arrange for the services of female attorneys specializing in women's legal issues (e.g., abuse, separation and divorce, child custody, pregnancy) as consultants to the program.

• *Arrange for financial assistance and counseling to ensure economic stability.* The program should have ongoing relationships with public and private agencies through which financial assistance for the clients can be arranged, including SSI, Medicare, Medicaid, AFDC, unemployment, and housing assistance. Other successful strategies that have encouraged financial independence include establishing a business (e.g., word processing) on-site so that women can learn marketable skills, increase self-esteem, earn income and, if possible, begin holding a job; arranging for career-oriented field trips to community and women's organizations and to local industries to explore the variety of jobs available; having successful working women who represent diversity in terms of race, ethnicity, age, disability, and sexual orientation serve as role models and mentors; and establishing self-help, job-seeking groups as a support network to help clients deal with the ups and downs of job searches. The power of these groups cannot be overestimated in helping women take the risks involved in finding employment. Working with the local state unemployment office to use its employment network and computers is also useful, as is setting aside time each week for a "resume roundup." During this time women can learn to develop job histories and to translate their life skills into data for their resumes.

It may be possible to have a representative of the local office of the department of labor or a vocational rehabilitation center assigned to the program to assist in vocational assessment and placements at the appropriate time in treatment. A representative of a local department of education and training may be available to evaluate needs, develop appropriate educational plans, and make arrangements for meeting the educational and training needs of clients. In addition, representatives from local financial institutions are often willing to conduct workshops about basic money management—budgeting, paying bills, saving money, and obtaining loans. Another effective approach is to hold training sessions on how to balance checkbooks, secure insurance coverage, find quality medical and child care, and shop wisely.

An example of a woman with economic difficulties presenting for treatment and strategies designed to address those difficulties is shown on the following page.

Example of Presenting Problem

Economic Status

A 40-year-old woman who is a single head of household with three children is referred to the program by the District Court. In lieu of incarceration for petty larceny, she is required to be in treatment for heroin addiction for 30 inpatient days with follow-up treatment for 6 months. The woman, who has a 20-year history of substance abuse, presents with symptoms of chronic obstructive lung disease and undifferentiated "women's problems."

Alternative Strategies

In addition to treating the woman's substance abuse problem itself, program staff should consider the following strategies to address other issues:

- The program should immediately arrange for care of the three children while the woman is in the inpatient program, preferably by the woman's family (if the living situation is positive), but otherwise through Foster Care.

- The program should ensure that the woman's health issues are immediately addressed. For example, a thorough physical exam should be conducted, including testing for TB, cardiovascular disorders, and STDs (in response to the complaint of "women's problems"). The program must ensure that all treatment procedures ordered by medical personnel are followed (e.g., medications).

- Before discharge from inpatient care, the program should arrange for economic assistance (e.g., SSI, AFDC, worker's compensation). The staff person should also arrange for housing, food stamps (or other access to food), and for the woman to be responsible for the care of her children, if this is appropriate.

- In the inpatient program, particular attention should be paid to economic self-sufficiency. This includes arranging for the woman to complete high school or her GED, if necessary, and/or to participate in other skills/job training, job readiness training, or job referral programs.

5.3.3   Addressing Relationships and Related Issues

The client's relationships with family, significant others, and friends can be critical to her recovery. Her sexuality (including sexual functioning and sexual orientation) is also important although often neglected by treatment programs. These issues have been addressed in Chapter 3. Strategies to address relationship and sexuality issues include the following:

- Provide time each day for women to talk among themselves about their grief; to share issues of grief related to giving up both alcohol and/or other drugs and the lifestyle associated with these; and grief related to their children, homes, and partners. Encourage women to talk about grief related to losing loved ones when they were drinking or using other drugs and to air feelings of loss that may have been buried during years of substance abuse. Develop a list of the stages of the grieving process for clients;

- Encourage clients to keep a journal to reflect on relationship and sexuality issues as well as on their substance abuse; this can help the client to disclose these issues during individual and group counseling. However, it is critical that these journals be protected to prevent disclosure;

- Arrange for the services of a member of the clergy or spiritual leader, preferably a woman, to act as a resource to the staff and clients to help diminish denial, fear, and poor self-esteem. This may be particularly important for women who have a history of sexual or physical abuse or poor family relationships (including with their own children or their parents);

- Help clients to view assertiveness as a social skill relevant to recovery. Emphasize that life can be easier if one knows how to get what one needs from others without hurting

The client's relationships with family, significant others, and friends can be critical to her recovery. Her sexuality is also important although often neglected by treatment programs.

them or becoming anxious. Conduct classes on assertiveness so that women learn to share, to make their needs known, and to protect themselves. Encourage women to identify and discuss well-known assertive women whom they admire;

• Advise women to take on more responsibilities as they move through the program to build self-esteem and to promote their ability to function independently of the program;

• Arrange for groups in the treatment program to meet regularly to address relationship and sexuality issues. During these sessions, encourage clients to accept that the treatment program is a safe place to explore relationship and sexuality issues, even if there is a threat of domestic violence at home;

• Arrange for clients to receive counseling from mental health professionals specifically trained and experienced in working with women's relationship and/or sexuality issues, including posttraumatic stress disorder (PTSD) resulting from child and/or adult sexual or physical abuse; arrange for clients to participate in self-help groups that address these issues; and

• Help women learn how to express and begin to trust their anger, and how to deal with it in stressful situations.

5.3.4 Addressing the Client's Spiritual Needs

Increasingly, the need to address the spiritual needs of the client is seen as an important aspect of substance abuse treatment. The concept of spirituality should not be confused with that of religion, which is the way we attempt to systematize belief in a higher power through specific definition and through rituals, rules of conduct and philosophical frameworks. In contrast, spirituality is not defined nor constrained by specific parameters. In the context of this manual, spirituality may be considered in terms of one's journey toward increasing awareness of oneself and one's relationship to the rest of the world. It is an empowering and healing process. Bjorklund has noted the variations in spiritual journeys, suggesting that "spiritual relationships evolve from how a person has experienced life and how he or she has come to deal with life situations."[7] Experience with alcohol and other drugs as a destructive force alters the degree to which one can address our basic human needs, including relationships with other people. The following is a definition of spirituality that has been used in substance abuse treatment:

> Spirituality has to do with the quality of our relationship to whatever or whomever is most important in our life.[8]

Given a broad-based concept of spirituality as focusing on personal empowerment and crossing cultural and religious boundaries, treatment programs can provide an environment that facilitates the clients' spiritual journeys. In fact, the psychotherapist Moore suggested that "psychology is incomplete if it doesn't include spirituality ... in a fully integrated way."[9] The important relationship between spirituality and substance abuse treatment was described by Bjorklund:

> Spirituality, because it has to do with what (whom) is important to us, is closely related to values, priorities, goals, and preoccupations. It has to do with whatever is at the center of our life.[10]

In fact, he suggests, "Just to stop [alcohol and other drug use] without other growth and change would simply frustrate a person who has not learned any other way to meet basic human needs... spirituality takes its place with the physical and emotional aspects of a recovery program as a necessary foundation for building a new way of life."[11]

Programs that implement the Comprehensive Model described in Chapter 3 (including attending to the woman's physical, psychological,

Spirituality, because it has to do with what (whom) is important to us, is closely related to values, priorities, goals, and pre-occupations. It has to do with whatever is at the center of our life.

social and spiritual needs) help the woman to move from a sense of fear, despair, hopelessness and isolation to one of trust and belief; improve her self-knowledge and self-esteem; and empower her to be self-sufficient and interdependent upon completion of treatment. These goals can be an important part of the recovery process.

5.3.5   Retaining Women in Treatment

To retain women in treatment, the most important task is to ensure that the program is gender sensitive and that the broad spectrum of women's bio-psycho-social needs are met. This includes, for example, addressing their physical and mental health, housing, child care, and legal needs. These topics are addressed throughout this manual. Other specific approaches for retaining women in treatment include the following:

- Ensure that, if possible, women have their own "private space" in the treatment setting. This could be, for example, a separate recreation room or meeting area;

- Involve partners and family members as appropriate to enhance women's recovery and reduce sabotage;

- Recognize the reality of women's lives and responsibilities;

- Find ways to help women take control of their own treatment so that they become invested in it;

- Help women feel successful as they move from one phase of treatment to another;

- Provide positive female and male role models; and

- Eliminate barriers to retaining women in treatment that are identified within the program itself. Feedback from clients—particularly from those who leave treatment early—can provide useful information to identify such barriers.

5.3.6   Discharge

In the treatment process, the discharge plan is as important as the initial assessment and treatment plan because this phase serves as a bridge between the treatment process (whatever the modality of care or duration) and continuing care. The discharge plan should be prepared before the woman completes or leaves treatment. The determination about whether a client is ready for discharge should be made jointly by the client and her counselor, or with the treatment team, if the program uses such an arrangement.

The discharge plan should include the following:

- an evaluation of the woman's progress in treatment, specifically

    - her treatment goals and the extent to which they were met;

    - reason(s) for discharge;

    - summary of successes and problems encountered during treatment; and

    - factors that facilitated and/or hindered her progress.

- a discussion of the woman's current status with respect to

    - alcohol and other drug use;

    - physiological health in general;

    - mental health;

    - employment;

    - living arrangements;

The discharge plan should be prepared before the woman completes or leaves treatment.

- vocational and educational needs;

- parenting ability and status of her children;

- other emotional support needs; and

- financial support needs.

• a summary of unresolved problems, which may include referrals for

- substance abuse counseling;

- medical and mental health services;

- family therapy, child care, housing, financial and other services; and

- sobriety support groups.

The program should make specific arrangements for continued contact with the client, including periodic visits to the program. This will reassure her that there is a "safe place" to visit in times of emotional, psychological, or physical distress and will also facilitate the follow-up process.

5.4   Cultural Sensitivity/Competence

All treatment program components and procedures should be reviewed regularly to ensure that they are culturally sensitive and culturally relevant. This includes outreach, initial contact, intake, the treatment process, discharge, and follow-up. Cultural competence and sensitivity as related to different ethnic and racial groups, age groups, disability groups, and sexual orientations should be reviewed so that appropriate responses can be ensured. For example, during client case presentations made to staff, issues raised by different population groups in treatment should be discussed. Staff should be trained to avoid discriminatory language and behaviors. Moreover, specific rules should be established and enforced with respect to such language and behavior on the part of clients and staff members.

To help ensure that the clients' culturally specific needs are met, the program should offer clients the opportunity to attend 12-step or other self-help meetings that are population-specific (e.g., for women of color or lesbian women). This could be accomplished through referral, by scheduling regular meetings at the treatment program's location, or by listing these meetings as part of the program's regular activities.

To help ensure that the clients' culturally specific needs are met, the program should offer clients the opportunity to attend 12-Step or other self-help meetings that are population-specific.

Examples of strategies that relate to specific populations of women follow. They are grouped within the following categories:

- Age groups (adolescent and older women);

- Ethnic and racial minority group populations; and

- Other specific groups of women.

5.4.1 Age Groups

Adolescents

- Arrange for role models and provide materials specifically geared to adolescent girls. Identification with appropriate role models is critical for adolescents to gain hope and to progress through treatment. It is also helpful to compile a book that will foster a sense of hope using letters written by young women in recovery.

- Conduct home assessments and encourage family involvement in the treatment process where appropriate. Meet various persons who are involved in the adolescent's life, including parents, grandparents, children, partners, other family members, probation or parole officers, social workers, guidance counselors, and teachers. During these meetings, program staff should try to ascertain if there appears to be sexual or physical abuse as well as substance abuse in the family. If possible, visit the young woman's last place of residence and meet the people; this should be done only with the knowledge and consent of the person in treatment.

- Pregnant teenage girls require special support while they are in treatment to help ensure that they remain in school. Strategies include day care services and special attention to nutrition.[12] In addition, girls who became pregnant as a result of rape also need to receive psychological counseling while they are in treatment.[13] Provision of services to address sexual abuse concurrent with treatment for the client's substance abuse "ensures that the young women are better able to remain drug and alcohol free." [14]

- Keep on hand personal care items (e.g., nail and hair care supplies, stationery, and pens) as incentives or rewards for the adolescent girls.

Pregnant teenage girls require special support while they are in treatment to help ensure that they remain in school.

Older Women

- Work with appropriate senior service agencies to provide safe, inexpensive, and accessible transportation options that bring older clients to the treatment facility for scheduled treatment activities. This is a critical first step in providing care to this population. Schedule groups during the hours that these agencies offer transportation.

- Work with a local senior center or an adult day care center to arrange for space to hold groups at that facility. Establish a relationship with the administrative personnel of the local hospital to arrange for space to hold groups within the hospital setting. The senior transportation program may provide regularly scheduled transportation to these locations, and the scheduling of groups can be coordinated around the available public and senior transportation schedule.

- Help train representatives of health agencies so they can identify older women with substance abuse problems and refer clients to the treatment program for services.

- Ensure that the facility (both its entrances and furnishings) is accessible to older clients, including those with physical disabilities and/or sensory losses. For example, deep seats that are low to the ground are difficult for some older people to use.

- The physical condition of some older people must be kept in mind. Frail older people bruise easily, their bones may be fragile, and their sense of touch may be diminished. Many older women have osteoporosis and generalized bone loss. For example, what might be a therapeutic hug to a young person could bruise or break the bones of some older women. Hearing and vision problems should also be diagnosed and recognized during individual and group therapy. Because thermoregulation does not occur quickly for some women who are much older, it may be appropriate to encourage some older women to wear sweaters during therapy and education sessions.

- For homebound older women, regular telephone therapy groups facilitated by a substance abuse counselor may be an appropriate approach. On a specific day of the week, at a specific time of day, the counselor makes a conference call that may include, for example, three clients and the counselor/facilitator. The phone group should be closed, have specific discussion topics, and be of a set duration. Assignments to be completed between sessions need to be developed for each of the members. The group members can decide at the end of the formal, facilitated sessions (eight to 10) whether they wish to exchange telephone numbers and maintain informal telephone contacts. This approach can be extremely valuable: sensitive subjects can be discussed openly, given the degree of anonymity that the telephone offers. The telephone therapy group should be followed up with regular telephone contact between the counselor and the individual group members. These individual calls are also scheduled for a set length of time.

5.4.2   Ethnic and Racial Populations

Designing and implementing successful treatment strategies requires racial, ethnic, and cultural knowledge; competency; and sensitivity concerning diverse issues. However, in attempting to describe cultural factors, it is important not to fall into the trap of unintentionally perpetuating stereotypes of ethnic and racial populations. It is also critical to understand that diversity exists within a racial or ethnic group as well as among groups: women of all races and ethnic groups vary by personality, geographic origin, socioeconomic class, religious upbringing, and other factors, all of which play a role in their individual "cultures."

Moreover, many of the cultural differences attributed to one population may apply generally—if somewhat differently—to many racial and ethnic groups. For example, communication styles vary considerably in terms of preferred space (physical distance) between the conversants; the degree to which contact (touching) is appropriate; eye contact (which is value-laden in most societies); and language styles (formal or "street" or other). Differences in communication style also can vary by personality type, socioeconomic class, and religious upbringing. An example of the latter is the "call and response" communication attributes applied by some to African Americans who are religious. They are equally applicable to Roman Catholics irrespective of their race or ethnicity. Therefore it is important for the counselor to assess each individual's cultural orientation carefully. The counselor should not presume the degree to which the various "cultural" factors—not only ethnic or racial background—are predeterminant.

Counselors and staff should be trained to recognize and confront their own biases toward clients of other ethnic, racial, and cultural groups; this helps them to be aware of their own nonverbal communication. They particularly need to be cognizant of nonverbal communication that is rejecting, insincere, or judgmental. If these messages, however unintended, are communicated to the client, her response whether verbal or nonverbal, may be inappropriately labeled as defensive or hostile. As with other judgements regarding the client's behavior, counselors and other staff need to be aware that such labeling can unfortunately become a diagnosis that may follow the woman throughout her treatment and severely impede her recovery.

For recent immigrants of any origin, at some point early in the treatment process, the counselor should question clients about citizenship status, degree of acculturation, country of origin, circumstances of move to the United States, country with which they identify, language abilities, literacy level in native and other languages, spiritual/religious base, educational level, housing, and legal issues. However, given laws of deportation, the staff must be very sensitive when asking these questions.

Counselors and staff should be trained to recognize and confront their own biases toward clients of other ethnic, racial, and cultural groups.

African American Women

- As with other ethnic groups, there are regional cultural differences in the behaviors of African American women that have often been shaped by or formed in response to the dominant culture. For example, some African American women may be more inclined to avoid maintaining eye contact because it has been perceived as showing disrespect or as defying authority—a carryover from segregation. In contrast, other African American women may have rejected behaviors that indicate deference to authority and may be perceived by some program staff as defensive or hostile. Staff need to be clear about the particular viewpoint of the individual client and be cautious about judging behavioral clues.

- "Touching" during conversation to convey empathy is typically welcomed and accepted by most African Americans only between those who are close and by intimate friends. However, if touching is secondary to an insult or an act of disrespect that the care provider is attempting to redress, it may be considered intrusive and insincere. It may not be appropriate for a therapist to touch the client unless there is an established level of trust and rapport that merits such intimacy. Touching should not be viewed as a therapeutic approach to gaining trust.

- African American women are often reluctant to engage in conversations with and seek assistance from health care professionals, particularly those who are not African Americans, because of negative and demeaning experiences that they have heard about or experienced. African Americans may perceive questions related to finances or sexual behavior as intrusive and as indicative of stereotypical thinking. Because some African American women are reluctant to "put their business on the street," staff should be aware that it may take some time before clients disclose information that the program requires or believes necessary for treatment.

American Indian Women

- The American Indian woman often experiences feelings of isolation from the rest of the American Indian community while in treatment. These feelings can be minimized by integrating traditional healers or other community leaders into treatment programs, if so desired by the client. This should be done early in the treatment process when making decisions about treatment placement (i.e., outpatient versus inpatient) and the length of stay. Include the family and/or tribal decision makers in planning the treatment and continuing care program if applicable.

- Culturally appropriate and community-specific conceptual processes, including an awareness of historical and contemporary factors influencing substance use and abuse, are critical. Also important is an awareness of the cultural concepts and definitions of health, illness, and substance abuse held by American Indians and how these beliefs can be used as the foundation for treatment. If possible, services in American Indian languages should be provided for those women not conversant in English. If the treatment agency is not nearby, the agency should make arrangements for providing transportation for clients and their families, if appropriate. Program staff members must acknowledge and promote clients' religious beliefs, values, and practices as a significant part of their empowerment and validation. Collaborating with American Indian health care programs and allowing for culturally relevant adaptation of treatment modalities (e.g., sweats, dances, and Talking Circles) are important ways to show respect for American Indian cultures. The Swinomish Mental Health Program manual suggests ways to develop appropriate services for American Indian women.

- American Indian female clients should, if possible, be referred to American Indian agencies, educational programs, and vocational training programs when outside resources are used.

Asian/Pacific Islanders

- It is essential for treatment providers to be aware that various Asian/Pacific Islander (API) groups have traditional methods and values for physical and emotional healing. Although some of these perspectives may seem contrary to mainstream recovery practices, they can help the API client. For example, the use of Chinese acupuncture and herbs are accepted by some as a viable means to help with detoxification symptoms, cravings, and physical imbalances. These healing approaches have, in fact, shown very favorable results in the early stages of recovery.

The value of spirituality as a source of strength and healing should not be overlooked.

- Recognizing the historical significance of spirituality and religion will help counselors understand the API client. Many API cultures have integrated Western religion with their indigenous beliefs and rituals. The value of spirituality as a source of strength and healing should not be overlooked. For example, some Native Hawaiians use healers and respected elders called "Kahunas" to provide and promote emotional and spiritual guidance and healing.

- The case manager should be responsible for locating culturally specific services that have bilingual/bicultural staff, or identify appropriate staff in mainstream service agencies.

Hispanic/Latina Women

- If the target population is predominantly Spanish-speaking, all materials should be printed in Spanish, including intake and assessments forms, treatment plan forms, discharge forms, and other documents. The program should also have available educational materials in Spanish. At least some clinical staff (part time or full time) members should be Spanish-speaking.

- Programs should establish a library of books and tapes in Spanish that present the stories of Hispanic/Latina women who have addressed (and overcome) similar problems and who can act as role models for women entering substance abuse treatment.

- It is recommended that the program host or arrange for referral to AA, Al-Anon, or other 12-Step meetings in Spanish for women only.

- Networking with programs and agencies serving Hispanic/Latina women and their families to arrange for cross-training is extremely helpful. Through this method, the program staff can explore how they handle substance abuse issues, share program information, and formalize communication.

- By providing access for Hispanic/Latina women to groups that address women's concerns or general concerns of their cultural community, clients can build confidence as women in roles other than those of addicted persons or mothers. Such groups can include, for example, those relating to expanding women's roles in the economic development of the community, generating housing opportunities, and helping to increase access to health care services.

- One avenue which may serve as an incentive for Hispanic women to enter treatment is to invite Hispanic/Latina women from the community to visit the program and explore services for themselves, their children, or other relatives.

5.4.3 Other Specific Groups of Women

Women in the Criminal Justice System

- Treatment staff should acknowledge and address the additional stigma that incarcerated women or women with criminal records face; this will be particularly useful during follow-up and continuing care.

- Criminal justice and treatment personnel should work together to ensure that each conveys similar messages to female clients, regarding the importance of ensuring that they access substance abuse treatment and determining the appropriate modality for each woman.

- It is important to involve women from different ethnic and socioeconomic backgrounds who have "graduated" from the criminal justice system as role models for those in treatment. Such involvement may include their participation in discussion groups at the program, having available written personal histories, or arranging for videotapes in which their personal histories are presented.

- The program should develop a referral system to provide legal assistance for such issues as custody and parole.

Women with HIV/AIDS

- Substance abuse treatment programs should provide an ongoing HIV/AIDS education, prevention, and treatment component that is fully integrated into the overall treatment system. Programs that are part of a medical center will likely have the appropriate resources to provide medical care to their clients who are HIV-positive or who have AIDS. Most programs will provide services through referrals to outside sources. The treatment program should have formal referral agreements with such sources, which should include case management to ensure that the treatment program is aware of services provided, their outcome, and the on-going health status of the client. In addition to the comprehensive services described previously in this chapter, the special parenting issues, self-care techniques, symptom management, medical needs, and the needs of family members and significant others should be addressed.

- Legal assistance should be provided to women with AIDS who may need help drawing up a living will or addressing other legal (or legal/financial) issues such as access to Social Security benefits and life insurance.

- The program should also offer appropriate psychiatric and psychological assessments and psychological support for women infected with HIV/AIDS to address the issues of death and dying and custody and care of children when it becomes necessary.

- The program should establish liaison with the many support groups that address parenting, general or sexual health, and other issues for HIV-positive and AIDS clients.

- Personnel must be prepared to help the women with AIDS and their families deal with the issue of medication for easing pain in the terminal phases of AIDS.

Women with Disabilities

- To serve women with disabilities, it is critical that information, policies, programs, and facilities are accessible to them. Providing accessible transportation, particularly in communities where transportation options are limited, is also essential. Women with disabilities who are staff members of the treatment program can facilitate the process of engaging women with disabilities in treatment for substance abuse problems.

- Staff members need to be careful not to view a client's disability as *the* cause of substance abuse, or even as a cause. Sometimes the disability may be the result of substance abuse. For example, a woman's disability could have been the result of an accident that occurred when she was driving while intoxicated. Sometimes the disability may be a minor or irrelevant factor. Counselors may find it helpful to obtain information on the extent, nature, cause, and age of onset of the disability, as well as the woman's assessment of the role of her disability status in her substance abuse problem. This information can be obtained as part of the intake process, but it should not be the first item on the intake agenda.

- Counselors should assess women with disabilities in the same manner that they assess women who are not disabled. They need to cover the same topics and issues during intake and avoid making limiting assumptions about the woman's sexuality or lifestyle. For example, sexuality should not be overlooked in the treatment of women with disabilities. It is also important to consider women with disabilities as the experts on their own disabilities.[15] They should be key participants in determining what types of accommodations and help they need to participate in the treatment program.

- The language of disability is rapidly changing. In general, the term "disability" is preferred to "handicapped," and "woman with a disability" is preferred to "disabled woman,"

It is also important to consider women with disabilities as the experts on their own disabilities.

since the woman comes first, before her disability. Language that suggests victimization and suffering should be avoided; for example, avoid the terms "suffers from cerebral palsy," "victim of polio," or "confined to a wheelchair." New terms such as "differently able" or "physically challenged" or "mentally challenged" have been rejected by disability rights activists as euphemisms. However, some people with disabilities may disagree. Thus, when in doubt, ask the woman what terminology she prefers.

References

1.   National Clearinghouse for Alcohol and Drug Information (NCADI). 600 Executive Boulevard, Suite 402, Wilco Bldg., Rockville, MD 20852.

2.   O'Neil, C., RN, PhD. (1993). Addictions. Nursing Network. 5 (1), 33.

3.   Center for Substance Abuse Treatment. (1993). Screening for Infectious Diseases Among Substance Abusers. Rockville, MD: U.S. Department of Health and Human Services, Public Health Service.

4.   Zweben, J.E. (1992). Issues in the Treatment of the Dual-Diagnosis Patient. In Wallace, B.C., Ed., The Chemically Dependent, Phases of Treatment and Recovery. New York: Brunner/Maze, 298.

5.   Kulewicz, S. (1990). The Twelve Core Functions of a Counselor. Somerville, MA: David and Goliath Creative, 39.

6.   Center for Substance Abuse Treatment. (1993). Pregnant, Substance-Using Women. Rockville, MD: U.S. Department of Health and Human Services, Public Health Service, 7.

7.   Bjorklund, P.E. (1983). What is Spirituality? Center City, MN: Hazeldon Foundation, 7.

8.   Bjorklund, P.E. (1983). What is Spirituality? Center City, MN: Hazeldon Foundation, 3.

9.   Moore, T. Care of the Soul. (1992). New York, NY: Harper Perennial, xix.

10.   Bjorklund, P.E. (1983). What is Spirituality? Center City, MN: Hazeldon Foundation, 4.

11.   Bjorklund, P.E. (1983). What is Spirituality? Center City, MN: Hazeldon Foundation, 10.

12.   Center for Substance Abuse Treatment. (1993). Guidelines for the Treatment of Alcohol and Other Drug-Abusing Adolescents. Rockville, MD: U.S. Department of Health and Human Services. Public Health Service, 15.

13.   Center for Substance Abuse Treatment. (1993). Approaches in the Treatment of Adolescents with Emotional and Substance Abuse Problems. Rockville, MD: U.S. Department of Health and Human Services. Public Health Service. x.

14.   ibid.

15.   See for example Linton, S., and Rousso, H. (1990). Sexuality Counseling for People with Disabilities. In Weinstein, E. and Rosen E., Eds. Sexuality Counseling: Issues and Implications. Pacific Grove, CA: Brooks/Cole, 114-34.

Chapter 6

Continuing Care and Follow-up

Photo by Ellen Shapiro

Today, it is well understood that no single system can provide comprehensive and effective solutions to the host of problems confronting women in recovery for substance abuse.

Chapter 6

Continuing Care and Follow-up

CSAT defines alcoholism and other drug dependencies as chronic, progressive disorders comparable to other chronic disorders such as diabetes and hypertension but often characterized by relapse. Thus, continuing care for women, which involves activities that support long-term rehabilitation and prevent relapse of female clients who have completed specific substance abuse treatment programs, is an essential component of effective treatment programs.

Given the effects of substance abuse on all areas of a woman's ability to function—physical, mental, emotional, social, economic, and spiritual–continuing care services must be both comprehensive and focused on individual needs. In fact, many believe that continuing care, which provides the support structures and services that empower women to live drug-free lives, should span a woman's lifetime, although diminishing over time. Support structures for women in continuing care may include frequent contact with other recovering women, individual and family therapy sessions, regular group support meetings, access to literature, life skills training, ongoing formal education, vocational training, job placement, and, when needed, respite or hospice care. These services must be culturally sensitive and competent, convenient, accessible, and affordable.

Today, it is well understood that no single system can provide comprehensive and effective solutions to the host of problems confronting women in recovery for substance abuse.

Today, it is well understood that no single system can provide comprehensive and effective solutions to the host of problems confronting women in recovery for substance abuse. In view of this fact, CSAT has taken the lead in establishing alliances with other programs in the U.S. Department of Health and Human Services as part of the Substance Abuse Linkage Initiative. These alliances facilitate new understandings in the field of substance abuse treatment and establish new directions in acquiring additional treatment services that offer more effective avenues for rehabilitation.

6.1   Issues Related to Continuing Care

Continuing care interventions, designed to address the complex issues in women's lives discovered throughout the treatment process, are often introduced during or near the end of the treatment process.

Services that programs should provide include the following:

- case management;

- the development of relapse prevention skills;

- assistance in accessing, and developing skills to access comprehensive services, including, for example, safe and affordable housing and child care; and

- the facilitation of women's entry into relevant education and job training programs.

The use of these services in the treatment process is discussed in Chapter 5. Their role in continuing care and in relapse prevention is described below.

6.1.1   Case Management During Continuing Care

Case management is essential to the successful continuing care of women recovering from abuse of alcohol and other drugs.

Case management is essential to the successful continuing care of women recovering from abuse of alcohol and other drugs. The case manager facilitates continuing comprehensive care and follow-up services. The case manager also helps the recovering woman develop a healthier and more productive life for herself and her family. For example, the case manager can help clients obtain benefits and entitlements; assist with and arrange access to health care, housing, child care, and transportation; and coordinate appointments with mental health service providers. The case manager also provides ongoing assessments of clients' recovery and responds appropriately to requests from clients for additional services. The case manager is specifically responsible for identifying women who have relapsed or who are in danger of relapsing and for helping them to return to treatment, if necessary. Ideally, the case manager should hold weekly case conferences to ensure that clients' ongoing needs are addressed.

6.1.2 Relapse Prevention and Recovery Skills

In examining issues of continuing care and follow-up for women, it is important to consider relapse and recovery. The path of recovery is as unpredictable as the process of addiction. Clinicians and program directors should be aware of CSAT's definition of alcoholism and other drug dependency as a chronic, progressive disorder often characterized by relapse. Given this definition, and the fact that women who relapse may be in particular need of the treatment program's continued support, reentry opportunities to formal treatment must remain open. Continued relapses may also indicate the possibility of serious psychiatric problems, such as depression or bi-polar disorders. Issues related to dual disorders are discussed in greater detail in Chapters 3 and 5.

The path of recovery is as unpredictable as the process of addiction.

Staff of treatment programs must acknowledge that recovery is a lifelong process and, therefore, should realize that chronic relapse—which is often viewed as the client's fault—should instead be viewed as a preventable part of the recovery process. The program staff should be prepared to accept women who relapse and respond to their needs. Judgmental reactions on the part of treatment personnel towards women who relapse must be reduced by providing staff training on appropriate methods and manners of dealing with women who relapse. They should also periodically examine the program's treatment modalities to improve their effectiveness. For example, the treatment and continuing care program may need to determine if its services are helping clients to secure the basic financial, emotional, and physical support needed to maintain recovery.

Largely because of financial constraints, formal treatment is often not extensive enough for a woman recovering from alcohol and other drug abuse. Issues related to substance abuse, such as past sexual abuse or incest, often require separate attention and may go beyond the scope of substance abuse treatment. Therefore, to prevent relapse, the client may have to continue addressing these issues long after leaving treatment. The program needs to help the client obtain services to deal with her specific issues at different times in her recovery.

Issues related to substance abuse, such as past sexual abuse or incest, often require separate attention and may go beyond the scope of substance abuse treatment.

For recovery to be successful, counselors must help the client identify stressful areas of her life and learn how to locate and use resources to deal with the stress. During discharge planning, the program builds on its efforts throughout treatment to empower the woman to handle stress.

Many programs include a formal relapse prevention component that offers mechanisms for early detection of relapse and mechanisms for intervention. Relapse prevention should in part focus on structured, supervised leisure time that will create a foundation for a client to handle leisure time more effectively after treatment.

Every member of a family can be affected by substance abuse, and this problem often extends across many generations. Therefore, continued family involvement and intervention are necessary to help the woman recover and become a more functional part of her family system. The history and current status of her family members—including significant other(s), children, and parents—are extremely important. For example, if a woman's significant other has been in recovery but relapses, the program should make an effort to help refer him/her to treatment and work closely with the client to help her avoid relapse.

Because many addicted women will need a constellation of services ancillary to direct treatment, the continuing care network must include all of the services that she used while in treatment. If any of these services were not available, it could create stressors that may lead a client to relapse. These services include housing, health care, employment, and child care.

6.1.3 Access to Services

Ensuring access to adequate comprehensive services following treatment is critical to successful recovery. This section briefly describes issues related to this phase of care.

Housing. Traditionally, housing has not been considered a treatment program concern. But today, the lack of affordable and safe housing has become a major obstacle for women leaving treatment and reentering the community. In addition, it is an added stress factor that can be related to relapse. Often, clients cannot go back to their previous housing because they are no longer welcome; they have lost their place in public housing communities by being in treatment; or they cannot return to their partners. The housing issue is important to all women who leave treatment, but it is a particularly critical issue for women who have been physically and/or sexually abused, women just released from prison, homeless women, and displaced or runaway teenagers. In most geographic areas, few halfway houses exist for women with children and for women who are vision- or hearing-impaired or who have other disabilities. Continuing care must include effective approaches to help all of these women and their children locate housing that is inexpensive, safe, and drug free.

Women in early recovery often need frequent, high-intensity reenforcement of their recovery efforts. During this time (e.g., the first year or two), it may be advisable for clients to live in halfway houses or

The lack of affordable and safe housing has become a major obstacle for women leaving treatment and reentering the community.

Women in early recovery often need frequent, high-intensity reenforcement of their recovery efforts.

group homes with other recovering women, rather than on their own. In this way, clients can develop support structures and positive peer relationships. For those who are too young to manage independent living situations and who do not have an intact home, long-term living arrangements, such as therapeutic foster care, should be developed. Program staff should try to identify a wide range of housing options in the community.

Some ways to help women who are discharged from intensive treatment to find suitable housing include the following:

- form an alliance with the Public Housing Authority and other housing programs to identify subsidized housing in safe, reasonably drug-free neighborhoods or recovery-oriented enclaves in high-risk neighborhoods;

- maintain a data bank on housing that is accessible to women with disabilities;

- network with Habitat for Humanity and similar nonprofit and church-related groups to locate houses where women in recovery and their families could live;

- hire a housing coordinator to connect recovering women with housing programs and group living facilities that are self-governing, self-supporting, based on recovery principles, and drug free;

- work with sister corporations that buy and rehabilitate apartment buildings and houses, and then sell or rent space to women in recovery and their families;

- target particular blocks of neighborhoods or streets which are safe for women and children and "zoned drug free"; and

- provide long-term halfway house services for women only, for women with children, and for women who are severely debilitated from alcohol and other drug abuse. (Providing graduated phases of decreasing intensity of treatment in these houses will help clients resume recovery more quickly).

Health Care. The program should make provisions for continued access to adequate health care services, as appropriate, before a woman leaves treatment. Some approaches include the following:

- network with existing women's health services, women's hospitals, medical colleges, university interns and residents, and public health nurses to identify primary health care services for women and their children;

- develop a directory of local physicians, dentists, and health care and medical facilities, including teaching hospitals, that can offer flexible payment plans, accept Medicaid, provide services for the indigent, or provide a limited number of free hours of service. This directory should include information on the accessibility of offices and the types of services offered to women with disabilities;

- meet with physicians, hospital administrators, and health clinic managers to develop agreements so that all women can receive gynecological care; pregnant and postpartum women can receive prenatal, delivery, and postnatal care; and parenting women can receive pediatric care for their children; and

- assist women who are eligible for Medicaid in preparing their applications.

Financial Independence. Economic self-sufficiency is an important goal in the recovery process for women. While job readiness should be part of ongoing treatment, it is essential prior to discharge and during aftercare. However, problems of illiteracy, inadequate job skills, and child care can exacerbate a client's difficulties in finding work and thus must be addressed in the discharge plan and by the continuing care program. The

Problems of illiteracy, inadequate job skills, and child care can exacerbate a client's difficulties in finding work.

program can help women overcome these and related problems in the following ways:

- teach women how to write resumes and develop job histories using all relevant skills and experiences, including house-hold, church, school, and volunteer work;

- conduct assessments of interests, capabilities, literacy, and bilingual skills for placement of the client in appropriate vocational and educational programs;

- teach basic skills and techniques needed to obtain a job; for example, rehearsing for a job interview;

- provide information on the Americans with Disabilities Act which offers protection against employment discrimination and other forms of discrimination;

- provide apprenticeships, job referrals, and job placements that are in environments supportive of recovery and where attention is paid to the physical and psychological exigencies of abuse/addiction and potential impairment; and

- establish small, for-profit, majority women-owned businesses in which recovering women can work as paid apprentices or employees, buy shares of stock in the business, and learn business management skills. Examples of potential program and/or client-run businesses include food cooperatives, bakeries, restaurants, clothing shops, building rehabilitation companies, information management services, and child care services. Some portion of the profits could return to the women's treatment program and continuing care program that helped to initiate the business. Start-up money for this type of business is available from sources such as the Department of Housing and Urban Development's Community Development grants and loans, Small Business Administration (SBA) loans, women's business associations, and minority business associations.

Women may have residual disabilities from their abuse of alcohol and other drugs that may not be taken into account by vocational and educational programs to which they may be referred. Women may be routed into short-term, low-paying clerical or other jobs while they still cannot read, write, concentrate, or coordinate eye-hand movements because of the aftereffects of drugs on the central nervous system. These effects may take a while to abate after a client becomes abstinent. Some women may need to be classified as "long-term disabled" to ensure they receive prolonged recovery treatment and continued care.

Child Care and Parenting Skills. Women in continuing care may need assistance to develop strong, nurturing relationships with their children and to access child care before and after discharge from treatment. Treatment programs can help women develop strong parenting skills and find appropriate child care in the following ways:

- support a woman's desire to be a full-time parent, if assessment shows she is able and prepared to assume the full-time care of a young child or of several children;

- continue to provide counseling and support or referrals for these services to women who feel they cannot cope with parenting and/or who believe that their children would be better off in the care of someone else;

- ask for assistance from the Center for Substance Abuse Treatment, the state or county office responsible for child and family services, or a local university to help develop a parenting curriculum for mothers in recovery;

- develop a resource directory of parenting assistance and child care agencies, foster home systems, private homes, nurseries, and schools in collaboration with a family service agency; and

Women may have residual disabilities from their abuse of alcohol and other drugs that may not be taken into account by vocational and educational programs to which they may be referred.

Women in continuing care may need assistance to develop strong, nurturing relationships with their children.

- investigate community-sponsored parenting and child care courses that are free or inexpensive and invite existing programs to provide their courses to clients on-site, if possible.

6.1.4 Provisions for the Terminally Ill

Until recently, services for women who are terminally ill were not considered part of continuing treatment. The advent of HIV/AIDS in communities with a high incidence of substance abuse has made this an urgent need. Continuing care for addicted women in terminal stages of any disease includes providing food, shelter, clean bedding, and clothing, access to personal hygiene facilities, assistance in addressing "unfinished business," compassionate interaction, and assistance in accessing spiritual guidance. The facility in which terminally ill clients are housed must be safe (insofar as possible) and clean, and must have room for women to visit with their children. HIV/AIDS support groups, Alcoholics Anonymous, Narcotics Anonymous, and other 12-Step programs should be made available on-site.

The substance abuse treatment program staff need to work closely with hospice program staff and with child protective services to keep families intact, if possible and appropriate. Funding possibilities for hospice care include charitable organizations such as the United Way, churches and synagogues, health insurance companies, private foundations, women-owned businesses, and county health departments.

6.1.5 Women with Dual Disorders

In addition to the general discussion of the prevalence of dual disorders among substance-abusing women (Chapter 2), issues related to assessment and treatment of women with dual disorders are described in

Chapters 3, 4, and 5. For those women who have dual disorders, the period of continuing care following structured treatment can be particularly difficult. Because formal substance abuse treatment seldom lasts long enough to address such problems thoroughly, women with dual disorders need continuing treatment not only for the substance abuse problem, but often (and as importantly) for the dually-diagnosed disorder as well. This is true whether or not the disorder is directly related to the problem of substance abuse (see discussion in Chapter 3).

To help ensure that the needs of the client with a dual disorder (or disorders) are met, the treatment program staff should prepare a mental health assessment for each client prior to discharge, make referrals for continuing mental health services, and arrange for follow-up on the outcome of these services, insofar as possible. The CSAT report, Assessment and Treatment of Patients with Coexisting Mental Illness and Alcohol and Other Drug Abuse advises programs that:

> An aftercare plan for patients with dual disorders is essential. This plan should integrate rather than fragment strategies for treating the patient. It should include methods to coordinate care with other treatment providers.[1]

With respect to relapse prevention for those with dual disorders, the same CSAT report suggests that:

> Relapse should be defined as engagement in any unsafe behavior such as alcohol and other drug (AOD) use, self-harm, and noncompliance with medications. Relapse prevention should focus on preventing AOD use and recurrence of psychiatric symptoms.[2]

For those women who have dual disorders, the period of continuing care following structured treatment can be particularly difficult.

6.1.6   Women, Violence, and Continuing Care

As has been noted elsewhere in this document, a high proportion of women in treatment have been adult or childhood victims of emotional, physical, or sexual abuse (including incest) and/or have been exposed to violence in their communities, or suffered the loss of a family member or friend as a result of a violent crime. Many may be vulnerable to continued abuse in their current or former relationships and to continued exposure to violence in their communities. Therefore, it is critical that the program staff help to ensure insofar as possible that clients have adequately addressed their issues related to past exposure to violence. Also, they need to have access to services to continue to address problems associated with injuries resulting from abuse.

The staff should be aware that relapse can be related to difficulties in coping with unresolved issues related to a history of abuse.

In the latter regard, arrangements should be made for clients to be referred to individual or group counseling as necessary and to support groups (e.g., those associated with rape crisis centers or women's therapy groups) in their community. They should also be provided with information that can be used in the event that they are exposed to abuse in the future (e.g., contact information for a local shelter for battered women). For women who may be in relationships in which they are vulnerable to abuse, the staff should, as part of a discharge plan, help them to develop a "safe plan" which includes strategies for immediately resolving abuse issues in the future. For women who are self-mutilating (which can be an outcome of abuse), this safe plan should include strategies for self-care.[3]

The staff should also be aware that relapse can be related to difficulties in coping with unresolved issues related to a history of abuse, or to concerns related to current vulnerability to either personal violence resulting from a relationship or exposure to violence in their community. Therefore, for women with a history of abuse or exposure to violence (and in particular for those vulnerable to continued abuse and/or exposure to violence), understanding the relationship between emotional and psychological reactions to such abuse is important.

Perhaps the most sensitive issue in continuing care of the woman who is involved in a relationship where abuse is likely to continue is the family reunification approach taken by the treatment program. While the safety of the woman is paramount, it is also important for the program to empower the woman to deal with the potential for exposure to abuse. In addition to the accurate assessment of women early in treatment, and addressing abuse history during treatment (see Chapter 5), the program should pay particular attention to providing these clients with information that can be used should abuse recur. Covington has suggested that such information include use of restraining orders, in addition to hotlines and contacts for shelters (see above).[4]

6.2   Community and Interagency Collaboration: Referrals and Resources

Interagency collaboration can be a powerful tool to ensure that recovering women receive necessary services during the transitional or continuing care phase of treatment and when they return to the community. It is important to form strong bonds with other agencies and community groups that have the expertise and capacity to provide services to these recovering women, such as departments of corrections and criminal justice (adult and juvenile), child protective services, the Department of Veterans' Affairs, domestic violence agencies, rape crisis centers, employee assistance programs, health maintenance organizations and other health service providers, women's resource centers, family centers and independent living centers as well as other disability advocacy groups. The program staff also needs to interact with community organizations and service agencies to establish a cohesive mechanism that will enable case managers to monitor a client's progress. An assigned individual within each agency can track the client's progress and provide her with access to services and programs.

During discharge planning, staff must ensure that a woman who is moving into continuing care has a comprehensive list of available resources and services, and they must provide clear directions for accessing these services. The counselor should discuss referrals with clients so they know exactly what services they can expect from providers. Staff members should make certain that if a client is not literate, is not English-speaking, or has other communication problems, she knows how to follow through with referrals. To prevent crises that could contribute to relapse after discharge, program staff should work with other community health providers to establish or expand a crisis/support hotline for women who have left inpatient treatment and are now living in the community or who have completed outpatient care.

Treatment programs empower recovering women by helping them gain access to appropriate supportive resources.

It is critical for a treatment program to establish, to the greatest extent possible, working relationships with groups in the community that provide safe and appropriate recreational resources for women reentering the community after residential or outpatient treatment. Treatment programs empower recovering women by helping them gain access to appropriate supportive resources. Identifying and involving women in activity centers (recreation, group meals, education programs, social events) facilitates the process of meeting and socializing with other women. Introducing recovering women to community-based volunteer programs in which they can participate not only benefits the community, but will improve clients' social skills and self-esteem and widen their circles of associations and networks of support. Every treatment program must evaluate its existing referral mechanisms. For example, because recovering women should be referred to continuing care programs that are culturally and ethnically appropriate, program staff should make sure that service providers have a successful record of working with women of various population groups.

Staff should not hesitate to identify and intercede in referral relationships that are clearly discriminatory or counterproductive to the client's recovery. Individuals in other organizations may misinterpret actions and behavior of people from different ethnic and racial minority groups and react in ways that discourage further contact. Also, to determine whether women are receiving needed services in a timely manner, programs can invite clients to join a focus group that will provide information to help evaluate the referral system.

Collecting accurate and up to date data on and conducting an analysis of community resources for serving women in recovery is also critical. Because such endeavors often require resources that the program itself may not have, these may be carried out in conjunction with other human service agencies. Working collaboratively, and forming consortia among the local providers to address accessing resources can be helpful. Identifying strengths, weaknesses, service gaps, duplications and capacity, and reporting these findings to policy makers, social service organizations, alcohol and drug associations, community leaders, and the media will not only improve the visibility of the program but could facilitate fundraising.

6.3   Support Groups

Recovery issues pertaining to self-esteem, sexuality, sexual abuse and violence, cultural roles/identity, communication skills, assertiveness, stress management, family and other relationships, and health, are ongoing for women and should be addressed during treatment as well as during continuing care. Women in recovery can address these issues by establishing connections with recovering women in self-help groups as early as possible during treatment and after discharge. A foundation or a new "family" of other recovering women can be created by holding ongoing support meetings and facilitating daily phone contacts. Peer retreats or weekend experiences that reunite treatment program participants can help women maintain treatment gains and provide positive experiences for their new lifestyles.

Programs can also develop networks of recovering people who will volunteer to serve as temporary sponsors and act as "big sisters" to women reentering the community after treatment. It would be helpful to have the clients meet these volunteers before they leave the treatment program. Women's organizations such as sororities, the Older Women's League, and support groups for abused women are good resources for such "buddy" activities. The program could also advocate for new or increased women-only 12-Step or comparable support groups such as Adult Children of Alcoholics, Codependency Anonymous, Women for Sobriety, as well as groups specifically designed for populations such as lesbian, adolescent, and older women. The program could offer the use of space in its facility when possible. Hosting social events for clients, alumnae, and their sponsors allows women to meet and socialize with other recovering women.

Another way to help a woman in this phase of recovery is to enlist the involvement of supportive persons within the cultural and geographic community as early as possible in the treatment process. Telephone chains among program graduates and others help ensure that women receive regular inquiries about their well-being. Some programs have established a 24-hour hotline for recovering women to help them with relapse problems. Some hotlines have a telecommunications device (TDD) to ensure access for women who are deaf.

6.4   Follow-up Strategies and Procedures

Follow-up of clients' status after treatment allows the program to respond to changes in the clients' physical and mental health and socioeconomic status during the continuing care phase of recovery. It also provides programs with information about the effectiveness of treatment. Follow-up conveys to clients that the program staff maintains concern about their welfare. To ensure effective follow-up, ongoing staff training in treatment, follow-up and tracking of women who leave treatment must be provided. To evaluate a program's effectiveness, follow-up data collected at three-month intervals for a year after treatment can be considered fairly reliable for clinical purposes. However, anything less will not be credible or useful in evaluating treatment programs.

Locating clients after they have completed (or terminated) treatment is essential. Follow-up procedures, which should be part of the treatment process, can make it easier to track clients after their treatment is completed. For example, information obtained at initial contact, such as employment status and current address, as well as the names and addresses of the client's landlord, close relatives, and friends, will facilitate locating the client for follow-up. This information needs to be updated regularly.

It is critical to the recovery process that treatment programs maintain contact with the client as long as is necessary. The program should devise general procedures to follow a client's progress either in person or by telephone until the counselor, case manager, and client feel that follow-up services are no longer required. These procedures must also be adapted to the particular needs and living environment of each client. To avoid abrupt graduations from formal treatment, counselors should schedule incrementally decreasing face-to-face contacts interspersed with regular telephone conversations. During these contacts, the counselor should, without fostering unhealthy dependence, encourage the client to talk with a trusted program staff member as frequently as she thinks necessary and make her feel welcome to return for consultations and other services.

It may be unproductive to begin follow-up counseling by directly questioning the client about her current status with respect to use of alcohol or other drugs. Rather, a more useful approach might be to address the issue indirectly, for example, by asking the client for her opinion about the quality of service she received and if she believes the service was helpful.

Confidentiality must be carefully observed in the follow-up process.

Confidentiality during client follow-up is also an extremely important issue. Confidentiality must be carefully observed in the follow-up process not only to comply with government regulations but to avoid adverse effects on the client's relationships with others who may not be aware of her treatment. For example, if it is necessary to contact a client's employer, substance abuse cannot be mentioned unless the client has given written consent for disclosure of this information. Similarly, the name of a treatment facility should not be mentioned to friends or family members of the client without her written consent. It may be necessary to construct a plausible cover story in some instances.

References

1. Center for Substance Abuse Treatment. (1994). Assessment and Treatment of Patients with Coexisting Mental Illness and Alcohol and Other Drug Abuse. Rockville, MD: U.S. Department of Health and Human Services, Public Health Service, 60.

2. Center for Substance Abuse Treatment. (1994). Assessment and Treatment of Patients with Coexisting Mental Illness and Alcohol and Other Drug Abuse. Rockville, MD: U.S. Department of Health and Human Services, Public Health Service, 60.

3. Covington, S.S. (1994). Violence and Abuse. Bethesda, MD: Policy Research Incorporated, 3.

4. ibid.

Chapter 7

Program Management Issues

Photo by Larry Crowe

The program staff should determine if the program's policies and procedures are respectful of the clients and based on valid treatment assumptions as well as the realities of women's lives.

Chapter 7

Program Management Issues

Treatment programs must address program management issues that cut across phases of care. Some of these issues have been addressed in other chapters of the manual that correspond to the phases of care (e.g., staff composition as it relates to outreach). The issues are either listed (if they have been addressed in detail in a previous chapter) or briefly summarized under the following categories: policies and procedures, staff training, staffing and gender sensitivity, legal and regulatory issues, linkages with other agencies, and financing mechanisms.

7.1   Policies and Procedures

The treatment programs' policies and procedures not only reflect their philosophies and standard procedures pursuant to public regulations and guidelines, but also their recognition of the importance of gender and cultural differences. A number of issues concerning program policies and procedures relate specifically to women in treatment and should be addressed by any program in reviewing its policies and procedures and when initiating treatment services for women. In doing so, the program staff should determine if the program's policies and procedures are respectful of the clients and based on valid treatment assumptions as well as the realities of women's lives. While it is important to have clearly defined rules and a structured treatment environment, it is also important that the rules not be so restrictive as to hinder the potential for clients to remain in treatment and realize successful outcomes.

Because the treatment program staff (especially the counselors) knows the particular needs of clients, it is important that program directors hold frequent staff meetings to review policies and ensure that they are appropriate and conducive to effective treatment. Program managers are urged to involve staff in decision-making with respect to organizational arrangements, policies, and procedures whenever possible. Women who

The program staff should determine if the program's policies and procedures are respectful of the clients and based on valid treatment assumptions as well as the realities of women's lives.

have completed treatment can also be a source of practical information and suggestions regarding program policies and procedures.

Many of the policies and procedures relating to women in treatment (e.g., ensuring access to comprehensive services) have been discussed throughout Chapters 4, 5, and 6. Key policies should address the following issues:

- duration of treatment, which may need to be longer for women, in view of their parenting and other caretaking roles, as well as the multiple presenting problems that may need to be addressed in treatment (e.g., history of sexual abuse); in any case, the length of stay should be individualized within the program's range;

- gender discrimination and harassment (Section 7.5);

- the need for flexible outpatient program hours based on clients' daily schedules. Nine-to-five weekday office hours are often unmanageable for working women and may be difficult for women with children if child care is not provided. Programs with evening-only hours but without child care do not meet the needs of women who must make babysitting arrangements and who are concerned about leaving their children in environments where illicit drugs and alcohol are used or where violence occurs;

- the degree to which documents used by the program in outreach, treatment, and continuing care reflect knowledge of and sensitivity to women's issues and are devoid of gender and cultural stereotyping;

- for outpatient programs, the number of appointments that a client can miss during treatment and still remain in the program. For women with children who must arrange for child care (if it is not provided by the program), this restriction may be seen as difficult or impossible for practical reasons;

- requirements in residential programs that there be "no naps during the day," which could be difficult and not medically appropriate for pregnant women;

- for programs that have "strip search" policies, these should be carried out only when necessary and then by same-gender staff specifically trained to perform the searches in the most sensitive and least intrusive manner; and

- decisions regarding establishment of a smoke-free environment in most of the program's facilities, if this is not the policy for the entire facility. For the programs that have children in treatment with their mothers, the entire facility should be smoke free.

7.2 Staff Training

On an ongoing basis, the treatment program should identify the training needs and requirements of program staff as they relate to female clients. Training needs to be more intensive when the program is initiating operations or when female clients are being recruited for the first time. Staff training should focus on ensuring that all staff (women and men) have an understanding of the particular needs of women in treatment and that they have the capacity to meet these needs.

On an ongoing basis, the treatment program should identify the training needs and requirements of program staff as they relate to female clients.

If the state licensing and credentialing agency has materials that are used to assess the competency of counselors, these materials can be adapted by the program for use as a partial basis for the training. The program should also prepare alternative model treatment plans that are appropriate for women under a variety of circumstances (e.g., with or without children, with or without a supportive spouse or significant other). The program should involve in the training as many local resources (individuals, organizations, and materials) as possible to strengthen relationships with potential referral sources in the area.

Program management also should provide periodic training for staff, identifying the topic areas through feedback from staff (with staff members specifying their own training needs) and from ongoing and structured supervision. In this regard, all treatment programs should have clearly identified and written guidelines for staff performance and treatment procedures, with periodic clinical supervision by either program staff or consultants. The program can use a variety of mechanisms to monitor the knowledge, skills, and attitudes of staff with respect to women in treatment. Management can include the use of role playing exercises, the review of treatment plans prepared for and by the women, review of aggregate outcome data, and the subjective feedback obtained through focus groups involving staff and invited experts knowledgeable about women in treatment.

Staff training needs can be met in several ways:

- involve in-house program staff who may have particular expertise in the topic areas for which training is necessary (e.g., treatment planning);

- invite external experts to regularly scheduled staff meetings or those specifically arranged to address a given topic;

- arrange for staff to attend workshops and conferences that address general issues relating to substance abuse treatment, treatment of women or other issues related to comprehensive services for women. Support staff members in participating in workshops and conferences and presenting papers whenever possible; and

- exchange training resources and sessions with other facilities or organizations (e.g., with the local medical or nurses association, particularly those with which the program has ongoing relationships). This can facilitate linkages and be a more cost effective method of training.

Many treatment program staff serving women may benefit from training in many topic areas, including the following:

- understanding of women's issues related to substance abuse, including physiological effects, dual diagnosis, social service needs (e.g., child care);

- gender role stereotyping in general and with respect to substance abuse in particular;

- family, parental, friend, and other relationship issues for women in treatment;

- approaches to addressing a client's history of sexual and physical abuse and other violence in the treatment process;

- intake, assessment, and orientation procedures and instruments appropriate for women (and for their children, if in treatment with the woman);

- cultural competency with respect to ethnic/racial groups, different age groups (e.g., adolescents and older women), lesbians, women in the criminal justice system, and women with disabilities; and

- ethical issues, including those discussed in section 7.5.

All of these issues also should be addressed as part of clinical supervision.

7.3   Staffing and Gender Sensitivity

Although the commitment to engage, treat, and retain women in treatment is the responsibility of all program staff members, it must originate with the program's administration and must be based on client needs and expectations. However, making a program gender sensitive (which

Making a program gender sensitive is challenging to many administrators.

changes the status quo in many treatment programs) is challenging to many administrators because addressing the specific needs of women requires a variety of changes in such areas as staffing, training, and treatment arrangements (e.g., treatment hours) as well as ensuring that there is ongoing clinical supervision. These changes also present a challenge to program staff who must participate in and adapt to these new arrangements. If a treatment program for women is to work, its board of directors, advisory board, administrators, and staff members, must all be committed to reevaluating program goals, policies, and services that are offered directly by the program or for which referrals are made.

Making a program gender sensitive is challenging because it requires all staff members to develop a commitment to and an understanding of the issues related to female clients. Some staff members may have difficulty accepting new approaches to treating women in recovery, particularly when such approaches address issues relating to sexual behavior and sexual abuse. Both female and male staff members who have been victims of sexual abuse may be uncomfortable talking with women about sexual behavior. To work effectively with female clients, all staff members need to explore their own feelings and experiences regarding sexuality and sexual abuse, either individually or in a group. In addition, all staff should be trained in program practices that relate to establishing and maintaining appropriate boundaries with clients. Program rules must be established and enforced to prevent the intentional and unintentional sexual harassment of female clients. However, it should be understood that "appropriate boundaries" can vary by culture. Through staff supervision, program management can identify particular knowledge, skills, and attitudes that need to be improved with respect to gender issues, both for individual staff members and for program staff overall.

A number of treatment providers have found that involving male therapists in the recovery process makes the male partners of the women in

Program rules must be established and enforced to prevent the intentional and unintentional sexual harassment of female clients.

treatment more likely to interact with the treatment center and their female partners in various activities, including family-related sessions.[1] Male therapists can also be healthy role models for women who will necessarily interact with men in work, social services, and other aspects of their lives after treatment. This may have positive long-term benefits on the recovery process for the women.

Both female and male staff members (as well as clients) must understand what constitutes sexist attitudes and behavior and be able to identify such behavior among the staff and clients. Staff members must also be knowledgeable about and sensitive to the issues and needs of the women in the treatment program, including those of heterosexual and lesbian women and women of different abilities, ages, ethnicities, races, and religions. Staff must receive training to improve their knowledge and sensitivity as necessary.

Staff members must be knowledgeable about and sensitive to the issues and needs of the women in the treatment program.

If at all possible, the program staff and the program's board of directors and advisory board should reflect in their membership the client population with regard to ethnicity, race, gender, disability, sexual orientation, and language.

7.4   Addressing Legal and Ethical Issues in the Program

In addition to the legal service needs of individual clients (e.g., concerning child custody or spouse abuse), treatment programs for women confront two types of legal issues:

1. gender issues concerning the relationship between the individual client and staff member, such as sexual harassment and job discrimination; and

2. institutional problems, such as the federal, state, and city regulation of substance treatment services.

Although the sexual harassment of women in substance abuse treatment programs is a known problem, many programs do not have policies to address such harassment.

Although the sexual harassment of women in substance abuse treatment programs is a known problem, many programs do not have policies to address such harassment. Strict and clearly delineated policies with respect to the potential sexual harassment of clients and the liability that the problem represents for the programs are absolutely essential. These can be developed with assistance from local legal aid programs or agencies, based on federal and state guidelines and legal statutes.

Institutional regulations affect the kind of treatment that can be offered to women and how it may be delivered. These include federal regulations that apply across states (e.g., the Americans with Disabilities Act, mentioned in Chapter 5) as well as state and local public health and safety and other regulations that necessarily vary by locality.

Before planning for establishment of a treatment program or adding services to an existing program, providers must be thoroughly familiar with the regulations that apply to them. These regulations may include licensing of the facility by the local and/or state health department(s) and accreditation by the state alcohol and other drug abuse agencies. Although these regulations will be applicable to most, if not all, treatment programs, those serving women and their children may also face requirements related to the care of the children (e.g., for child care and for early childhood education). The program should obtain all required licenses and certifications as quickly as possible. This will help ensure the safety of the facility, build credibility with funding sources, and may be necessary to obtain third party payments.

In addition to legal issues, ethical issues need to be of concern to all treatment staff. The most commonly known are those related to client confidentiality, fraternizing between staff and clients, and sexual harassment. Most programs have policies that include ethical standards related to these issues. However, staff of treatment programs must also be aware of and seek to ensure adherence to basic ethical principles which are considered to apply across cultures and which can be used to guide substance abuse treatment. These principles—in particular justice and nonmalevolence—are of increasing interest to those concerned about civil and human rights and liberties. Jillson has described four ethical principles as they apply to health policy in general; their applicability to substance abuse treatment is as follows:[2]

- The principle of autonomy is the capacity to reason and to alter one's decisions and plans based on such reasoning and to act on the basis of one's decision. Client autonomy is an important goal for the client and the treatment staff to work toward during the recovery process. As the client becomes physically and emotionally stronger, her ability to reason and make decisions must be respected and strengthened as it aids in her recovery. It should be noted that this ethical principle may be difficult to apply early in the treatment process. However, when the client's judgement is likely to be impaired by recent and/or extensive use of alcohol and/or other drugs, such impairment does not absolve the treatment program from its obligation to ensure that the woman's autonomy is protected in the treatment process.

- The principle of beneficence is related to goals held by people and social institutions on their behalf. This is seen by some as the most important moral obligation of health and social service programs. When beneficial goals can be agreed upon by program managers, staff members, and clients, they should be pursued. For example, both the program and the woman might agree that an appropriate treatment goal is for the woman to be employed within a certain period of time. However, beneficial goals can be particularly difficult to implement in substance abuse treatment because there is an assumption that there is an agreed-upon definition of what is beneficial, to whom, and under what circumstances. For example, the treatment program may have treatment goals (and related general outcome indicators) that are not appropriate for every

Client autonomy is an important goal for the client and the treatment staff to work toward during the recovery process.

woman in treatment; moreover, the policy-related goals of funding agencies may differ from those of individual treatment programs receiving funding. Finally, the beneficial outcome for a woman's child(ren) may conflict with treatment approaches designed to ensure a beneficial outcome for the woman herself. For example, while it may be preferable for the woman to have time to recover without having her children with her in treatment, it may be preferable for the children to be with their mother throughout the duration of treatment.

- The principle of equity holds that each person must be given her/his due and that equals must be treated equally. While the treatment program cannot be responsible for ensuring justice and equity in all aspects of their clients' lives, it can ensure that all clients receive equal access to its services, that all are treated with equal respect by program staff, and that attempts are made to provide equal access to services outside of the program. This is critical to women in treatment, particularly to disadvantaged women because services have been disproportionately lacking for them and available services may not address their particular needs. The paucity of related health and social services for disadvantaged clients (and for some populations of women in particular) is also an issue related to distributive justice.

- The principle of non-malevolence, or "first, do no harm," holds that social institutions — in this case, treatment programs — should not impose harm or evil upon those affected by their actions. This is an apparently obvious virtue which, in practice, raises difficult societal issues. An example of how this principle applies in substance abuse treatment is the importance of ensuring that research and evaluation (whose intent is, ostensibly, to obtain data and information for use in improving the delivery of treatment services in general) does not in any way violate the integrity of the woman in treatment. Another is the need to ensure that protecting (as well as improving) the basic physical and mental health of the client is a focal point of service delivery; for pregnant and post-partum women in treatment, difficult trade-offs may be required of treatment staff. For example, the program may need to determine when it is necessary to make arrangements for placement of a newborn or young child in other living arrangements when the mother continues to abuse drugs and is deemed incapable of caring for the child.

7.5   Linkages with Other Agencies

The importance of establishing relationships with other community-based agencies to ensure that clients have access to comprehensive services has been addressed in Chapters 4, 5, and 6. If the treatment program is part of an umbrella agency that provides services not offered at the program site (e.g., health services), these services can be arranged through the umbrella agency. For freestanding substance abuse treatment programs, the arrangements may either be permanent (e.g., the service provider is part of the staff, either full-time or part-time) or arrangements can be made for regular or as needed consultations at the program site or the site of the service provider.

The program should establish and maintain a network of agencies that can meet the broad range of women's needs. To do so, the program staff should compile a list of health and other social service agencies that are resources for client services. This list should include the name of the agency, the service provided, its location, the telephone number, hours of service, the cost of service, information on accessibility to women with disabilities, and the name of the contact person. This list should be updated frequently and should be accessible to all staff members for use in referral to comprehensive services.

There are many opportunities throughout the treatment process for contacts with organizations that do not refer clients. For example, the program staff could collaborate with a local school/community college, university, or other organization that houses a media center to produce a professional quality audiotape or videotape on women and substance abuse treatment and mental health. Such materials would be useful to the program itself, to other providers in the community and to use in prevention and outreach by a broad range of organizations. Some collaborating agencies provide such production services free of charge, if they are assured proper credit for their efforts. Involving the clients in the process of planning for and producing the tape can be a challenging and rewarding experience for both clients and counselors; it is also likely to enhance the tape's usefulness. Other examples of contacts include exchanging training resources (mentioned previously in this chapter), setting up coalitions to exchange information on changes in health systems delivery and financing and its effect on substance abuse treatment programs, and exchanging written and audiovisual materials.

7.6   Financing Mechanisms

Because women need more and different compre- hensive services than are generally provided to men, it is likely that additional costs will be incurred.

Because women need more and different comprehensive services than are generally provided to men (e.g., child care, perinatal care, injuries resulting from sexual abuse and violence), it is likely that additional costs will be incurred to provide and arrange for the services for women that are described and recommended in this manual. Creative strategies must be employed to secure public and private money to fund the essential services that recovering women require. Examples of funding sources for treatment programs include the following:

- direct grants from federal agencies (e.g., CSAT, NIDA, NIAAA, Office of Minority Health);

- funding from the state alcohol and drug abuse authority, including the Substance Abuse and Mental Health Services Administration (SAMHSA) block grant funds, five percent of which are set aside for women's programs;

- grants from local and national private foundations that support substance abuse treatment programs specifically or health services for women and/or children generally; and

- state Medicaid agencies.

Ongoing and one-time donations from women-owned businesses, businesses targeting female consumers, and women's organizations can help to support nonprofit women's alcohol and other drug treatment programs. By involving these organizations either through defined collaborative arrangements or by having representatives serve on the program's board of directors, programs may be establishing relationships for potential financial support. Treatment programs can also sponsor community-wide symposia of issues directly and indirectly related to alcohol and other drug abuse and invite representatives of potential funding sources to speak or participate. In addition, programs can design and implement income generating projects to help ensure that the programs are economically self-sufficient to the degree possible.

To help gain their support for treatment of women, (including their economic support) community leaders need to be educated about treatment of women. Program staff, either independently or in coalition with other organizations, can encourage third party payer organizations to have insurance and managed care coverage reimbursements more in line with realistic costs for substance abuse treatment and intervention. If these efforts do not elicit an appropriate response from insurance companies, managed care providers, HMOs, and public medical assistance programs, it may be necessary and desirable to join with other agencies and community groups providing services for substance-abusing women to advocate for local and state legislative and administrative changes. Pennsylvania, for example, has successfully begun to mandate Medical Assistance reimbursement for long-term, halfway house services and to require insurance companies to provide at least minimal coverage for treatment of alcohol and other drug problems.

Each treatment program should have a development plan that includes identification of resource needs, potential sources of funding, and strategies to ensure financial sustainability. CSAT has issued a guide entitled "Funding Resource Guide for Substance Abuse Programs" that programs can use to assist them in preparing and implementing such a development plan.[3]

References

1.   Personal Communication: Senella, A.M., Bachrach, K., Star, K., and Zinn, I. (1994). Review of Practical Approaches in the Treatment of Alcohol and Other Drug Abusing Women. Tarzana, CA.

2.   Jillson, I.A. (1989). Towards a Framework for Consideration of Ethical Issues in International Health. Invited Presentation: National Council of International Health Annual Conference: Toward a Healthier World: Influencing Policies and Strategies. Washington, DC, 8-9.

3.   Center for Substance Abuse Treatment. (1993). Funding Resource Guide for Substance Abuse Programs. Rockville, MD: U.S. Department of Health and Human Services, Public Health Service.

Reflections

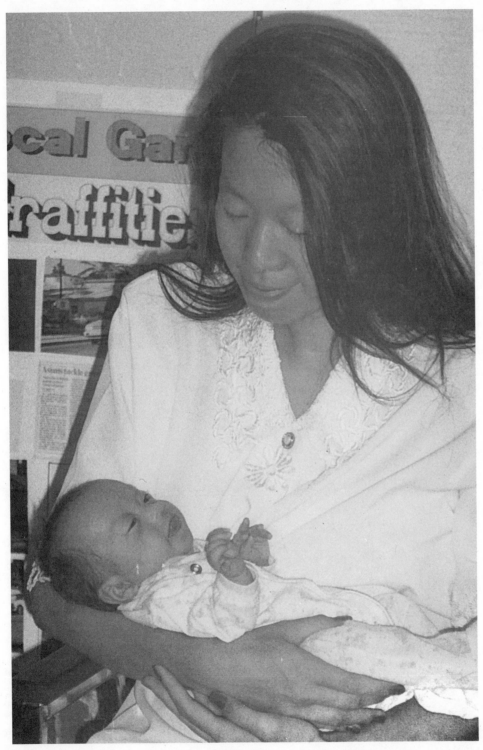

Photo by Walter Philips

From the perspective of the staff member of the treatment program, the millions of American women who have substance abuse problems become the one woman in treatment.

Chapter 8

Reflections

This manual was developed in response to an awareness at CSAT that women's needs have not been adequately addressed by most substance abuse treatment providers. The underlying assumption of this manual is that women have, to some degree, different physical, psychological, social, economic, legal, and behavioral treatment issues than those experienced by men. As a result, substance abuse treatment modalities and strategies have to be adapted and/or developed to meet the needs of women. It is also important to recognize that differences among women in ethnicity, culture, race, age, ability/disability, economic status, educational attainment, and sexual orientation necessitate different treatment strategies.

The manual described strategies for three stages of the treatment process: outreach when the program attracts the woman to treatment, comprehensive care when the program must address the woman's needs and retain her through the full course of treatment, and continuing care when the program helps to ensure that the recovering client's needs are met, as much as possible. Many of the strategies presented in the individual chapters (e.g., discussion of comprehensive services) apply across the continuum of care, as do discussions of particular issues related to special populations (e.g., older women). Moreover, because addiction is a chronic condition that is characterized by relapse on the part of many clients, many of the basic premises apply across the stages of care. Some of these have been highlighted in one section of the manual (e.g., the need to use screening and assessment tools that are gender-specific and culturally sensitive) rather than being repeated throughout the stages of care.

The underlying assumption of this manual is that women have, to some degree, different physical, psychological, social, economic, legal, and behavioral treatment issues than those experienced by men.

8.1 Two Key Themes: Comprehensive Services and Linkages

The issues addressed in this manual have been varied, reflecting the complex nature of substance abuse and many of the problems faced by women in treatment. Increasingly, substance abuse treatment programs must address the physical and mental health problems of women in treatment for which they may have received little attention, if any, prior to treatment. The consistent theme of the manual has been recognition of the need to provide comprehensive services for women in treatment. However, few programs have sufficient resources to provide a complete range of services in-house, nor should they be expected to do so. Most communities have public and/or private sector organizations which provide services directly or which facilitate access to them. Treatment programs, therefore, need to establish strong contacts with other organizations to refer clients for services and to receive referred clients.

Contacts and linkages are another theme of the manual. The ability of treatment program staff to establish successful relationships with the staff of health and social service agencies is critical to meeting the comprehensive needs of women in treatment. It is also essential to establish linkages with community-based organizations which represent women of color, adolescent and older women, lesbians, women in the criminal justice system, and women who have differing physical and mental abilities. These linkages help to ensure that treatment program staff have an increasing understanding of and sensitivity to the wide range of differences in women needing treatment; they also serve as an important source of referrals and resources for speakers and facilitators.

A number of sensitive issues that need to be addressed directly in the treatment process have been raised in the manual. These include for example, the increasing incidence and prevalence of HIV, AIDS, and sexually transmitted diseases among substance-abusing women, and the connection between sexual and physical violence and addiction. However, as has been noted in the manual, there are a variety of approaches to providing services to women who present with these problems. For example, opinion varies regarding the point at which counseling regarding prior history of sexual abuse should be initiated during the treatment process and how it should be addressed. Moreover, cultural and other values play an important role in terms of what is acceptable to the female client and what is permissible by local norms as expressed in public policy or the law. An example of the impact of cultural values is the divergent opinion concerning HIV and AIDS (e.g., counseling concerning safe sex practices and ensuring that condoms are available for clients). Although these are difficult and contentious issues, programs need to face them directly if their services are to meet the needs of their female clients. Program management and clinical staff should be sufficiently knowledgeable about the advantages and disadvantages of alternative strategies in terms of their client population. It is important for the staff to discuss these strategies with their clients and delineate a clear rationale for selecting the approach which is recommended for each client. If changes are made, all staff need to be made aware of the changes and the treatment protocol should be adjusted accordingly.

8.2   Do We Know What Works for Women?

The manual was prepared using both published and unpublished research and the experiential knowledge of women who are noted experts on the treatment of women for alcohol and other drug problems. However, it must be emphasized that there are many theories and approaches to the treatment of alcohol and other drug use in women and that the wide range of treatment programs reflects that diversity. Do we know with any certainty what works for women in treatment? If we think certain specific strategies work, are they more effective for certain populations under different circumstances? These questions apply in general to the treatment for alcohol and other drug abuse as well as the treatment of women specifically. It is important to coordinate efforts between funding sources, programs, and researchers to evaluate empirically approaches to engage and retain women in treatment. To facilitate recovery, research and evaluation

To facilitate recovery, research and evaluation are needed to determine which treatment modalities are most effective for women in general and for specific groups of women.

are needed to determine which treatment modalities are most effective for women in general and for specific groups of women.

The diversity of theoretical views and biases hampers the development and implementation of research and evaluation studies that could identify differences in treatment outcome. For example, the underlying concept of addiction serves as an explicit or implicit foundation for the design of research and evaluation. Many in the general public (and some in positions of leadership) still support the view that in general, alcohol and other drug abuse is a moral condition, particularly where women are concerned. Many others support the medical model perspective, defining substance abuse as a disease in the physical sense. But if the field is to address successfully the complex problems of alcohol and other drug abuse among women and to evaluate the success of treatment programs, it must develop successful, replicable treatment models. The focus should be on what treatment models and specific services are effective for which group of women in a variety of physical, psychological, social, and cultural circumstances.

In identifying what treatment approaches successfully engage and retain women in treatment and result in their recovery, it is important to look at specific aspects of the treatment process, examining the combination of treatment modalities and services that is most effective under different circumstances for diverse populations. For example, to consider the appropriateness of requirements (or standards) for the duration of residential treatment and frequency of outpatient visits for women in varying circumstances, the following types of questions should be addressed:

- Are twice weekly outpatient counseling sessions sufficient for a poor mother of four children without a job or job skills who is living in a temporary shelter?

- Will long-term residential treatment work best for a pregnant mother currently living with a violent spouse, whose children are in foster care under order of child protective services?

- Will a five to seven day inpatient detoxification treatment work best for a married woman with two children who is experiencing co-occurring symptoms of post traumatic stress syndrome, depression, and alcohol abuse?

The treatment program should consider these issues in defining its treatment philosophy and determining the scope and level of services, including treatment modalities. It should also consider these types of questions when preparing or reviewing the program's policies and procedures manuals and when reviewing the program's achievements.

8.3   Other Treatment Design Considerations

In addition to the issues raised in this manual, there are other important concerns in the design and adaptation of services for women. While some of these are applicable to both female and male clients, there are particular aspects that impact specifically on women. These issues are not addressed in detail, but are listed for consideration by the programs:

- Treatment programs are operating in a health care system that is in the midst of major changes and reform. How will alcohol and other drug programs fit into the overall plan? What is the current financial impact on the programs of the changing health care industry?

- Process and outcome evaluation are increasingly important to the viability of alcohol and other drug abuse programs for women. Programs that are funded in the future may be those which can document successful outcomes that are replicable in different environments. How can treatment programs serving women with complex health and socio-

Programs must have community partnerships and must receive funding from sources other than the government in order to survive.

economic problems document activities and outcome and for what outcomes will they be held accountable, whether or not they have "control" over the outcome (e.g., employment)?

- Programs must have community partnerships and must receive funding from sources other than the government in order to survive. However, there is increasing competition for scarce resources in both the public and private sectors. This can result in a competitive environment rather than a cooperative one. What are the possibilities for generating income on joint fund-raising efforts and for sharing of services to make the best use of scarce resources?

- Cultural competence does not just mean having racial and ethnic diversity among the staff and board members. It means ensuring attitudinal and behavioral change, incorporating understanding, and respecting a diverse client population and target group. It must be acknowledged that there is no consensus regarding cultural "norms" and accepted practices and language, even among a particular group of women. Program staff must be aware of the diversity within and among their particular client and target populations. In this regard, staff training is critical.

- Participatory decision-making is key to ensuring that a program meets client needs and is well managed. These programs will more than likely identify, target, and treat clients using strategies that have been successful with that client population. Feedback from staff and clients is part of an on-going program assessment and is an important part of program operations.

- Safety of the treatment environment is important for all clients, but particularly for women and their children, if the children are living with their mothers. However, for a number of reasons, substance abuse treatment programs are often located in areas that are not safe: they are accessible to potential clients, the facility is affordable, or other communities are not amenable to having substance abuse treatment facilities in their neighborhood. To protect client safety, some treatment programs take precautions that make them appear to be impenetrable and therefore uninviting. Programs need to strike a balance between client safety and accessibility.

8.4   We Do This Because...

In reflecting on the strategies for providing treatment services, it is often easy to get lost in the detail, to lose sight of the fact that those who provide substance abuse treatment services for women do so because there is the possibility of recovery. However, on a daily basis, from the perspective of the staff member of the treatment program, the millions of American women who have substance abuse problems become the one woman in treatment for whom services are provided, care is demonstrated, and in whom hope is invested.

The following case study is the true story of a woman who completed treatment in a program funded by the CSAT Division of Clinical Programs' Women and Children's Branch. "Anita's" story is a reminder of why we devote our energies to each woman who is in our care.

From the perspective of the staff member of the treatment program, the millions of American women who have substance abuse problems become the one woman in treatment.

One Woman's Story

Today Anita is healthy and happy. She is taking care of her three children. She is employed. She is a college student. But she didn't always live her life this way...

Anita was admitted to treatment for crack cocaine use in November 1989, when she was three to four months pregnant. During the course of treatment she delivered a substance-free baby girl, Stephanie. After successfully completing treatment in April of 1990, she returned to her mother's home.

Approximately two months later, Anita relapsed and was once again hooked on crack cocaine. Her mother would not tolerate her lifestyle nor allow Anita to live in her home. She notified the local child protective services office, which removed Anita's infant daughter from the home. Anita's life continued to deteriorate. On one occasion she was choked to the point of unconsciousness and was left in a vacant lot. Another time she accepted a ride with two men who promised her drugs. When she realized that they both had guns, she escaped from their car. They became angry and fired at her. Fortunately, Anita was not hurt physically. At this point, she "had hit bottom" and decided to seek help again.

Anita admitted herself to a treatment program in January 1991. She was two months pregnant. The program has a detoxification center, a residential care facility, and an outpatient continuing care program. Anita was first admitted to the detoxification center. She remained there for one month until bed space was available in the residential facility. Anita completed the six-month course of treatment in May. Treatment included direct attention to her substance abuse, prenatal care and other health services, counseling to address her problems with relationships, and referrals for social services, including job training. After completing this treatment phase, Anita entered an outpatient continuing care program and attended support groups. She remained in the outpatient program until September 1991. When she left the residential treatment program she had a full-time job and a stable living environment in her mother's home. During this time, Anita delivered her baby, Shauna, who was substance-free. After three months, she moved into her own apartment with her infant. Once she completed all the required treatment phases, the program's advocacy department assisted Anita in regaining custody of Stephanie.

In April 1993, Anita was hired as a program assistant for the treatment program. She wanted to be a role model and provide hope to those, like herself, who are still in treatment. Since then, she has been promoted and is working on her bachelor's degree in social work. In the year since she has been employed by the treatment program, Anita has married, and all three of her children—Eric, Stephanie and Shauna—live with her and her husband, who is adopting the children.

Today, Anita continues to participate in self help meetings, is drug-free, and committed to recovery.

Glossary of Terms

abstinence: nonuse of a specific substance.

abuse: harmful use of a specific substance.

addiction: a disease process characterized by the continued use of a specific psychoactive substance despite physical, psychological, or social harm.

AIDS: acquired immunodeficiency syndrome. A disease characterized by opportunistic infections (e.g., Pneumocystis carinii pneumonia, candidiasis, Kaposi's sarcoma) in persons whose immune systems are weakened; caused by the human immunodeficiency virus (HIV) and transmitted by exchange of body fluids.

at risk: term used to identify individuals based upon a composite profile of various risk factors.

case manager: one who defines, initiates, and monitors the medical, substance abuse treatment, psychosocial, and social services provided for the client and her family.

cross training: to be trained in several disciplines to facilitate broader coverage in a treatment unit.

dependence: abuse of alcohol, tobacco, or other drugs, such that to stop using would result in physical and/or psychological symptoms of withdrawal.

dual disorders: denotes the coexistence of two independent, but invariably interactive disorders.

early intervention: a strategy to identify problems early in the development cycle, to minimize risk factors, and to prevent progression to more serious problems.

epidemiology: the study of the relationship between various factors that determine the frequency and distribution of diseases in human and other animal populations.

fetal alcohol effects (FAE): diagnosis given to a child who shows signs of prenatal exposure to alcohol but who does not meet all the criteria for an FAS diagnosis.

fetal alcohol syndrome (FAS): a syndrome caused by prenatal exposure to alcohol through maternal use. Characterized by small head size, mental retardation, heart or other organ defects, and facial features including small eyes, drooping eyelids, flat midface, and a simple philtrum (underdevelopment or absence of the indentation in the upper lip).

gonorrhea: a sexually transmitted disease manifested by an inflammation of the genital mucous membrane.

HIV: human immunodeficiency virus. Retroviruses that become incorporated into host cell DNA and result in a wide range of clinical presentations varying from asymptomatic carrier states to severely debilitating and fatal disorders. AIDS is a secondary immunodeficiency syndrome resulting from HIV infection and characterized by opportunistic infections, malignancies, neurologic dysfunction, and a variety of other syndromes.

incidence: the number of new cases within a particular period of time.

maternal alcohol and other drug use/abuse: use or abuse of drugs or alcohol by a woman during pregnancy.

morbidity: pertaining to severe illness.

mortality: pertaining to death.

perinatal: clinical definition—the period from the 20th-28th weeks of pregnancy through four weeks after birth. Program definition (e.g. Healthy Start)—the period from conception through the first year of life.

polydrug use: use of multiple drugs.

postneonatal: the period from six weeks after birth to the end of the first year of life.

postpartum: the period after childbirth (up to a few weeks); usually refers to the mother.

prenatal care: refers to health promotion, risk assessment, and intervention linked to the risks and conditions uncovered. Prenatal care begins when conception is first considered and continues until labor begins.

prevalence: the total number of cases at a particular point in time.

problem use: use of alcohol, tobacco, or other drugs that does not fit the criteria for abuse or dependence, but that does bear significant risks.

psychotropic: pertaining to drugs used in treatment of mental illness; affecting the mind.

recovery: a process that supports abstinence from alcohol and/or other drug use, involves changes in social, physical, and psychological functioning, and that may or may not have an end.

relapse: is any occasion of alcohol or other drug use by a recovering person when such use violates her/his own prior commitment to recovery.

resiliency: the ability to withstand or minimize the effects of an illness, exposure to alcohol and other drugs, continued use or abuse of alcohol and other drugs, or to social and environmental factors contributing to such conditions.

risk: the association between an exposure and the likelihood of an outcome or effect.

service delivery system: the full continuum of health and other care providers, alcohol and other drug prevention and treatment providers, and public and community-based organizations involved in providing services to women, children, and families.

stabilization: the accomplishment of a steady, nonvarying physical state.

STD: sexually transmitted disease; venereal disease. Any of several diseases that can be contracted through sexual intercourse, for example, gonorrhea, chlamydial infection, herpes, syphilis, genital warts, and human immunodeficiency virus (HIV).

syndrome: the combination of signs and symptoms associated with any morbid process, which together constitute the picture of the disease.

syphilis: a chronic, contagious, often congenital, sexually transmitted venereal disease caused by a spirochete. If left untreated, it will usually progress through three stages of increasing severity over many years and may eventually lead to death.

treatment: a broad range of services for persons who have abused alcohol and/or other drugs; may include detoxification, inpatient or outpatient care and counseling, methadone maintenance, rehabilitation, and long-term residence in supervised housing.

Appendix A

CSAT's Comprehensive Treatment Model for Alcohol and Other Drug-Abusing Women and Their Children

The purpose of this model is to foster the development of state-of-the-art recovery for women with alcohol and other drug dependence and to foster the healthy development of the children of substance-abusing women. The model is a guide that can be adapted by communities and used to build comprehensive programs over time. The goal of alcohol and other drug treatment is to support a woman's journey to a healthy lifestyle for herself, and for her family whenever possible. Because alcohol and drug dependent women tend to have few economic and social resources, comprehensive treatment is extremely important. The purpose of comprehensive treatment is to address a woman's substance abuse in the context of her health and her relationships with her family, community, and society. These relationships are influenced by gender, culture, race and ethnicity, social class, sexual orientation, and age.

Treatment that addresses the full range of a woman's needs is associated with increasing abstinence and improvement in other measures of recovery, including parenting skills and overall emotional health. Treatment that addresses alcohol and other drug abuse only may well fail and contribute to a higher potential for relapse.

Confidentiality and informed consent, as well as the establishment of universal precautions against the spread of STDs, are essential throughout all aspects of treatment.

Although this treatment model has been designed specifically for women and their families, many components apply to men as well.

I.   Program Structure and Administration

- Develop joint cooperation among substance abuse agencies, schools, courts, probation officers, health and mental health providers, job training programs, and human service agencies. Create inventory of local, state, and federal resources available to the treatment program.

- Establish an advisory board to assist the treatment program in collaborating with other resources and organizations, and to advocate on behalf of the program. This board should reflect the cultural and socioeconomic diversity of the women and include recovering persons as well as community leaders. Training and support are necessary.

- Cross train staff in collaborating organizations to develop an integrated continuum of care for each woman in treatment and to address differences in philosophy, experience, and style of various disciplines.

- Staffing should include individuals who are culturally competent and sensitive to and knowledgeable about treating substance-abusing women.

- Substance abuse treatment in correctional facilities should be delivered by trained and certified personnel.

- Staff training should encompass the guidelines generated in CSAT's TIPs that relate specifically to perinatal substance abuse.

- Clinicians and program managers should participate in staff training. Such training should help lead to an understanding of the impact of psychological and psychiatric disorders, incest, physical and sexual abuse and their impact on recovery, and readiness for treatment, family dysfunction, multi-addiction, and the importance of flexible treatment approaches.

II.   Clinical Interventions and Other Services

Intake Screening and Comprehensive Health Assessment

- Admission priority must be given to women who are known to be pregnant, HIV-positive, or who have AIDS, and/or TB. Pregnant/postpartum women should be referred immediately for obstetrical care. (See TIPs.) Immediate referrals must be made if the program cannot provide appropriate care for these women. It is essential to document all referrals and admissions.

- Assessments for possible pregnancy, HIV status, and exposure to and/or existence of TB should begin immediately.

- Same-day intake services should be offered whenever possible.

- Assessment may occur over a period of time. A complete health assessment must be conducted, and must include a physical examination, psychosocial evaluation (including psychiatric assessment where indicated), as well as an assessment of a woman's reproductive, oral, and nutritional health status.

- Other assessments must include a substance abuse history; physical, emotional, and sexual abuse history (past and present); educational level and intellectual functioning; work history; family assessment; current living situation and childcare responsibilities; and racial/cultural/ethnic factors that are relevant to treatment. There should be an assessment of patient eligibility (and subsequent registration) for Medicaid, Medicare, SSI, public assistance, and other health and human service benefits.

- An individualized treatment plan, including a plan for relapse prevention and continuing care, must be developed in collaboration with each woman entering treatment.

Medical Interventions

- <u>Medical assessments</u> and subsequent care should be provided through arrangements with healthcare facilities accessible to individuals in the community or on-site, and should include the provision of preventive and primary medical care (including prenatal care, if appropriate); medical or medically supervised detoxification services, where clinically indicated; linkage to psychiatric care; provision of or established referral linkages as needed for acute medical care; testing and treatment for hepatitis, tuberculosis, HIV and HIV disease, sexually transmitted diseases, anemia and malnutrition, hypertension, diabetes, cancer, liver disorders, eating disorders, gynecological problems, dental and vision problems, and poor hygiene. It is preferable to have a healthcare professional available to consult directly with the program.

- <u>Women's Health Services.</u> Preconceptional care should be provided either on-site or through referral, for nutrition, family planning, and general gynecological services.

- <u>Pharmacotherapy</u> intervention should be provided on an as-needed basis and should include provision of, or established referral linkages, for concomitant assessment and monitoring by qualified medical or psychiatric staff. Interventions should promote equal access to treatment for all women based on assessment of their ability to participate in treatment.

- <u>Urine testing</u> should be used where clinically appropriate, and should be conducted on an initial and random basis. (See TIPs.) The program should follow informed consent guidelines responsive to State reporting requirements, if applicable.

- <u>Infant and child health services</u> should be provided either on-site or through referral and should include the following: primary and acute healthcare for infants and children, including immunizations, nutrition services (including assessment for WIC eligibility), and a developmental assessment by qualified personnel. For treatment programs without medical personnel on-site, a back-up medical plan that identifies a protocol for pediatric emergencies must be in place.

• Early Intervention Services for children should be available. Access to an age-appropriate, comprehensive developmental assessment by qualified personnel, including an assessment of learning and developmental disabilities, should be provided to all children, beginning at birth. On-site provision of, or referral to, early intervention and remedial programs, and linkages with State Individuals with Disabilities Education Act (IDEA) should be encouraged.

• Home-Based Support. Public health nursing and/or social work visits should be provided to high-risk postpartum women and their infants, especially to new mothers and those who are discharged within 24 hours after delivery. Linkages and referrals should be established with home care agencies.

Counseling for HIV-positive/AIDS Patients. The program must provide for pre- and post-test counseling for HIV-positive/AIDS patients as well as individual counseling and support groups. Staff should be properly trained to intervene on behalf of those who are HIV-seropositive, whether symptomatic or asymptomatic. Appropriate care for HIV-positive children must also be assured.

Linkages and Collaboration

• Appropriate linkages to local, state, and federal programs must be maintained for those services not provided on-site.

• Linkages with outreach, outpatient, and residential programs should be maintained as a means to assure appropriate matching of women to substance abuse treatment. Similarly, linkages with parental/child programs (e.g., Head Start) should be encouraged.

- Support should be offered with the criminal justice system where appropriate, and should include intervention with juvenile or adult justice authorities, TASC (or related case management/tracking systems), Legal Aid, and/or Bureau of Indian Affairs. Access to needed legal services should be provided if not available through Legal Aid, probation, immigration, child welfare, foster care, and legal service.

Substance Abuse Counseling and Psychological Counseling

- Substance abuse education and counseling, psychological counseling (where appropriate), and other therapeutic activities should be provided by practitioners who are licensed or certified to provide these services and matched in competency to the populations served.

- Services should be offered in the context of families and relationships, including individual/group/family therapy. Counseling for partners and fathers of babies should be promoted/provided at critical times throughout treatment.

- Counseling should address low self-esteem; race and ethnicity issues; gender-specific issues; family relationships; attachment to unhealthy interpersonal relationships; inter-personal violence, including incest, rape, and other abuse; eating disorders; sexuality; parenting issues; grief related to loss of alcohol and other drugs, children, family, partner, work, and appearance; creating a support system that may or may not include family and/or partner; developing a vision for the future and creating a life plan; and therapeutic recreational activities for women alone and with their children.

- Parenting Education. Counseling, including information on child development, child safety, injury prevention, and child abuse prevention should be provided. Parenting education should be integrated with substance abuse counseling in order to be recovery-oriented. A woman's family issues that affect parenting should be addressed in a way that supports rather than compromises her stage of recovery.

- Relapse prevention should be a discrete component or phase of each woman's recovery plan.

- Flexibility and creativity should be stressed in the use and timing of therapeutic approaches. Accusatory, judgmental, and humiliation techniques are inappropriate and have not been proven to be effective.

Health Education and Prevention Activities

- Health education and prevention activities should include HIV/AIDS education; the physiology and transmission of sexually transmitted diseases; reproductive health; understanding female sexuality; preconception care; prenatal education; child birth education; childhood safety and injury prevention; physical and sexual abuse education and prevention; nutrition and smoking cessation classes, especially for pregnant women; and general health education.

Life Skills Education. Life skills education should be offered and should cover practical life skills such as parenting (where appropriate); vocational evaluation; financial management; negotiating access to services; stress management and coping skills; and personal image building.

Educational Training and Remediation Services

- Educational training and remediation services should be provided, with on-site provision of or case-managed referrals to local education/GED programs and other remediation issues identified at intake.

- English language competency and literacy assessment programs should be facilitated.

- Job counseling and training should be provided, if possible, via case managed/coordinated linkages to community programs.

Transportation. Transportation to programs is needed to access treatment and related community services.

Housing. Access to safe, drug-free housing to the maximum extent possible throughout treatment is all-important.

Childcare Services. Age-appropriate care of infants and children should be provided at treatment facilities using a developmental model. Respite care should also be available. If space or licensing requirements prohibit on-site care, contractual arrangements with local, licensed childcare providers should be provided.

Continuing Care. Continuing Care should be provided, planned for, and should include sustained and frequent interaction with recovering individuals who have graduated from the intensive or primary phase of treatment.

- Provision should be made for graduate re-admission to more intensive forms of therapy in cases where relapse has occurred.

- As women complete the intensive phase of treatment and move into the community, the effects of domestic violence, rape, and childhood sexual abuse must continue to be addressed.

- Socioeconomic issues (e.g., jobs/educational deficits) require long-term remedies and must be included in relapse prevention planning.

- Public assistance and housing must be addressed in the continuing care plan.

- Ongoing transportation assistance must be provided for attendance at self help groups (AA, NA, and other support meetings).

- Continuing provision of primary healthcare services and medical assistance as needed for women and children.

Appendix B

Consent, Confidentiality, Principles of Conduct, and Client Rights Forms

CONSENT FOR THE RELEASE OF CONFIDENTIAL INFORMATION

I, _____hereby authorize

_____ to release to

_____for the purpose of _____

_____the following information:

_____

_____

_____

    I understand that my records are protected under the Federal and state confidentiality regulations and cannot be disclosed without my written consent unless otherwise provided for in the regulations. I also understand that I may revoke this consent at any time except to the extent that action has been taken in reliance on it (e.g., probation, parole, etc.), and that in any event this consent expires automatically in 90 days unless otherwise specified below.

Other expiration specifications:_____

Date executed: _____

Signature of client:_____

Signature of witness:_____

CONFIDENTIALITY OF ALCOHOL AND DRUG ABUSE CLIENT RECORDS

The confidentiality of alcohol and drug abuse client records maintained by this program is protected by Federal law and regulations. Generally, the program may not say to a person outside the program that a client attends the program or disclose any information identifying a client as participating in an alcohol or drug abuse program UNLESS—

1. the client consents in writing; or

2. the disclosure is required by court order; or

3. the disclosure is made to medical personnel in a medical emergency or to qualified personnel for research, audit, or program evaluation; or

4. the client commits or threatens to commit a crime either at the program or against any person who works for the program.

Violation of the Federal law and regulations by a program is a crime. Suspected violations may be reported to the United States Attorney in the district where the violation occurs.

Federal law and regulations do not protect any information about suspected child abuse or neglect from being reported under state law to appropriate state or local authorities.

I have read, understand, and received a copy of the above statement.

_____   _____
Client signature   Date

_____   _____
Witness signature   Date

PRINCIPLES OF CONDUCT

As a client of this program, you are expected to behave at all times in accordance with our Principles of Conduct. If for any reason you fail to follow these principles, you may be asked to leave the program so that your behavior does not become a barrier to the recovery of others.

Our Principles of Conduct are as follows:

1. I will be honest about matters related to my recovery.

2. I will sincerely attempt to understand my addictions problem.

3. I will follow the directives and advice offered by the staff.

4. I will not use drugs or alcohol at any time during the program. (Clients taking prescribed medications will be allowed to participate in the program with the approval of the Director.)

5. I will submit to breath tests or random urine drug screening or searches when asked.

6. I will honor the confidentiality and rights of other clients, staff, and volunteers.

7. I will be considerate and respectful of other clients, staff, and volunteers.

8. I will not engage in or tolerate violence, threats of violence, and/or antisocial behavior.

9. I will not engage in sexual contact of any kind—physical or verbal—with others in the program, the staff, or volunteers.

10. I will be on time for all meetings and sessions assigned by my Counselor, except when excused for good reason in advance by the Director of the program.

11. I will not smoke during group sessions.

12. I will not eat or drink during group sessions.

The Principles of Conduct have been clearly read and explained to me. I have been given a copy for my own use. My signature below is an acknowledgement that I understand and agree to abide by these Principles of Conduct.

_____   _____
Client Signature and Date   Staff Person Signature and Date

CLIENT RIGHTS

1. You have the right to treatment without regard to race, religion, sex, ethnic background, age, sexual orientation, physical disability, employment status, insurance coverage, or any other nonclinical reason.

2. You have the right to professional, committed, and qualified services.

3. You have the right to be informed about all program policies which affect the course of your treatment.

4. You have the right to confidentiality of your treatment record, except in case of medical emergency or court order.

5. You have the right to participate with your Counselor in your treatment plan and in other decisions that will establish your treatment goals.

6. You have the right, with specific limitations, to see your own treatment record.

7. You have the right to be treated with dignity and respect.

8. You have the right to question any aspect of your treatment experience.

You have the responsibility to protect your rights. If at any time you believe your rights have been violated, please contact the Director of the program immediately.

My rights have been clearly read and explained to me. I have been given a copy for my own use. My signature below is an acknowledgement that I understand my rights.

_____   _____
Client Signature and Date   Staff Person Signature and Date

ISBN 0-16-045254-6

9 780160 452543

90000